A PATCHWORK OF BROKEN PIECES

My Story

Elizabeth Swords

To Naomi
FROM
Betty

ORIGINAL WRITING

ISBNS
PARENT : 978-1-78237-003-1
EPUB: 978-1-78237-009-3
MOBI: 978-1-78237-010-9
PDF: 978-1-78237-011-6

A CIP catalogue for this book is available from the National Library.

Published by ORIGINAL WRITING LTD., Dublin, 2012.

Printed by CLONDALKIN GROUP, Glasnevin, Dublin 11

I dedicate this book to my three beautiful daughters. Valerie and Pamela who are truly a blessing in my life, and our beloved June who went to heaven too soon.

Also to my five grandchildren, who gave me a reason to smile again.

CONTENTS

PREFACE

I thought that when we got to our sixties, after forty years of marriage, and three adult children, that it would be hand in hand for the rest of the journey. We had no financial problems, and lived very comfortable for all of our forty years together. My story goes through the journey of love and marriage, childlessness, the wonderful joy of adopting two children, then giving birth to a disabled child after ten years of marriage.

There was a time in my life that I thought I could join all the broken pieces again like a patchwork quilt, and get myself together. But now this can never be, because one of the main pieces is now gone forever, my beautiful youngest daughter June.

There is nothing in this life that prepares you for the loss of a child, even an adult child. In the natural course of events, we bury our parents, not our children. The worst part was that she suffered so much, always with dignity, never complaining.

She was the youngest of my three beautiful daughters, so the older two spoiled her rotten. They grew up best friends as well as sisters. The memory of the laughter and the giggles, as they grew up will always bring a smile to my face. When my husband left me after 40 years of marriage for another woman, my world fell apart, but it was my three girls, who gave me strength to keep going.

I now had to face the ultimate betrayal, dumped, for a grandmother of similar age as myself! June still lived at home as her sisters were now married. It was difficult at times, but with everyone's help we got through it. Although June was in a wheelchair, she held down a full time job in the public service.

She was the one who had to listen to my tears during the night while I tried to come to terms with the rejection. Many times she got into her wheelchair in the early hours to sit with me and talk me through it. I found it hard to accept that he didn't want me anymore, after struggling through some real hard knocks in our life together. I believed the loss I felt could not be worse. But I was wrong. The loss of losing a child rips you apart like nothing you've ever known. I miss her so much. I miss the fun and the laughter that was part of our lives for 34 years. We could laugh together at our limitations, with her lower limb paralysis, and my Rheumatoid Arthritis. She had great patience teaching me how to use the computer with my crooked fingers so that I could write my story.

I contacted Rheumatoid Arthritis when I was 28 years old so the years since then have been very painful. But the most painful of all was, as the years went on my husband changed towards me. I could no longer be the glamorous dress designer that I once was. Was this the reason for the change? I don't know, but he constantly criticized me and the way I looked, from then on.

I had no clue that he was seeing another woman, in fact it was my children who found out first. I remember thinking that it was the worst thing that could happen to me, after all we knew each other since I was 5 years old. My children were 36, 31, and almost 30, at that time. They too were devastated, their Daddy had turned into a stranger.

June never felt close to her dad, and told me so many times. I tried telling him how she felt, but his answer was always, 'Ah that's silly'. But no matter how many times I said it, he never seemed to talk to her on a one to one basis. He would have the odd joke with her when she playfully jeered him combing his hair. But there was never any serious conversation, so he had no idea of her feelings and worries. Consequently, she was closer to me.

When my two older girls got married, she witnessed the constant verbal attacks and took up for me many times. Sometimes for peace I let it go and didn't answer him, but she wouldn't let him away with it. I hated when she got upset on my behalf, so I avoided confrontation most of the time.

In spite of the difficult time I had, I tried to remain cheerful for my children's sake. When they were smaller I thought that I was successful in hiding it from them, but the oldest girl heard more than I thought.

She recently found her diary from when she was 13/14 years old, where she had written about 'Mammy and Daddy's row'. I was so disappointed to hear this, because in my mind I never answered him back in front of the children. Clearly on that day I had. The main reasons for the rows were my appearance, the arthritis, and the housework not up to his standard. We had no financial problems, as I worked all my life as a dress designer and he had a well paid job. I was never good enough no matter how hard I worked, and just when life should have been easier for us, he left.

Later when June's health deteriorated, I soon realized that there was nothing worse than losing a child. When the end was near, I rang him and he came to see her during her final weeks.

There were days she would do her best to talk to him. She told me that she felt uncomfortable in his company, but I think it was because she didn't want him to know that she was so ill. He missed out on so much, and now it was too late.

The kind words and letters to us since have been a great comfort, and we read them over and over again. I started this book as a fun thing at June's suggestion to show my grandchildren what life was like growing up in Dublin in the fifties. June laughed as I got going with my one straight finger! But the events that happened since changed the whole story. June read quite a lot of it before she passed, and I promised her that I would try to get it published. Besides she told all her work colleagues of South Dublin Council to watch out for it, and also the staff of Tallaght hospital!

Anyone who knew June loved her, and she genuinely cared about people. She loved life, animals, especially dogs. Her favourite charity was The Guide Dogs for the Blind. Every year they went into South Dublin County council collecting, and she would spend her time rubbing and talking to the dog!

The intense loss that I feel never goes away, the pain in my heart is invisible. But often, I allow myself to wallow in the warm memories, that are mine alone and I can smile.

I have changed some of the names so that I don't hurt anyone.

Chapter one

A RUDE AWAKENING

I sat beside my disabled daughter June as she drove along in her specially adapted car. She kept talking, trying to stop me crying, while keeping her eyes on the road.'Mam, it's his loss, and he's not worth your tears'. I looked at my beautiful daughter, so capable, so level headed, and in my misery I was in awe of her. Here she was, almost thirty years old, on dialysis three times a week, and still held down a full time job. We made this journey every Saturday and, like today, bank holiday Mondays, always in great form. Sometimes I drove as her car had dual controls.

But today was different. My life as I knew it had changed drastically. It was coming up to my fortieth wedding anniversary, and I had just found out that my husband was seeing another woman. My loyal hardworking husbandwho had no time for anyone cheating on their wives, was in fact, cheating on me. He was almost 63 years old, I was 61.

We pulled up outside of Tallaght hospital, parked easily in the disabled section, with June insisting that I sit for a while to get my act together. I tidied up my face as best as I could, before taking out her wheelchair and facing the dialysis nurses who knew me well. Normally we would have a laugh while June waited her turn, but today, we didn't feel like laughing. Instead we sat quietly in a corner consoling each other, and texting my other two daughters. Life for them would also change.

June held my crooked hands in hers and continually rubbed them. She did this often in the privacy of our own home to give me relief from my arthritis, it was a comforting thing. Today I needed comforting, and yet my heart was breaking for June, she had so many health problems, and never complained. Her biggest concern today was for me. She hated that for the next three hours, she would be on dialysis, when she only wanted to comfort me. When the nurse called her name, I helped her up on to the bed and waited until they connected her up and checked her blood pressure. She had low blood pressure so I held my breath each time as the dialysis machine stopped if the pressure went too low. As it happens, today it was fine. She gave me another few words of advice before I left and we promised to keep in touch by text until she was finished. No phone calls were allowed in dialysis.

I went back to the car with pools in my eyes. It was getting harder to see where I was going. I pulled into the car park of Lidl shopping centre in Walkinstown rather than go home, and sat in the car for what seemed like hours. I kept going over and over my life in my head, wondering what went wrong. I loved this man deeply and always did, even though he was hard to live with. Yes, we had a lot of hard knocks during our forty years of marriage, but I thought we came through them well. I thought back to the beginning of the journey that now led to this. My head was racing, nothing was making sense. I was an ordinary wife and mother, nothing special. I came from a poor background as did my husband, and we both worked hard to give our children a comfortable life. I first met him when I was five years old, I was his sister's best pal, and we are still good friends. I thought back to my own parents, how they also did their best for us, and I found myself reflecting on my whole life.

Chapter Two

IN THE BEGINNING

The evening of January 15th 1945 was dark and snowy. It was coming into the last few months of the war, but here in Ireland we were still governed by the "blackout" rule so, there wasn't a light to be seen out on the streets. According to my Dad, he walked for over an hour in cold weather to get the midwife as my mammy was in heavy labour. It was just before midnight when I was born, the third daughter of what was to be a family of daughters, five to be exact. My Daddy loved to tell the story of 'losing a bet' every time mammy was pregnant.

Each time he was convinced that it would be a boy, but alas he was to be the only male in the family until the grandchildren came along!

My Dad Michael Foley married my Mam Annie Kelly on April 11th 1939, a few months before world war two broke out. They came from a humble background so there was no lavish wedding. My Mammy told me that she wore a grey suit and hat, as did her bridesmaid. After church, it was back to her parents small house on Monesterboice Road Crumlin, were they dined on current cake and sandwiches. The men had bottles of porter, and there followed a great 'hooley'.

There was not much work in Ireland at that time, however, Daddy worked in the Capital Cinema as a maintenance man. Two years after they were married, my sister Kathleen was born. She was christened Catherine Mary, but called Kathleen after our maternal grandmother. 14 months later, my sister Marie was born. Christened Marie Theresa, and called Marie.

I was christened Elizabeth Ann, but called Betty. The Queen of England was Princess Elizabeth at that time, so I have always believed that I was called after her. There were a lot of Elizabeths born that year, so it must have been one of the most popular names, and later there were four Elizabeths in my class in school! My sister Joan was born four years after me. She was christened Josephine Mary, but called Joan. Joan too was born in the house on Monasterboice Road. It amazes me to think that I woke up one morning and dad said 'You have a new sister!' Imagine, here was a two bedroom house, with Mam's five brothers, one sister, plus our little family, and I never woke for the commotion! However I was delighted with my new baby sister, and believed my Daddy when he told me that he found her under a head of cabbage!

A few weeks after Joan was born, I fell in the back garden and got a deep nasty cut on the bridge of my nose. Mrs. Mac was duly sent for. Mrs. Mac was in fact Mrs. McDonald, an expert on all things medical but on reflection, probably no real qualifications at all. Her advice was to dress it at home rather than go to the hospital because she said, they would stitch it and I would be badly scarred for life. So Mrs. Mac, dressed it every day until it healed. To this day I still have a slight scar, but she was probably right, as the hospital stitches in those days were rough. Many years later, as an adult, I met Mrs. Mac, and she insisted on inspecting my nose! She was quite pleased with it and knew that she did the right thing.

I started school when I was four years old. My two sisters were pupils of St. Agnes' School in Crumlin, so it was natural that I would join them. I remember that I was very frightened on the first day. We were learning how to draw a straight line with chalk on our mini blackboards. I was scared of doing it wrong so I asked the girl beside me to do it for me, which she did. The teacher saw us, but she was nice about it and encouraged me to try it myself. Of course I was well able to do it but this was my first day, and I was very nervous.

When I got over my nervousness, I loved school after that. I was interested in every subject and practised everything at home, even when I was too young for homework. I was a reader from very young. Daddy used to cut out the cartoon strips from the newspapers, paste them into a scrap book and I would read them over and over again. In those days (late forties) it was safe for us young children to play on the street. We had few toys, but we made our fun ourselves. I remember playing shop with 'chainies'. Chainies were bits of broken delph and coloured glass, that we used for money. I was only four or five years old at the time. When I think about it now, I would not allow my grandchildren play with broken glass! And yet, it was a game that most of my generation played in Dublin, without cutting themselves!.

We also played with our 'potato dolls'. These were dolls made from potatoes. A small potato for the head, a large one for the body, joined together with a match stick. The arms and legs were made from more match sticks. We had great fun with them. Rag dolls were also very popular back then. I remember my Aunt Rita, mammy's sister making me one out of an old tea towel. I treasured it, and thought I had the best doll on the street!.

My Aunt Rita was in her late teens at that time. Even at that young age, she loved children, and was very kind to us. I recall that at one time she worked in some sort of electrical factory. She would bring home lots of beads, and us children would have endless fun threading them, making necklaces and bracelets. I was to discover years later, that the 'beads' were coloured wire used in electric cable! The actual wire was removed and the outer part was cut into tiny pieces, thereby making beads!

There were no expensive toys, so we made up our own little games. We made our swings on the lamp posts, with a rope. The tallest among us would be chosen to go up the lamp post to secure the rope. She would spit on her hands, then rub the inside of her thighs, and climb up the post! Some were more skilled at it than others, the higher the rope, the better the swing. We spent long hours swinging around the lamp posts. Many years later when Daddy made a real swing for our back garden, it just wasn't as exciting as the lamp post swing! There was a field at the end of the road where most children hung out. Bonfires were a regular occurrence and potatoes thrown on to cook. I clearly remember the taste of the burnt potatoes, which I loved, and blame them for my love of almost burnt toast today! Needless to say, anytime that I was found at the fires, mammy took me home.

The house on Monasterboice Road was a corporation house rented out to Granda Kelly. Granda Kelly was affectionately known as "Daddy Kimmage". Probably because there were two Daddys in the house (mine and granda). My Granny died when I was 2years old so I cannot remember her. She was just 49 years old when she died from a kidney related illness. Today, it may have been easily treated, but back then, more knowledge and dialysis was yet to come.

My uncle Mikie left the house and joined the navy. Two more uncles Eddie and John got married within six months of each other and also left the house. That left uncle Jem , Aunt Rita and the youngest, uncle Peter. And of course, us four girls and Mammy and Daddy.

I don't remember any discomfort, but where on earth did we all fit?. I do remember us six sleeping in the one bedroom, but my memory is only of fun. The two bedrooms were so small. Downstairs consisted of a sitting room with a fire place and what we called a coal hole. This was a space with a door where the coal was kept The only other room was a small kitchen with a bath in it. There was a bath board over the bath to give a kind of work surface, during the day, although us children were put into a tin bath in front of the fire one at a time. The toilet was outside, and I do remember the cold sitting there. Looking back now, I wonder what genius designed a house with the coal room inside, and the toilet outside! Some of our neighbours were dealers, who sold fruit from a stall outside of their houses. My friend Patsy Furlong's mother also sold fish on Fridays. I remember sitting on the step with Patsy and her grandmother playing jack stones. This was played with five stones and you had to throw one up while picking up another. It wasn't easy for four year old hands to catch them, so I never mastered it.

I used to watch Granny Furlong, with amazement as she put 'something' on the back of her hand and sniffed it. At home I asked Mammy what it was, and she told me it was scent. It wasn't until many years later that I found out it was snuff!

In 1950, the corporation gave mammy and daddy a house in the new suburb of Ballyfermot. This, at the time was the most exciting thing ever! Our very own house with a toilet INSIDE! We all went out there to have a look before we moved in. The corporation were still building, but there was our house, among others in the middle of a very long road, ready for us to move in.

It was a mild evening when we left Crumlin for Ballyfermot. We children went on the bus with mam and Aunt Rita. We had to get two buses to reach our destination. The furniture went with daddy and friend on a horse and cart. When we arrived at our new house, it was getting dark, and daddy was there with the furniture still on the cart. He looked worried as he told mammy that he couldn't find the key. Mam reminded him that he put it in his overcoat's inside pocket. But where was the overcoat? It was in the wardrobe still on the horse and cart! Carefully, Daddy and friend lifted the wardrobe into the garden and mam was right, it was there.

Chapter Three
A NEW SUBURB, BALLYFERMOT

We were tired after the journey to Ballyfermot and only wanted to get into the house. Oh the excitement running around it , checking out all the rooms. It seemed enormous at the time with rooms everywhere. We had two bedrooms now, and a bathroom with toilet upstairs. Downstairs there was a parlour, and kitchen cum dining room. To us it was pure luxury. There was a black gas cooker in the kitchen that worked only when a single shilling was put into a meter that was situated under the stairs. I cannot remember how much time we got out of the shilling but I do remember mammy's frustration when the gas went off in the middle of a meal.

We settled in well to our new surroundings. There was a lovely front garden with a gate, and a large back garden. We had nice new neighbours, the Fays on one side and the Bruntons on the other. Because everyone at that time was poor, neighbours helped each other. Although we were poor, we always had food on the table. It was a time when you didn't keep up with the Jones's as they too were poor. Nearly all mothers worked in the home back then, in fact I do not remember one who went out to work.

But then there was very little work at that time. If your dad had a job, you were lucky! My dad was now working at building. Seemingly, he worked on the building of Holdens wool sorters, on the Long Mile Road, in Walkinstown, and when it was finished, he got a job working in it. This was where he was to work for the next sixteen years.

All the people who moved to Kylemore Road were young families like ourselves, so we soon made lots of friends. There were no schools in Ballyfermot then, so we had to get a special bus to Baggot Street school. At first there was only one bus, but in no time, they had to supply a second. There were two buses also bringing children to Whitefriar Street school.

So at 8 o'clock every morning, my sisters Kathleen and Marie and myself, would go to the end of the road to wait for the bus. It returned again after school at 3.30pm. Baggot Street was a Catholic school run by the Sisters of Mercy. There were some lay teachers there too, but mostly nuns. Teachers and nuns in the 1950s were quite strict ,and corporal punishment was still allowed. Even so, my memories of Baggot Street are happy ones. Perhaps it's because I was a willing student and loved learning My sisters on the other hand, had some very cross teachers. I remember Marie was terrified of Sister Immaculatta. She was a small thin nun with a cross face. I was never in her class, but I was always afraid that I would be, after all the tales Marie told me! But I was lucky with all my teachers, they were strict but fair. However I have one bad memory of Baggot Street school. It happened one day when all the classes were lined up in the yard ready to go down the long lane to board the busses for home. I was caught talking, so an older teacher Miss Sheppard who was a friend of mammy's, ordered me to stand in the middle of the yard on my own. She then ushered the classes down the lane and left me there. I was in a real panic wondering if I would catch the bus home. She waited until the bus was ready to go before ordering me out. Well I ran as fast as I could to catch the bus gasping and crying in the process! Weeks later, she spoke to my mammy and she told her that I was a very stubborn little girl. I could never figure out how that episode made me stubborn, but my mother was to repeat it to me many times during my childhood, when I misbehaved, ie 'Even Miss Sheppard said you're stubborn!'

The school building was an old one, but always clean. There were open fires in most of the class rooms that were in full blaze when we arrived every day. The cleaning lady was affectionately called Molly, although perhaps that was her real name.She was a small thin woman with no teeth, and her black hair caught up in a hairnet.She worked very hard and did every thing from lighting fires to giving us lunch.The lunch was free, and everyone availed of it, at twelve noon each day. How I remember the time is, that we would have to say the Angelus first along with our

'Grace before meals'. The lunch was a sandwich and a small bottle of milk. On Monday we had a cheese sandwich, Tuesday corn beef, Wednesday a currant bun, (very dry), Thursday corn beef again, and Friday, our favourite, jam sandwiches. If there was any leftovers, Molly allowed us have seconds, much to our delight! Every Friday, fifteen minutes before we went home we had to cleen our desks. Those who could afford it brought in brasso and polish. We shined our inkwells with the brasso, until they gleamed, and the same with the desks. There were no ball point pens then, only nib pens and ink.

Back on Kylemore Road, I made lots of new friends. There was Mary Boland, Pauline Henderson, and my very best friend Connie Swords. Connie and I were the same age and shared the same interests including our love for Irish dancing. We played all the street games that were popular at the time. Everyone had a skipping rope, but Connie's one was the best. It was what we called a Guinness's rope, I don't know where she got it, but she was the envy of everyone. Her mam used to stand at the gate and turn it for us. We would spend many hours skipping and singing the rhymes of the day.

(Keep the kettle boiling,
On the glimmer,
If you don't you'll get no dinner,
North south east or west,
Cadbury's chocolate is the best,
If it cracks, send it back, to north south east or west).

Everyone loved Connie's mother. She was the only mother who sat for hours telling us stories. Alas, we were to learn in later years, that she had multiple sclerosis and was in a lot of pain at that time. But as children, we were just having fun, so we had no idea of her suffering. Connie had one sister and three brothers. A baby sister Irene died at six months.

She was the second oldest, and so had to do a lot of housework. Her older brother was Laurence, whom I married many years later, but right now he was a shy young lad who hated girls!

We played from early morning until we were called in for food. There was no church in Ballyfermot, so we had a long walk down to Decies Road where we got mass in a large converted hut. Yet, us children never complained. In fact, we frequently made the trip in the evening as well, for devotions to Our Lady. Connie and I also walked down to Decies Road for our Irish dancing classes to Miss Cadwell. We were good dancers and would practice regularly out on the street. I made my first holy communion on 31st of May, 1952. It was a lovely time for me but a traumatic time for my mother. Daddy had an accident in work. He lost a finger and damaged two more badly. He had to stay out of work for a couple of weeks, and on top of that mammy gave birth to my baby sister, Rita, who was christened Margaret, probably after our great grandmother.

Because my mammy wasn't 'churched' it meant that she could not go outside of the door. Up until the early sixties women had to be 'churched' to cleanse the body and soul after having a baby. It was a rule of the catholic church that has since been abolished, and rightly so. My godmother Aunt Kathleen, brought me to St Michaels Church in Inchicore to make my Holy Communion and afterwards brought me back to the school for a party. I remember seeing cream cakes for the first time at the party. We were all hungry as in those days we would be fasting from the night before, to receive Holy Communion. So the cream cakes disappeared very quickly, but I managed to grab two! After the party Aunt Kathleen brought me to see all my relations, where I collected money in every house. I had a great time on the day, but poor Aunt Kathleen was exhausted. I wanted to leave on my pretty dress and veil going to bed and had to be coaxed into putting on my nightdress!

Daddy went back to work a couple of days after my Holy Communion. He was still in a lot of pain but in those days, if you didn't work, you got no money. My memory of my new baby sister is that she was very quiet. Indeed she was also shy growing up, always hiding behind mammy's leg when anyone visited us.Mammy had her work cut out trying to get her to start school. She tried two schools before she eventually settled.

I smile when I think of it now, as in reality she never left school after that as she went on to become not only a teacher, but also a school principal! How mammy would have enjoyed that!

Our childhood days were filled with games and hobbies. There were very few toys on Kylemore Road so we made our own. We played piggy beds, this was a game with a tin, such as an empty polish tin or our favourite, an old Vaseline tin. It was our favourite because it would slide better than any other. The beds were made by drawing out squares on the ground with chalk. You then hopped on one leg and kicked the tin into each square, but if it fell on a line, you were out. We had no 'real' chalk then, but we used anything from bits of plaster, to broken statues! There were many happy children if a statue fell, and broke! The unfortunate saint would be headless while we used the head for our chalk.

At home Daddy would bring home jigsaw puzzles from work which we loved putting together. I was to learn many years later that these were old square tiles that he painstakingly cut into odd shapes! Then he would have riddles for us to find an answer to. We would come up with all kinds of answers but never the right one! He loved playing games with us, and could keep us entertained all night with a piece of string!

My sister Joan also came with Connie and I to Irish dancing lessons. On Saturday nights there was a programme on Radio Eireann called ' Take the floor' in which they played traditional Irish music. So daddy would move the kitchen table to the side to let us practice our dancing to music. Not many people had a gramophone back then, so this was our only chance to practice with music. To us children, we lived in a make-believe world on Saturday nights, pretending our little kitchen was a big stage. Looking back, the house seemed big with lots of rooms. But when I think about it now, it was tiny. Mammy and Daddy were so proud of their new house, that they never stopped cleaning and polishing. They were probably the only ones among their friends and relations who got a house. Everyone was invited and we had many a great 'hooley' there. Dad bought a piano on hire purchase. He could not play it, but we never noticed.

He had a great singing voice and so he hit any and every key to accompany himself singing. You would be so taken in by his voice that you never noticed the piano! I don't think anyone who had no musical knowledge realised that he couldn't play. In fact many years later, I met an old woman who had known my father well. She said to me, ' Your father was a great hard working man, and a great singer, and, he could make that piano talk!'

Meanwhile, my Aunt Rita got a new boyfriend who COULD play the piano. So on Sunday afternoons they would visit, and we would have a great sing song around the piano. We looked forward to them coming every Sunday. Aunt Rita and Uncle Joe eventually married and the sing songs got fewer as new cousins were born! But we continued our own sing songs with Daddy belting away at the piano!

There were no shops yet near Kylemore Road at that time. Then a 'house shop' opened around the corner from us. The houses on the road were all painted blue, so the shop was known as The Blue Virgin, but it was owned by Mr. Hannon. It sold everything from groceries. to cigarettes and sweets.

It was just a little house like ours and they sometimes sold from a van outside their house. They did good business as it was a long walk to the real shop.

I loved when mam asked me to get something for her, that is except cigarettes! In those days you could buy them at any age and so, I was often asked to get them.Mam and dad smoked at the time, but I absolutely hated the smell of them. And to this day I still do! Even now I would not clean out an ashtray for anyone. I would get someone else to do it.

In 1955 when I was ten years old I made my confirmation. It was February 28th and very cold. I wore a green coat, a beautiful pink nylon dress, a lovely pink cardigan that my friend Mary Boland's mam knit for me, a new yorker brown hat , brown bag and gloves, but my favourite was my black patent hornpipe shoes! They did not match my brown accessories but I had pleaded with my mother for so long, to buy them for Irish Dancing, that she promised to buy them for my confirmation. I couldn't stay still in them, I only wanted to dance. Going into Westland Row church in the city, mammy had to warn me to stop dancing! Archbishop McQuaid conducted the service, that took almost two hours. During the service a couple of children were randomly picked to answer a question on religion. I was one of those chosen, so I was convinced it was because of the hornpipe shoes! After the service, we visited all the relations again, and collected what seemed like a lot of money at the time. Of course mam took it and gave me back a shiny sixpence! In early childhood I developed a love of needlework. I would watch my mam as she hand sewed the holes in our socks. From the time she showed me how to thread a needle, I began to make clothes for my dolls. There was no spare fabric in those days, but mam would let me cut up old clothes. I also loved knitting. All my friends would sit around crocheting square shawls. I remember sitting on my own in our back yard wondering how to start a shawl. I kept trying different ways and eventually I figured it out. I was amazed that I figured it out all on my own, at eight years old! After that there was no stopping me. It was beg, steal or borrow, wool from anyone. Mammy even gave me old thick socks belonging to Dad to rip up! I made quite a few shawls that were used on our beds. I got to love crochet and many years later was to eventually to crochet the top of my wedding dress. But sewing was my first love and I never missed an opportunity to practice. In school, we were learning to hand sew an apron. Not many in the class liked sewing, they just did it because they had to. But I loved it and was delighted when the teacher would hold mine up to show the class. Truthfully, I was a bit of a show off so to be good at it as well was a bonus. I always wanted to be the best at everything. I just loved learning new things. I joke with my children, and grandchildren these days, that I was the best in the class and on reflection, I probably was! In those days of corporal punishment, I never got a slap or a telling off for not doing my lessons.

In 1956 when I was eleven years old, my parents decided to ask the housing authority to re house them in the Walkinstown area. By then Dad was cycling in all weathers from Ballyfermot, to Walkinstown every day. In those days there was no shortcut like there is today. So, many a time he came home at midnight, soaked to the skin.It wasn't easy to get a change of house from the Corporation, unless you knew someone with 'pull' like a T.D. Yes, even in the fifties, it was all about knowing the right person. Daddy didn't, but he knew someone who did! So, he was brought to the T.D.'s house in Walkinstown, and weeks later, we got the key. I don't think money change hands, in fact I'm sure I it didn't in our case, as Daddy hadn't any.

Moving this time we didn't use a horse and cart like before, we were very 'posh' with Uncle Peter's van! Although it took a few trips on account of the van being small, it did the job in style, and like before, us children got the bus with mammy.It was exciting moving to a new house, but sad leaving all my friends.

Chapter Four

WALKINSTOWN, AND BACK TO
ST. AGNES' SCHOOL

Walkinstown was nice, and I quickly made new friends, as children do, but there was no school. The local school was still under construction so it was back to St. Agnes s for me by bus. My sister Joan and I walked to Walkinstown Cross every morning to catch the 55 bus to Crumlin. We enjoyed the short journey as it was no great hardship. We got one and a half hours for lunch, so we went to Granda Kelly on Monasterboice Road, the house were we were born for lunch.

We loved going to him every day. He told us stories of his young days that fascinated us. We would tell him all our news, and he told us his. He always made us laugh. He was a real Dubliner and his favourite saying when he didn't believe you was 'gerraway' (get away). He was in his early sixties when I was eleven, and I thought that he was very old. Now that I'm a similar age, I do not think it's old at all! One day he told us the story of a watch he found. Apparently, sometime in 1948/49 he and uncle Jem were walking through town when they found a lady's gold watch in a leather case. They had no luck tracing the owner, in spite of an inscription on the back. There was no name on it. The inscription read: Presented by the pupils of Colehill national school 1924. So they kept it, hoping that someone would claim it eventually. Well no one did, and he showed us the watch. Myself and Joan were fascinated looking at it. Remember this was a time when only 'rich' people had a watch! Certainly, no children had one. It was real gold with roman numerals. He allowed us to hold it, so we felt very special.

Almost every day after that, we would ask him to show it to us again. Sometimes he would, but more times he would fob us off until another day. I suppose he got tired of us always asking. In my childish cheekiness I asked him to give it to me. He just laughed and said ' I will leave it to you in my will'. Well, in a kind of way, he did, and to this day I still have the watch. Granda died when I was 23years old and married. My Auntie Rita gave the watch to Uncle Jem, as he was with granddad when they found it. I asked Uncle Jem would he give it to me for sentimental reasons, and he gladly gave it to me. Many years later, I tried to trace the true owner of it , even writing to Colehill School, but they couldn't help me. I haven't given up hope of finding the true owner or relatives, although I know it will be difficult.

When I was about eleven, we got our first television set. I had seen one in my uncle John's house, and was amazed at this 'radio' that showed pictures! An aerial had to go on the roof to pick up the signal from the BBC. So in some areas, the reception wasn't good. Oddly, whenever it was foggy out, our picture was clear. But a lot of times we would watch whole programmes through a snowy screen! It was something you got used to, and it never detered us from watching our favourite programmes.It didn't start until five o clock in the evening, but we kids were so excited that we would watch the test card for an hour before!

Meanwhile, school was good and I was studying for the primary certificate. This was the big exam at the time, that you had to pass before you could start work. The amount of pupils going to second level school were small, mostly because there was no free education then. There was a scholarship available to the two top pupils in the primary examination results. I got the highest marks. It was a bitter sweet moment for me because I really wanted to start work at sewing. I remember Sister Mary Frances calling me into her office. She tried to convince me to stay at school. 'Just imagine,' she said., 'if you stay at school, you will get a lovely job where you can wear a nice suit and shoes!' 'On the other hand if you go to a factory now, you will be wearing ragged clothes and sloppy shoes!' But she couldn't convince me. I left and went to work in a local factory. Besides, money was short at home, although mammy was great at budgeting. She could make a wholesome stew out of very little meat with a marrow bone and vegetables. I remember her making brawn from a pigs cheek. It was made by boiling the cheek until it soften and the bones fell off. Then the meat was pressed into a loaf tin along with onions, herbs and spices. A plate with a weight on top pressed it down until it cooled. After that it was turned out and we had a delicious meat loaf that could be sliced not only for dinner, but also, tea, and lunches. Mammy always seemed to run out of money on Thursdays, and so wouldborrow 5 shillings from the bread man, then pay it back on Saturdays.

I recall the same bread man cashing a post dated cheque for her that she borrowed from a money lender. Clothes were expensive, so they were passed down in turn to the five of us, but unfortunately I had the biggest feet, so my footwear was limited! One incident stands out in my mind and still saddens me now when I think about it. I was about thirteen years old and had only one cardigan, which I wore almost daily except when it was getting washed. One day I must have been misbehaving, and mammy dragged me in from the garden and gave me a few clatters. In the process she tore a hole in the sleeve of the cardigan so big that it was beyond repair. I felt humiliated, and devastated over my only cardigan. Later that evening when dad came home, the first thing he said was 'What happened to your cardigan?'

I told him that mammy did it, and there was a sudden silence as they looked at each other. Nothing was said in my presence but after wearing my 'holy' cardigan for a few more days, they bought me a new one. Did I deserve the punishment? I cannot remember what I did, but the memory still hurts, especially as I always wanted to please my Mammy and Daddy. Perhaps mammy was having a bad day, because these were the early years of her rheumatoid arthritis. Anyway, I feel mammy was more strict on the three older children than the youngest two, but maybe they have a different memory of that time. My favourite memories of mammy was sitting by the fire as she told us stories of her childhood. She grew up in what was then tenement houses in Holles Street in Dublin near where the hospital is now. There were whole families lived in one room, with one toilet outside that was shared by everyone.

She too went to Baggot Street school but dropped out very young to work as a house servant in a 'posh' house. She often laughed telling us that she was thrown out of school for cutting off a girl's plait! I don't know if that was true or if she was just trying to make us laugh, but we believed her. She was the second eldest of the family, so she helped out with the five younger ones. The hardship they must have endured through poverty, like most families of the time, didn't affect her sense of humour. She made it sound like fun, which I'm sure it wasn't. I'm not sure if mammy could write. Most times Daddy would do any writing that was necessary in the house, but very occasionally I recall Mammy signing her name on a form. She could definitely read, as she was in the local library and always had a book on the go. I think she may have been a bit disappointed that I didn't take up on the scholarship to secondary school, but in later years I know she was proud of my chosen career in fashion.

Chapter Five

MY FIRST SIGHTING OF A SEWING MACHINE

The first morning at work, was amazing with the buzz of the sewing machines, and dresses everywhere. Although the work was hard I loved it. We worked a 44 hour week for £1-6-8, which, in today's money would be less than 2euro! I had to hand it up to mammy and she gave me back enough to spend on the cinema and a few sweets. But the money meant nothing to me. I just couldn't take my eyes off the sewing machines. I lay awake at night thinking about nothing else. So, imagine my delight when a month later, the supervisor Mrs. Moore instructed me to go over to a vacant machine. I had no idea how to thread it up, but she showed me and gave me pieces of waste material to practise on. I practised real hard and within a few days, I was making sleeves for the girl beside me, who was making the dresses. She was a nice girl called Mary, who taught me how to make other parts of the dresses.

So, just like school, I was eager to learn as much as I could. Within a year, I was making full dresses, and I trebled my wages. By now I couldn't get enough of sewing. I sewed all day in work, and until bedtime at home. I had no sewing machine at that time, so I hand sewed. Once, a neighbour, Mrs. McGinley let me use her machine to make a skirt. My whole family were so proud of me, that everyone was shown the skirt. It was at that time, that they all got together to buy me a sewing machine on hire purchase.

My new sewing machine became my best friend. I made clothes for all the family and did alterations for friends and neighbours. In no time at all, I was earning good money, much to the delight of my parents. I still handed up my wages and most of the money earned at home.

The sewing factories at that time were indeed like sweat shops. Where I worked there were two long rows of machines, about twenty each side facing each other and what they called a 'well' in between, for placing finished dresses. Eight dresses had to be made every day by each machinist, and if you made one over, you got paid half a crown (about 15 cents) extra. The emphasis was on speed as well as quality. There was no time for chatting, just heads down and work. There was a sign on the wall that read; 'Any girl caught talking after being corrected will be suspended for three days'. We got an hour for lunch so because I lived close by, I went home. Mammy loved to hear how my day went as I ate lunch, and would frequently give me advice on how to handle different situations. I loved work as much as I loved school.

The walk home was less than ten minutes, but the Long Mile Road was just a dirt road, with blackberry bushes each side at the time. My friend Chris and I would often be up to our knees in muck by the time we got home. Chris made the buckles by hand from fabric and metal. I clearly remember the welts on her hands from making them.The factory had only one heater, that everyone stood around at break time to get a heat. Alas, you couldn't get much of a heat with fifty of us around it, so it was easier to generate heat by working harder. Perhaps the employers knew this!

Although we could not talk, we were allowed sing, so there would be a a regular sing song going on throughout the day. When a new song came out, someone would know all the words, and we would share them so that we could all join in. When we all sang together, it sounded good, but individually there were few of us that had a good voice, certainly not me! But it made the day go quicker when we sang.

After a year, one of my workmates asked me if I would join night time college with her for fashion design. I was eager to learn more, so we enrolled together. From the day I entered, I knew that this was what I was waiting for.

I then studied fashion design for six years, soaking up information like a sponge! I remember asking if I could do the City and Guilds intermediate certificate, after the first year! My tutor, Mr. Hatfield, said that normally its done after two years, but if I was that confident go for it. Even he was surprised when I got it with honours! I put my head down then to study for the final certificate as it was much more advanced and would take two more years. So, I worked until six every evening, and got the bus after work to Parnell Square in the city centre four nights a week. The college The Institute of Tailoring and Textiles had a brilliant library so I brought home lots of books to study at the weekend.

Alas, this left me very little time for socialising and, as my mother would say for cleaning my room! My room was full of books, bits of fabric, buttons zips etc. How my poor mother put up with it I don't know. She yelled at me a few times to clean it up, and I did, but in no time it was back to messy again. But secretly I know she was glad that I was happy and making extra money.

The college closed in June and July every year, so I picked up with my friends again. We went dancing once a week, firstly to the local tennis club 'hop' and when we were older, to the dancehalls in the city centre. The 'hop' was great fun as we knew everyone there. It was on until 12 midnight, but I had to be home at 11pm. I hated leaving before everyone else, but a young lad, my own age occasionally left with me to walk me home. He was a neighbour and we were to become very good friends. His name was John and everyone thought that we were an "item" In fact we really were just good friends, often chatting for hours telling each other what we wanted to do with our lives. His ambition was to be a drummer in a band. When we were at the 'hop' he continually drummed his hands on the table to the beat of the music. I told him of my plans in fashion design. We were real pals until he went to England to work. We wrote to each other for a while, but it was never the same as our chats.Meanwhile my new best friend Joan Staines and I, began going into town to the big dance halls We felt real grown up at eighteen. We met lots of nice lads, but we were having too much fun to hook up with anyone. One night we were standing on the queue outside the Ierne ballroom when we noticed that a couple of English girls were getting great attention from the Irish boys. In a moment of madness we decided to pretend that we were from Australia! So in our best imitation Australian accent we chatted to each other. Immediately all the boys were 'chatting us up!' We were enjoying it so much that we kept it up all night. Two lads that were pals came over to us and asked if they could buy us a mineral. There was no alcohol allowed in dancehalls then. So off we went upstairs to where the café was. They asked us what life was like in Australia and we told them a pack of lies! They were fascinated with us and hung on to every word we said. I had a coin on a silver chain around my neck medallion style. It was a half crown that I got my dad to put a hole in weeks earlier. They asked where I got it as it was an Irish coin. I said an aunt of mine sent it to Australia to me, and I didn't know it was legal tender!

Well then the night was over, and it was time to say goodbye. So our two friends wanted us to double date with them the next night. We agreed to meet them at Nelson's Pillar the next night at 8 pm. Joan and I debated all next day deciding if we should go or not. Alas, we realised that we could not keep it up for a second night, so we never turned up, but felt ashamed of leaving them waiting.

The following week, we did not go to our usual dance in the Ierne just in case we met them again. So we went around the corner to the National Ballroom. So there we were just settling in when the band started a new set. Out of nowhere, our two friends whisked us on to the floor for a slow dance! Now, we were in a worse predicament because I didn't know if Joan was telling her lad the truth, and she didn't know what I was saying! My lad asked why we didn't turn up. With a serious face I told him that we couldn't find Nelson's Pillar! I was feeling sick worrying what Joan was saying. We met up with them when the music stopped, and much to my relief I heard Joan telling her lad that we got lost! We had one more dance with them, and we then went out to the ladies. We agreed that we couldn't keep it up, and so, discreetly we left. It was a long time before we went dancing again in that area! It was a lesson for us never to tell lies again, and we didn't.

At home, my eldest sister Kathleen, got married when she was nineteen years old. That wasn't unusual as many people got married young in those days. I was fifteen years old at the time and Marie was eighteen. It seemed to me that Kathleen was a rock of sense from very young. She took everything in her stride, and was great at giving advice. Her boyfriend Tommy was a kind lad and very quiet. I would spend hours talking to him at the hall door when Kathleen wasn't home. I loved Elvis at the time, so he got me loads of photos of him. We were all happy when they got married.

They lived in a flat as most couples did when they first got married. But they were told that they would have a better chance of getting a house from the corporation if they lived with us, on the grounds of overcrowding. Six years and three children later they got their house!. While mam and dad were delighted for them, I think deep down they missed them when they moved, especially the grandchildren.

Marie, the second born was more outgoing. She loved a laugh, and she was very popular with the girls and boys. She was a good cook from very young. I clearly remember coming home from mass on Sundays, to a fry up. She just loved to cook. We all had our little jobs to do in the house and we did our best The older ones learned to make 'bread and milk' to feed the younger ones. It was made by breaking up white bread into a cup, adding boiling water straining it when the bread softened, one spoon of sugar, mixed well, then topped off with milk. It was also a comfort food for sick tummies. Many older people called it 'goodie'.

I remember mammy teaching me how to mix arrowroot biscuits, to feed our baby sister Rita. Two biscuits were put into a cup with boiling water, strained when softened, and mushed up with milk. It was the first solid food for babies, following breastfeeding. I used sneak a spoonful myself when mammy wasn't looking!

Marie was always up to mischief. She was the only one of us five girls who smoked. And she started very young, probably about ten years old! I remember one day Mam was gone out somewhere, and Marie was sitting at the fire smoking cigarette ends. She kept asking me to have a go, but I couldn't stand the smell! She laughs now when I remind her of that. I was seven years old and she was ten! In later years she loved to go out enjoying herself, but many times ended up in a row with Daddy for coming home after eleven o'clock.

I think she was fifteen when she started going out with Liam. He was a nice lad the same age as herself. Us smallies, used to love the nights that they went out, as she always brought us home Double Centre sweets. They eventually married when they were both twenty years old. They lived with Liam's parents at first but were lucky to win a house in the 'newlyweds draw'. This was a raffle held every year by the government whereby they gave a house to the first two hundred names picked out of a drum, but they had to be newlyweds.

Meanwhile, I continued to go to college almost every night after work. My whole life revolved around fashion and sewing. I made lots of friends, male and female in college. Boyfriends didn't interest me. But because many of my pals were in relationships, I started to go out on dates. If I liked the lad, I would go on a second or third date, but I never met anyone that I wanted to stay with. That is until September 1964.

Chapter Six

LOVE AND A RAINBOW AROUND THE MOON

I had heard that my childhood best friend's mammy had died. I had never forgotten Connie and frequently wondered how she was, now that we were all grown up. And I remembered her mammy with great fondness. So I decided to visit her. There were very few house phones in those days, so I arrived unexpectedly at their door in Ballyfermot. I was nervous after so many years and wondered would they remember me, as I would have been about eleven years old when I last saw them.

Her dad opened the door and of course, he did not remember me. I asked for Connie, but he said that she was gone out. Just as I was about to walk away, her sister Ann came to the door. 'Are you Betty Foley?' she asked. I laughed and said yes, amazed that she remembered me. ' Come on in' she said, 'Connie will be disappointed that she missed you'. So, in I went and her Dad apologized for not recognizing me. They were so nice to me that night. They made tea and we talked about old times, and in particular about there lovely Mammy who had recently died. As we enquired about each other's family, I asked about Lar. (the shy young lad who hated girls). His dad said that he was fine, but he wished that he would go out more and get himself a girlfriend!

'I keep telling him he won't meet a girl sitting in every night' Just then we heard the front door opening. 'Oh this is him now' said his dad.

So in walked this handsome guy and my heart missed a beat. 'Hello' he said shyly.

His sister Ann asked if he knew who I was. He had no idea, and guessed, 'Are you a cousin?' 'No' Ann said, 'this is Betty Foley'.

I could sense that he felt as I did. And for the rest of the night through hours of conversation, I could feel his eyes on me. At the end of the night, I stood up to catch the last bus home. But his dad insisted that Lar drop me home on his motorbike. I was terrified getting on in my tight skirt, but delighted to have to hold on tight! When we got to my house, we chatted for a while, and he said that he would come over on Tuesday night to bring me back over to see Connie. I went to bed that night with a smile on my face! To see him again on Tuesday meant I had to miss college, so I knew for me to do that, he was special.

Tuesday came, and this time I was more prepared for a motorbike trip. He was on time and my parents were delighted to meet him again after all the years. Mammy was very impressed with him and agreed that indeed he had grown into a handsome young man. I was 19 and a half years old, and he was 21.

Our evening with Connie went great. It was amazing to see her again as a beautiful nineteen year old. We promised never to lose touch with each other again. Lar left me home that night and asked me out on a date. I counted the days to Friday and spent hours getting ready. We went to the cinema and chatted through the whole film! I had a wonderful time and when we got home, he kissed me. This was my first ever kiss. Although I went on lots of dates with other lads, I refused to kiss any one of them. So now I knew that Lar was special.

I was now missing college on Wednesdays and Fridays. I worked extra hard the other nights because there was lots more that I wanted to do in the fashion industry. But I kept Wednesdays, Fridays, and Sundays for Lar. I remember coming up to our first Christmas together, I was invited to an evening of fashion with visiting designers to the college. I put my name down for it, so I told Lar that I would have to miss our Friday date. He was fine with it but said he would miss me. On the evening of the show, I got a bad migraine headache. I couldn't open my eyes it was so bad. So my mam said forget about the show, and go to bed.

About 10oclock that night, the headache lifted and I got up out of bed. I was now sorry that I didn't go. I had a bath and felt better. Next thing a very angry Lar knocked on the door. I was more worried about how I looked with my wet hair etc. at first. Then he told me that he met a girl from college and there was no fashion night on. It took me a while to calm him down, but when I explained that it was by special invitation only, and not everyone was invited, he relaxed. He said that he had paid dear for a watch for Christmas, for me and he wanted to make sure I wasn't two timing him. I was disappointed that he would think bad of me, so after that, I made sure that he knew everything I did when I was not with him.

I told myself that he was a little insecure and needed reassurance.

Meanwhile I went from strength to strength in college and passed every exam with flying colours. The more I succeeded the more Lar, and my parents were proud of me. In April 1965 I won the young dress designer of the year award.

It was an exciting time for me, and I enjoyed all the attention. My picture appeared in the newspaper, and also in 'Futura' fashion magazine. When everything settled, I was offered a very good position in London, in one of the fashion houses. I was flattered to be asked, but I was a home bird, and never seriously considered taking it up, besides, I didn't want to leave Lar. Also I was loyal to the company I worked for (A.G.Ireland Ltd) because I had worked for them from school and they had given me first class training.

Subsequently, I was promoted and life was wonderful, at least for now. A week after I won dress designer of the year, Lar and I got engaged. He had asked me to marry him when we were only two months together, but we decided to wait before buying the ring. It was Easter, and I made a new outfit to meet Lar to buy the ring. I was to learn many years later, that he had borrowed the money for the ring. I felt bad about that, because I was earning good money at the time, nearly twice as much as him. However, I did not have expensive taste, and chose a simple ring that cost £25. That would have been about two and a half weeks wages, for a man back then. I remember feeling strange meeting him on the day of the engagement, because up to then, we never saw each other during the day. We started seeing each other the previous September, and now it was April. We were only together Wednesday, Friday, and Sunday nights each week, so daytime was a strange experience for me! I felt very shy when we met in town, but kept talking, out of nervousness all the way up to the jewellers shop. I chose the ring quickly, studying the price as much as the ring! I bought Lar a ring too, but I was to find out in later years that he hated wearing jewellery. Still, he did wear it for a few years. Anyway, it was Easter Saturday, so he bought me an Easter egg and we got the bus home to my house. We showed everyone the ring, then went into the kitchen and Lar officially placed the ring on my finger, and we kissed. We were blissfully happy that day.

Around the time of our engagement, Lar and his family moved from Ballyfermot to Raheny. His dad worked on the north side of Dublin, and after the death of his mother, it made more sense to move nearer his work. His sister Ann didn't want to go. Indeed she asked me to try talking Lar out of it as she felt that he instigated the whole thing. I talked to him about it but he said the house in Ballyfermot held too many memories. Ann was real disappointed, and the move went ahead.

I think Connie was okay about the move. She was working in town at the time, so distance wise, it made very little difference. She too worked at sewing, but absolutely hated it! I think to this day, she still does.

Ann left school early to keep house and look after her younger brothers, Leonard and Noel. She was a great housekeeper and a great cook. It was hard for her moving in among married couples, when she was only seventeen or eighteen, and at home all day. But she made friends with a nice neighbour next door Mrs. Simpson, who was married with children. She settled in, at least for now.

Connie was also engaged to be married at the time to Brian. They were together from fifteen, so it was a natural progression that they would get married.

They made a lovely couple, fun to be with, and still together to this day.

When the family moved to Raheny, I would occasionally go out to Ann during the day when the college was closed for holidays. I loved going on Tuesdays, because that day Ann always made stew, and that was my favourite dinner. We would chat for hours while Lar was still at work. At that time he worked in a foundry with his dad. One week I thought that I would surprise Lar, so I went out on a Wednesday. Anyway there were no phones at the time so I had no way of telling him I was coming. However, I arrived early, and Ann and I chatted for hours. Just then, Ann looked at her watch, and said , 'O my God look at the time, Lar's dinner won't be ready and he will go mad!' I said ' Ah surely not, I cannot imagine him getting angry over a dinner'. Ann suggested that I hide behind the door when he comes and listen. So, there was I hiding as Lar walked in tired and hungry. I heard Ann say 'Sorry Lar, your dinner is not ready yet' Next thing I hear is a very angry and aggressive voice shouting 'What? Why? Where were you?' I appeared from behind the door and gave him a shock. I was the last thing he expected. His voice softened and he made a joke of the whole situation. We all laughed, but I was to learn in later years that this was a glimpse of what was to come.

Our courtship continued in blissful harmony. We had so much in common, and we seemed to want the same things in life. We talked about marriage and children. We wanted lots of them and in our fantasy world, we could see ourselves living happily ever after. In those days there was no sex before marriage. So I was one of the 'good girls' refusing anything more than kissing, and Lar respected me for that. Besides my mother and father kept a close eye on us and sent him home at eleven after every date, yelling at us the minute the clock touched eleven.

We still went to the cinema on Wednesdays, Fridays and Sundays. We had a similar sense of humour and saw the funny side of everything. I remember one night we were walking home from our local cinema (the Apollo in Walkinstown). There was a drunken man standing, looking up at the sky, talking to himself. He called us over, while pointing to the sky. 'Look', he said pointing at the full moon, 'You will never see the likes of this again, see? There is a rainbow around the moon!' Of course we couldn't see any rainbow, but in his drunken haze, he obviously did! How we laughed that night. After that, every time there was a full moon, we would say 'There's a rainbow around the moon'. Even throughout our married life, if there was a full moon out when Lar was coming home from work, he would announce it when he came in 'There's a rainbow around the moon tonight!' Alas, over twenty years later, I would write in my diary;

"One time before the bitter snows
Life was oh! So easy then
How proud you were to be with me
But life was oh! So easy then
Young and fresh the world was mine
My dream was yours and love divine
An evening walk, a summer rose
Long before the bitter snows
The happiness you gave me then
Was equal only to the sun
But ripples on an ebbing tide
Creeps away from everyone
Starry-eyed we looked at life
But bitter snows came too soon
For now I know that as a wife
There is no rainbow around the moon".

Chapter Seven
LOVE AND MARRIAGE

We decided to set the wedding day for February 19th 1966, but Mammy talked me into waiting until May. So we changed it to Saturday, May 21st. We had to start saving hard as our parents were in no position to help us. Also, we did not know where we were going to live. Not many young couples could afford houses back then. Besides, the mortgage was given on the strength of the husbands wages only. The wife wasn't expected to work after marriage. Indeed, at that time it was unusual to do so, unless you were widowed. At that time, Lar got work in Rentel, a company that rented out televisions and erected aerials on roofs. His wages improved, as he was never afraid of hard work, and he had no fear of heights. Sometimes he was allowed keep the van home if he was working late. I was in awe of his expert driving skills. He had been in the British Army, and learned to drive properly. He loved his motor bike, but two months before our wedding it was stolen from outside of my house while we were at the cinema. He was heartbroken because he only had third party insurance on it. Also, he had bought it on hire purchase and it was a long way from being paid off. It was a lesson to both of us, and we made a vow that when we got married, we would never get anything on hire purchase.

He gave me money to put in the bank every week for our wedding and made me promise that I would only put in the same amount to keep things fair. I did what he asked, so the 'marriage money' was equally 'ours'.

My twenty first birthday was four months before our wedding. Lar asked me what would I like for a present, and being the practical person that I am, I asked for a hairdryer. So that's what I got. But Lar told me this story afterwards.

He went shopping on his own to buy it. He was walking down Capel Street when he saw some nice ones in a window. So in he went, and asked the assistant how much they were. " Four

Books" she said. Lar thought she said four bucks, (American style) so asked her 'How much is that in Irish money?'
The girl replied 'Four books of green shield stamps!' He was in a Green Shield stamp shop! They were very popular here in the sixties and seventies, but because Lar had been living away for a few years, he had never heard of them. How we laughed every time we recalled that story.

We talked endlessly of our forthcoming marriage. In fact many times in the cinema people would turn around and say 'SHHHHH' We would giggle and keep quiet for another few minutes! Looking back, it seems that there was always a rainbow around the moon in those days. We were madly in love and thought it would never end......

My sister Marie offered to let us live with her and Liam, in the small maisonette that they won in the newlyweds draw, and we accepted.

We decided to have our wedding reception at my home, as did my sisters Kathleen and Marie before me. I enjoyed making all the dresses for the occasion . My sisters Joan and Rita were to be my bridesmaids, and Lar's pal Shamie Keating best man, with my cousin Richard Kelly as groomsman.

We were to be married at eleven o'clock, and so I was awake at six. I began to feel very nervous, and my stomach turned over! My sister Marie held me over the sink as I vomited my guts up! She tried in vain to get 'milk of magnesia' down my throat. I never said a word to anyone, but I realised that I was getting married to someone that I didn't know well enough. I remember thinking to myself, that for the year and eight months that we were together, we mostly only saw each other three nights a week! And only occasionally, during the day. I had never seen Lar in swimming togs, or even without his shirt! Also, he had never seen me in a swim suit. All these things frightened me on this, our wedding day. I was nervous too about sleeping with him for the first time.

However, I bravely faced the day with a smile on my face, and hope in my heart. We were to be married at 11 o'clock that morning, but Lar was late arriving to the church. Apparently, there were road works, and the taxi driver got lost! Luckily, I lived across the road from the church and I didn't leave until I saw him arrive.

My Daddy joked with me all the way, to keep me smiling. Having all daughters, he joked about wearing out the steps of the church giving us all away! So, nervous but smiling I walked down the aisle with dad. My soon-to-be sister-in-law and best friend Connie, turned around as I passed and whispered 'You look beautiful'! I have never told her how much that meant to me. It was so reassuring, when I was feeling so fragile.

Lar smiled, looking equally nervous, but happy. Fr. Rochford conducted the service, and as it went on, I began to feel very special. After we exchanged our vows, The priest said prayers for us. There is one line that stuck in my mind at the time, and still does today. He said ' May you live to see your children's children'. I remember thinking at the time that it was two lifetimes away! But many years later I stood outside the labour ward as my daughter gave birth to my first grandchild, those words kept coming back. So, thank god, I did live to see my 'children's children' but like I said, that was two lifetimes away!.

The reception in my parents house went well. My godmother Aunty Kathleen along with my Aunty Maisie helped Mam prepare the food. Daddy wished us well in his speech, and joked to Lar that it wasn't too late to change his mind, he would give him a note for the priest! Daddy was a real joker and kept us amused throughout the day.

We hired a little cottage in Courtown Co. Wexford for our honeymoon. The plan was, that we would catch the six o'clock train from Westland Row that evening. The taxi came on time to take us there, but when we got as far as Dolphin's Barn Lar realised that he forgot his guitar, so back we went for it. That's when I realised for the first time, how much his guitar meant to him. It was very awkward going back, as it was only 15 minutes since our tearful goodbyes!

At last we were on the train sitting facing each other, chatting and reflecting on our day. In quieter moments, I was scared of what lay ahead. When I think of the way it is to-day with young couples, I smile at my innocence. Anyway we arrived at our little cottage at about nine thirty. We had a good look around and found a beautiful bedroom up a riccady stairs. There was no bathroom and the toilet was out in the back yard. The kitchen was more like a small scullery, with a table and two chairs. We made tea, laughed and sang with Lar playing the guitar. Finally we couldn't put it off any longer, it was bedtime. Neither of us drank that day to keep it special, but we weren't drinkers anyway, at least I wasn't and Lar took an odd pint of guinness. Lar suggested that I go up first and call him when I was in bed. So, looking all sweet and innocent, I called him. I remember him telling me how beautiful I looked, as I turned my head while he got undressed. We just hugged each other and kissed for most of the night, nothing more.

He was clumsy, and I was tense and terrified. Finally, we fell asleep in each other's arms. About 3 o'clock in the morning I was awkened by Lar sitting up and shouting "Daddy Daddy there's blood everywhere!" I jumped out of bed looking for a light switch in the black dark. When I turned on the light, I realised that Lar was fast asleep! When I woke him, he had no recollection of what just happened, nor did he recall a bad dream. Then I remembered, his sisters, Connie and Ann had told me that they used to stand outside his bedroom door and giggle at what he used to say in his sleep. This provided much entertainment for the years that followed!

Anyway the next morning, I woke before him. I grabbed my clothes and ran down to the toilet in the back yard. I quickly dressed myself, and put on my makeup before going back in and making breakfast. When he got up, there was I, the dutiful wife smiling and making breakfast. I had never cooked before but I made a good attempt and besides, I thought this was the way it was suppose to be.

We had fun on our ten days 'honeymoon' but alas, our nights and mornings remained the same. I came home from Wexford, still a virgin. We were too shy with each other to talk about it, but we knew it wasn't right. It continued at home for six more weeks, with me, still running to the toilet to get dressed every morning.

Finally, Lar got frustrated, and said, 'How are we going to get anywhere if you won't even get undressed in front of me?'. I knew he was right, but I was so shy that I couldn't even look at my own naked body. So that night, I shyly undressed in front of him, not naked, but down to my underwear. I was afraid of what he might think of my body. But Lar was so kind and gentle that I began to relax. Unfortunately , I wasn't relaxed enough to go all the way. So, I remained a virgin for two more weeks before we were successful.

It happened the night Connie and Brian got married. I found it painful at first, but with practise, over the next few weeks, we got better. Finally, everything was wonderful again. The courtship that we didn't have, was now in full swing. We were blissfully happy and we were going to love each other forever. In my youthful innocence I had no idea that there was an end to forever...........

We lived with my sister Marie, for six months before moving to a bedsit on Walkinstown Road. After two months we moved again, to a three room flat on St. Joseph's Road in Walkinstown. I had, like most wives back then, given up my job when I got married. But after staying home for six months longing for babies, I soon got bored and went back to work. I was now earning the princely sum of £16 a week which was big wages at that time for a woman. Lar's wages was £10 a week but he did a lot of "nixers" erecting television aerials to supplement his income. So, we were now in a position to save for a house.

Lar was a pessimist, and could never see himself owning a house. He had very little confidence in his ability. Besides none of our friends or relations had bought a house, he thought that applying to the corporation was the only way. I, on the other hand am an eternal optimist! Even at the tender age of twenty one and he was twenty three I took control of the money, putting all spare cash in the credit union.

Meanwhile, we bought our first car. It was an eight-year-old mini, pale blue in colour registration number, EZA 937. Of all the cars we bought after that, this is the only registration number that I remember, because I thought it was specially for me (Elizabeth). But then, there was still a 'rainbow around the moon' at that time. Lar didn't drink or smoke back then and I was glad, because I hated smoking and drinking terrified me. But I remember one Friday night, his sister Ann visited us in our flat. Lar wasn't home yet so she said that she would stay until he came home.

Finally he arrives home three hours later, drunk. I was embarrassed and Ann, like me was disgusted with him. He laughed foolishly, and fell around the place. Ann tried talking to him, but I was soon to learn that there is no point trying to reason with a drunken man. Eventually Ann had to leave to get two busses home. Before she left she called me aside and whispered 'He gave me this, but I'm sure it was meant for you'. She handed me his weeks wages, still in the envelope except for what he had drank. I was very angry with him the next day when he sobered up. We had our first row. I told him that I would not tolerate such bad behaviour again. He told me in no uncertain terms to loosen up!. I remember feeling hurt and disappointed over the whole episode.

But we were still madly in love , so it blew over and I forgot about it.

In the sixties in Ireland, on the music scene, there was a ballad boom. We both loved music, so we went to all the ballad sessions. It was about this time that we changed our car for a four-year-old beetle. Lar suggested that he teach me to drive. I was nervous, but he kept on at me to give it a go. His words to me at the time were 'You should learn because you never know in years to come you might need to be able to drive'. How prophetic those words were in the years that followed. So I did learn, from the master! He had the most rigorous driving tuition in the army, and taught them to me. I learned quickly, and within a couple of months, I was on the road. We went to all the music sessions, sometimes with friends, and sometimes on our own. I always drove home, because Lar would have a few drinks on him. The drink driving laws weren't out then, but I drove because I was nervous when Lar had a few drinks. Even though he kept reassuring me that he was quite capable, I still refused to let him drive. When we were out with friends or relations, I drove them home too.

Some of the time, we would have a sing-song in the car on the way home, with me, the only sober one. When we came home, I would make supper, and then we went to bed. We would laugh, chat, make love if he wasn't too drunk then fall asleep in each others arms. Oh! Life was wonderful then.

We nearly had enough money for a deposit for a house, so we started to look around. We both wanted to live in Walkinstown, but it had to be a new house to avail of the housing grant. With the price of houses at that time, we needed the grant, to keep within our budget. There were new houses under construction in Greenhills, Walkinstown, so we tried to get one, but they were all booked out.

A couple of weeks later we were driving down Parkgate Street in Dublin, when Lar said to me, 'There's Brid Cotter, she is married to my cousin Pat. I asked him to stop the car, as I had not met any of his relations. Brid was so warm and friendly to us, and she invited us for dinner the following night.

When we arrived for dinner, we were made so welcome by Brid and Pat. We had a great night chatting away. Then in conversation, we talked about trying to buy a new house in Walkinstown, but they were booked out. Pat said that he played golf with the guy that was building those houses, so he would ask for us. Just then he looked at his watch and said 'As a matter of fact, I might catch him now, as there is a crubeen (pigs feet) night at the golf club, and he will be there'. He left in a hurry, and was back within the hour and, not only did we have our house, but we had a choice of location! I could not believe the kindness of these people who would put themselves out for us. We were to become life long friends.

Chapter Eight
OUR NEW HOUSE

Our new house was just around the corner from where our flat was, so we watched almost every brick that went up! In fact we took many photographs of the house under construction. Finally it was completed in September, 1968. Lar borrowed a van from my uncle Peter and we moved in. We were so excited with our new house, and we didn't mind having such a few items of furniture. We stuck to our promise, never to buy anything on hire purchase and so we had a lot of empty rooms. We were only two years married and already we had worn out two beds! The one we had on moving, had three legs! You can imagine our delight when a brand new one was delivered as a present from Pat and Brid. They were such kind people that we were at a loss of how to thank them.

Indeed, a few weeks later we went into business together manufacturing ladies clothing. We named the business Paula Fashions after Brid's beautiful daughter Paula. Pat put a lot of money into it to get it off the ground. Lar left his job and came into the business too. In the first year, we struggled but we all got a wage out of it. Getting decent staff was difficult, but eventually we got eight or ten reliable girls. There were another three pals, only one of whom was any good. But we had to keep the other two, as the good one would leave if we let the two useless ones go! The second year was much the same as the first, as far as money was concerned. We were busy but we didn't seem to be making much more money. Pat felt it was going nowhere and wanted out. Where as we wanted to keep going because we had no family and therefore, no responsibilities.

So, our lovely friends, Brid and Pat allowed us to keep the business with a small financial settlement to be paid over twelve months. After that we continued to work hard at the business, making lots more new friends along the way.

Our staff increased, and we also used homeworkers. Even Connie who hated sewing, helped us out! We were now busier than ever, making friends with Ben Dunne senior, the founder of Dunnes Stores. Lar met with him and his daughters Therese and Elizabeth regularly either in Stephen's Street or at Paula Fashions. We had a good social life too. Lar had been in a ballad group The Wild Geese during the first year of our marriage, and we made friends with the banjo player Paddy and his girlfriend Ann, now wife. They visited us regularly and we had many a good music session in our house. Lar's Dad loved coming with us every Saturday night to the ballad sessions. I loved when he came with us, especially if he stayed over night . He, along with Lar would have a good few drinks, so I would drive home. I have fond memories of him sitting in the back of the car, 'well on' saying 'You're a great girl Beth', Lar is very lucky to have you!'.

He was a wonderful man who had a hard life, but just got on with it. Meanwhile we were trying to furnish our house without getting into debt. I still managed the money, saving as much as we could. Lar became brilliant at D.I.Y But in the beginning he wasn't very good. He had no confidence in his ability at all. However I encouraged him, praising every effort he made. Eventually, we were able to furnish all the rooms in the house. We thought we were great. Life was still wonderful. We socialized a lot but enjoyed our nights in as well. On winter nights, we had fun lying on the rug in front of a cosy fire, watching telly, among other things! Oh yes, there was still a rainbow around the moon! We made friends with another manufacturer Mrs. Melia, from Leedel Modes One day we were in Francis Street visiting her, when a friend of hers called. The friend was a guy our age who drove an oil tanker for a leading oil company. He had the oil tanker parked outside and he was talking to Lar. Of course Lar was real impressed. He knew that he was an excellent driver (and he was) and this is what he wanted to do. Later after we left, he said that it was always his ambition to drive an oil tanker. For the first time he admitted to me that he hated working with women! His feelings coincided with the fact that I now wanted babies. We both loved children and wondered why all our friends were having babies while we had none, in spite of trying every morning and night! It was now coming up to Christmas1969. We made a decision that after Christmas, we would have investigations, as to why I was not getting pregnant. And also, Lar would apply for a job in the oil company. As it happens, our factory was broken into during the Christmas holidays. There was quite a bit of damage, and all my new children's samples were stolen. We made up our mind there and then to sell the business. We did not claim from the insurance, because we didn't realise that we could! I realise now that we had no business sense at all! We were paying big premiums every year, but it never occurred to us that this is what it was for.

So, early in 1970, when we wound up the business, we did what we promised. I made an appointment with a gynaecologist. Lar hated writing letters, so I wrote his application for the oil company. Weeks went by, and it was March by the time I was taken into hospital for investigations. As luck would have it, Lar got an interview at the same time that I was in hospital. I remember the disappointed look on his face when he came to visit me that night. 'I had the job', he said 'until they looked at my licence'. Seemingly, as Lar learned how to drive in Germany, when he renewed his licence here, they stamped visitor on it. At that time there was no EEC agreement, on European driving licences. I tried consoling him but he felt that he had lost his chance. I vowed, when I got out of hospital, that I would move heaven and earth to fix his licence, and get back on the company's books. The only way out of the driving licence situation, was to do a new driving test. It ended up that he had to do two tests, one for the car, and one for the truck. He passed the one for the car, but he said it would cost too much for to do the truck test as he would have to hire out a truck. Meanwhile, we were finding it hard to sell the business as a going concern. So we gave back the key to the landlord, and sold the contents separately. We lost money because we had to sell quickly to vacate the premises. Lar picked up a truck driving job. The wages weren't good but as he didn't have the right licence, he had to accept it. I was at home all day so I started dressmaking again. When we saved another bit, I kept pushing him to do the truck test. Eventually, to shut me up he did it. He passed like I knew he would. I applied again to the oil company for him. But there were no vacancies at that time. He was real disappointed. But we had something else to look forward to. We had decided that if nothing came of the investigations into our childlessness, that we would adopt a baby. We both loved children so, to us it was the most natural thing to do. Besides, my sister Marie had adopted two gorgeous little boys and we were real impressed!

Chapter Nine
OUR FIRST BABY

Sometime during April 1970, we applied to the R.G.A.S, here in Dublin for our baby. In those days there was a choice of a girl or boy. We chose a girl. We were put through many hours of interviews by a social worker, and also a nice priest Fr. O'Neill. We also had to supply references from people who knew us, and our local parish priest. Less than a month later, we got a call from Fr. O'Neill to say he had a baby girl for us, and we could collect her the next day!

Oh! the excitement. I was so sick with excitement that you would think I was going into labour! But wait! I had no baby clothes! We didn't expect to hear from them that quick so we had very little prepared. I went shopping like mad grabbing everything I could in the short space of time. I had to borrow a carry cot. How sorry I was that I didn't get things sooner, but anyway everything worked out well. We were to arrive at 7 o'clock with a set of clothes. Of course I chose pink. I had pink dress, cardigan, frilly pants, socks, blanket and booties. The only white thing I had was a nappy!

We were both nervous when we got to Temple hill in Blackrock. The front of the hospital was like a big rambling house. Inside the floors were so shiny that you could see yourself walking. A nice but very efficient nun greeted us. When we identified ourselves, she took the clothes and disappeared into another room. She never told us to sit down, so we stood on the spot, waiting anxiously, watching the door. After about 15 minutes the nun came back with our first daughter. She placed her in my arms, and we were both overcome with emotion. She was a beautiful baby, with big blue eyes and dark hair. The nun was talking to me and giving me information on her feeds, but I didn't hear a thing. I could not take my eyes off this little miracle in my arms. I felt that this was so right and that already she was a part of me. Lar also bonded instantly. We proudly walked out of the door as a family! We got into our old beetle and drove around the corner where it was safe to pull in. We then opened up the blankets and marvelled at every tiny finger and toe. She looked at us from one to the other, smiled, then put her thumb in her mouth and cuddled in to me. She was three months old.

When we were choosing a name for her I liked the name Valerie. I did not tell Lar because I wanted to hear what he liked. I couldn't believe it when he also said Valerie. So we named her Valerie Mary. She had been already christened Mary by the nuns, so it was only right that we left Mary in her name.

When we got home, all our friends and relations were there to see our new daughter. There was great excitement in the house, but we were both delighted when everyone left and we had her all to ourselves! The feelings we had could not be described with mere words. This was special, and we would live happy-ever-after with rainbows around the moon.............

This was a new chapter in our lives as parents. We were loving every minute of it. Meanwhile, I continued to send in applications to the oil company for Lar. He told me to give up, that I was wasting my time, but all the 'not at the moment' letters would not put me off. Finally, in November of 1970, the letter we were waiting for came. This time he sailed through the interview, having the right licence now. So began another chapter in his life, the career he had always wanted.

I continued to take in dressmaking, but only sewed when Valerie was in bed. Still, I earned good money, and with Lar's job, we were doing well financially. My sister Joan babysat every Saturday night, so we still went to the music sessions once a week. We soon made friends with another worker and his wife, Sean and Áine. We became close friends as we were both young, and married with one daughter. We had a lot in common and loved a laugh.

By now the ballad boom was declining in Ireland, and was slowly taken over by the cabaret scene. But we continued to have our one night out a week, either with Sean and Áine, or Granda Swords. I loved being with Lar's dad. He was great company. Very often he would sleep over much to the delight of Valerie, who, like me adored him. We would stay up late chatting, laughing, and talking about the old days. Sean and Áine and their daughter Katy, visited us once a week. Katy and Valerie were good friends. Lar and Sean would go to the local pub, while Áine and I made supper as the children played. Áine was a hairdresser, so sometimes she would give me a new hairdɔ in return for dressmaking. Life was still wonderful.................

My mammy developed Rheumatoid Arthritis when she was 36 years-old. I remember she was in constant pain. Over the years she gradually got worse, and by the time Valerie came along, she was struggling to walk with a stick. I called into to her a few times a week with Valerie. She was on her own at that time while daddy was in work. It was heartbreaking to see her in so much pain.

When Valerie was three years-old I was to find out just how painful Rheumatoid Arthritis really was. My index finger was swollen and very sore. I thought it might be a splinter so I had Lar examine it under a magnifying glass. He couldn't see a thing, so with great difficulty I continued on for weeks. Then Valerie got measles, so I called the doctor. After ten days she recovered, and I brought her to the doctors surgery for a final check up. She got the all clear so before I left, I asked the doctor to look at my finger. He studied it, bending it in all directions while I squirmed in pain. Finally he asked if anyone in my family had Rheumatoid Arthritis. I was shocked as I replied yes, my mam has, but she is 54 years old! I am only 28! But then I remembered that she was 36 years old when she was diagnosed. The doctor told me that even small children get it, so he had to send me to a specialist, to confirm.

I felt shattered when I got home. Lar too was upset. This was indeed a sad day. Next day I visited mam, and told her the bad news. I looked at her pained face and thought, is this what's ahead of me? But she was so re-assuring and said, 'Don't worry, they will find a cure for it in your lifetime'.

Two weeks later it was confirmed. By now all my joints were hurting. Lar cried when he heard the news. He thought I was going to die. He remembered when he was small, he was told his mother had arthritis, when in fact, she had multiple sclerosis. But in his head, it was all the same thing.

It was hard for me to come to terms with it, but worse trying to console him. I desperately tried to hide the pain, but it was written all over my face. The hospital prescribed gold injections. So off I went to the rheumatology clinic in Mount Street Dublin, the same clinic that I went with my Mammy when I was ten years old. That is when she started on the gold.

Ordinary everyday things became difficult. My fingers were stiff and I could not grip very well. My knees and feet equally as bad. I had trouble with shoes. My whole world was falling apart, and Lar was in deep depression. Oddly enough, I could sit at my sewing machine and still sew! But I was still in pain. I struggled through every day but tried to continue as much as normal. We still went out every Saturday night, most of the time in pain. After six months the gold began to give me a bit of relief. But it made no difference to Lar. He was still depressed. He would go along for weeks in great form, but then he would have black moods. I knew nothing about depression at the time and didn't know what to do. His sister Connie, was always very close to him so I hoped that he would talk to her about how he was feeling, but he refused. He wouldn't go to the doctor and so, I was at a loss. Eventually, I confided in Connie. She was great. Without telling him that I told her, she brought up the conversation about depression in general, and got him talking about it. After that he went to our family doctor who prescribed medication for a while, so we got on with our lives and made the best of it.

Meanwhile I broke out in a rash from the gold injections and had to be taken off them. They tried a new drug that worked as well as the gold, at least for now.Valerie started school in September 1974. On her first day I was feeling very emotional looking at her in her little uniform. I held her hand and we bravely walked to school together. When we got there, mothers were crying, children were crying, and teachers were sighing! Valerie seemed happy, so I was determined not to be one of those crying mothers! So I kissed her goodbye and wandered home alone . I made a cup of tea, and turned on the Gay Byrne show. 'Now' he said, 'For all those mothers leaving their offspring to school for the first time this morning, I would like to read this poem by John D. Sheridan'. Then he read it. It was about your child's first day at school, letting go the little hand etc. Well before he got to the end of the poem, I was in floods of tears! Damn you Gay Byrne! I was doing well up to now!

I ended up watching the clock, and counting the hours. Like an eejit, I was the first mammy waiting outside the school, an hour before they were due out! I gave her the biggest hug ever when I saw her. This was a new chapter in her life.

Valerie loved school, from day one. The teachers in St. Paul's National school, in Walkinstown were lovely. The head nun's name was Mother Claude. Valerie thought it was Mother Cloth! One day we were walking to my Mammy's house when we saw two nuns on bikes. Valerie said 'Oh look, there's two Mother Cloths!!!'

Oh what happy memories. She was a happy child, always chatting , and playing with her dolls. She had a favourite teddy bear, that went everywhere with her, especially to bed. One day, she was out playing with her friends, as I was cleaning the knobs and knockers on the front door. She was wheeling teddy in her little pram when quite suddenly, there was a downpour of heavy rain. I ran out to get her and as I approached, she had her coat off to put over teddy so that he wouldn't get wet! This memory sums up the kind of child she was, caring, loving, and a willingness to help others. Teddy is still alive and well, living with Valerie, now age forty plus!

During her first year in school, Lar and I talked about more children. I went back to the hospital for more investigations. Lar was also tested. Finally the doctor told me that it was unlikely that we would have children. I was heartbroken, but I kept my feelings to myself, accepting that it was just one of those things that happened in nature.

Chapter Ten
CUDDLES, OUR SECOND BABY

In April of 1975, we decided to adopt another baby. Lar was still having black moods from time to time, but I was coping better with them now.
We went back to the R.G.A.S. and made our application. Two weeks later a social worker made an appointment to call out to our house. I was on edge, because Lar was in a mood all day. No amount of talking to him helped. My heart was in my mouth as I opened the door. In walked a very young social worker. We were now 30 and 32 years old, and the social worker looked about 21!
All of a sudden, Lar's mood changed as he stood up to greet her. He is normally very shy, but he was in great form now, much to my relief! The social worker could see that we were good parents , and that we loved children. We were asked once again to choose a boy or girl. We had already decided on another girl.
Later, when the social worker left, I confronted Lar about his change of mood when she arrived. He couldn't explain it. I was very annoyed with him and took it personal. I could not under stand how he had one mood for her and a different one for me. Clearly I had a lot more to learn about depression.........
However, two weeks later, on May 17th 1975 all three of us went to collect our new baby, whom we decided to call Pamela. This time we were to collect her from the office of the R.G.A.S. beside the Pro Cathedral in Marlboro Street in Dublin. It was just as exciting as when we were collecting Valerie, but this time Val was with us.
Nervously we sat in the waiting room, waiting. The social worker told us that she wasn't here yet, because the evening traffic was heavy. Then she told us a little bit about Pamela's biological parents. We weren't expecting this as we were told nothing about Valerie's. Lar wasn't listening, clearly he didn't

want to know. I suppose I didn't either, but out of courtesy I listened.

She said that the girl was very young, the boy was older, and they were still together but they felt that this was the right thing to do.

I felt a bit uneasy, but put it to the back of my mind, as we waited in anticipation. Finally, after half an hour our Pamela came into our lives. As I held her in my armsI got that that same overwhelming feeling that I got with Valerie. Yet again I knew that she was part of me. I felt the bond immediately, as did Lar and Valerie. This was indeed another beautiful moment, that would stay with me forever.

She was so tiny and cuddly that Lar nick named her 'Cuddles'. We had all the friends and neighbours in again like before but this time, I was better prepared, with everything ready. After everyone left, Lar walked around with her in his arms and much to the frustration of Valerie, he wouldn't, let anyone else hold her. I had to laugh when she said to me 'Ah Mammy, he won't give us a go!'.

And so began a close bond between Lar and Pamela that was to last over thirty years, one that I thought could never be broken...........

But for now, in spite of his depression, and my never ending pain, life was still wonderful. Yes, there was still a rainbow around the moon!

Pamela was a joy to look after, and even at five years old, Valerie was like a little mother to her. We were a close, happy family.

Lar worked long hours, so any spare time he had was spent with the children. I still liked to sew, when the children were in bed. Besides, the money was good for our growing family. We continued to go out to the music sessions every Saturday night, sometimes with Sean and Áine, other times with Granda Swords. We now had a new trusted baby sitter, as my sister Joan and Noel were now married with children.

Every Tuesday, Joan and I went to swimming lessons. I found the swimming helped the pain of the arthritis. The pain was getting worse, along with the stiffness, and an incredible tiredness. But

I battled on, refusing to let it get the better of me. I tried to continue doing what I had always done.

I remember one time on our night out, Lar wanted to see a folk group that he liked, in a pub in Aungier Street. We had never been to that pub before, and so, when we arrived and saw that it was up a large flight of steep stairs, I knew I wouldn't make it. But Lar really wanted to see this group, so he lifted me up in his arms and carried me up. I laughed and made a joke about it afterwards when telling my friends. But if I was to be honest, I thought Lar would have just gone somewhere else that would have been more comfortable for me.

I began to notice that on our nights out, we always went to where he wanted to go. I was in so much pain that I would have sat anywhere. The first thing I would do when we went into a pub, was check how far of a walk it was to the toilet. Many a night I held on to a full bladder rather than make that walk! Yet I was always able to drive home, much to his relief because now he had a job that required a clean licence. I think Lar enjoyed having the children all to himself on Tuesday nights when I went out with Joan. I would leave them in their pyjamas, ready for bed. He kept them up late and spoiled them. They loved Daddy, and would squeal with delight when he came home from work!

The swimming lessons were going so well that Joan and I decided to try another swimming pool. We went to the Burlington Hotel where they had a beautiful pool and leisure centre. So we made that our weekly session. We had never seen a sauna before, so each week we would promise ourselves that we would give it a try. The weeks went by before we had the courage to venture in! So in we went with our swimming costumes, swimming cap, and Joan, being short sighted left her glasses on! At first we were met with a burst of steam, so couldn't quite make out what we were supposed to do. Next thing we saw two young ladies lying naked on the bench!

We, in our innocence were totally shocked. They were spread out like nude models with their hair cascading down there backs! Clearly Joan and I had never seen the likes of this before.

In our confusion, we didn't realise that we were standing there holding the door open. Next thing one of the nude ladies yelled. 'Will you make up your mind and come in or out!' With fright we went in. Picture the scene, us sitting on the edge of the bench with our caps and costumes on and Joan constantly wiping the steam off of her glasses! I think we stayed for three or four minutes, then graciously left! Oh the innocence of it all. It was all too much for two convent educated girls! But that story has provided us with many a laugh since.

Another night we were in the pool on our own as no one turned up that night. After our swim we were alone in the dressing room drying ourselves, when in marched a tall skinny guy. We grabbed our towels and screamed with all our might. When we stopped to catch our breath the guy said 'What is wrong with you, why are you screaming?' It was only then we realised that the guy was in fact a girl! We didn't have the heart to tell her that we thought she was a guy, so we just apologised.

In September of 1975, we were swimming again, when I remarked to Joan that my swimming costume had shrunk. 'It must be that chlorine in the water', I said. Joan laughed and said 'Maybe you are pregnant'. I laughed with her knowing that deep down that it was impossible.

The following week, I realised that I was ten days late with my periods. At first I would not say anything to Lar, because I knew he would be so disappointed with a let down. But I eventually told him that I had an appointment with the Coombe hospital to investigate.

When I saw Dr. Greene, he was more surprised than I was. Remember this is the doctor that told me that as a couple, we had no chance of conceiving.

I brought a urine sample with me. In those days there were no magic tests that you could do at home. You had to leave a sample, and wait a few days.

However, Dr. Greene asked could I wait an hour, and he would get the lab to do the test urgently. After what seemed like forever, the test came back positive. The doctor gave me a big hug, and I just cried and cried and cried.......

Lar was delighted when I told him, and he couldn't wait to tell everyone. I looked at my beautiful Pamela who was only seven months old, and I thought this was wonderful. Two babies, and by then Valerie would be six years old. Life was perfect just then, and the bonus was, that the rheumatoid arthritis left me for the whole nine months!.

In October I realised that we hadn't heard from the adoption board about signing the final papers for Pamela. My sister Marie advised me not to tell them that I was now pregnant, in case it delayed things so I rang the social worker and asked about the delay.

She told me that this was a most unusual case. Apparently, the couple were still together. I was to learn thirty years later that they had got married six weeks after Pamela was born! And also she was pregnant again.

She said that Fr. O'Neill had travelled to the South of Ireland to speak to them again, making sure that this is what they wanted to do. I shook when I put the phone down. I never expected this. What if they took her back? I looked at my baby in disbelief. She was sitting in her baby chair with Valerie chatting to her. Clearly Valerie adored her little sister. I wouldn't allow myself think about it. And yet all sorts of scenarios came into my head. How could I explain it to a five year old? No! No! No! it wasn't going to happen. Like Valerie, Pamela was now a part of me. A part that I wouldn't let go. Lar refused to talk about it. Cuddles was his and he wasn't letting her go either. Our days and nights were focused on only the one thing. I had forgotten about my pregnancy for now. I had many sleepless nights, as did Lar.

What if? was going round in my brain day and night. Would God be that cruel to us?

Finally we got a letter to sign the legal papers on November 12th. Oh! The relief! But I was still holding my breath until the day came.

Excitedly we set out for the adoption board premises in Merrion Square Dublin I had knit Pam a lemon dress for the occasion, and made Valerie a pink one. We were ushered in to a room with a large table and about four people sitting at it. They made general conversation first, chatted to Valerie, then got down to the business in hand. We signed with the biggest smile on our faces. Valerie was smiling too. It would be many years before she would hear the story of the what happened in the weeks leading up to this day.

The very next day, on Friday the 13th. disaster happened. I started to bleed, and was taken into hospital with a threatened miscarriage! What was God doing to me? He knows how much we love children, so what is He thinking of?

Besides, we now had to have our beautiful children minded while I was in hospital. Dr. Greene insisted on a months bed rest. So my lovely neighbours, Evelyn and Peter Maguire took Valerie and my sister Marie, took Pamela. I was heartbroken being separated from the children. I made all sorts of promises to the doctor about resting at home, but to no avail.

I knew they were well looked after and Lar saw them everyday, but the hospital only allowed me out of the bed once a week to go down stairs to see them. I think I cried for them every day while I was in, and the time went so slow.

Four weeks later, I was home and feeling great. I had no arthritis pain, and in my ignorance thought it was gone forever. I loved being back in full swing as a wife and mother. I walked to the school every day wheeling Pamela, with Valerie in tow. Valerie was still loving school and made lots of new friends. I made friends too with many of the mothers. One day I was talking to another mother with a pram. We were comparing babies, ages, etc. when she asked me what road I lived on. I told her St Bridgets Drive, and she said 'I will be knocking on your door this afternoon with my collection box'. I asked what she was collecting for. She told me that it was for the Spina Bifida Association, and that her baby in the pram had it. I had never heard of it and asked her all about it. I looked at her baby again but couldn't see any thing different than normal. She was just a beautiful smiling baby to me!

However, we met every day at the school and became friends. Christmas came and went, and I started to put on weight. I thought I looked beautiful the fatter I got. I bought every book

I could get my hands on including ones on breastfeeding. I had waited almost ten years for this, so I wasn't going to miss out on anything!

I made lots of nice maternity tops so that I looked my best. Lar never passed comment on how I looked, good or bad. I had a feeling that he didn't like the look of me, but I refused to let it bother me. Besides he was still depressed from time to time so I felt his focus was on himself.

I would spend long hours after the children were gone to bed, just talking to him. He would go over his childhood over and over again. I tried encouraging him to look forward rather than back. Sometimes he felt much better after our chats, so he would be alright for another while. But in my opinion, he couldn't let go of his childhood.

One day he came home from work feeling terrible. He sat down for dinner and said he was very depressed. My heart ached for him, but I tried to be cheerful and talk him through it, but most of all I listened, so that he could get it out of his system, at least for now. He said that he felt like his head was going to explode. He also said that he didn't know how he got through the day. As I listened, I prayed to God that I would say the right thing to comfort him. After an hour, he was exhausted, so he took one of the tablets the doctor gave him weeks before, and went to bed.

The next day he was up early for work, like nothing had happened. He gave Pamela her bottle, like he always did, and kissed me goodbye. I asked if he was feeling better and he just said, yes, much better.

He was in good form for a while after that episode, so I thought he was over the worse. Meanwhile we were busy making plans for our new arrival. We talked about names as you do, but we couldn't agree on anything. If it was a boy I wanted to call him Laurence after him. He would not agree to it at all. For a girl he liked the name Gillian. But this baby was due in the month of June, so I wanted the name June. In the end we gave up arguing and hoped for a compromise when it was born.

He started to talk again about his down days and read every book written about depression. I read them too in an effort to help him. Then we heard about transandental meditation. We thought it was worth a try. I remember on the day of his first sessions, he wanted to back out of it.

He had to bring a bunch of flowers, and a white handkerchief , for the induction ceremony. He wasn't a man for carrying flowers, so he hid them under his coat on the way out!

I anxiously waited his return, praying that this would work. I tried really hard to understand what he was going through. At first it was difficult to understand. After all I knew what it was like to be in severe pain every day. I couldn't imagine waking up depressed, if I had no pain!. But I was to learn that depression was very serious.

He came home in great form, telling me all about it. To meditate he was given a "mantra", that he would repeat over and over, until he was in a better place in his mind. He said that he felt it working. He was told, under no circumstances was he to tell anyone his mantra, he was to keep it secret for it to work effectively. However as I mentioned earlier, Lar constantly talked in his sleep, so within days I knew the mantra. But I was so concerned about him that I never told him that he was saying it while sleeping. It was not until he gave it up that I told him and he couldn't believe it.

As I said, it only lasted about six weeks, then the moods started again. But for now they were bearable. That is until I was eight months pregnant. One night he got that feeling again that his head was going to explode. I felt so sorry for him as he held his head in his hands.

When I realized that it was getting worse, I left the children with Evelyn next door and we drove into A&E in Baggot Street Hospital. I remember there was a lovely caring lady doctor there, who carried out tests. She could not find anything physically wrong with him. So she gave him two strong seditives. It was a large dose and it worked. She also gave him a prescription for a smaller dose, to be taken for three weeks. When we got home, he was a new man. He felt much better but sleepy, so he went to bed. Life got back to normal again, and he was his usual cheerful self.

I was now attending the Coombe hospital weekly for the forthcoming birth of our baby. I was told from about six months that the baby was breach. But the doctor said that there was plenty of time for it to turn But now I was eight months, and it wasn't turning. At one visit I was sent for a blood test with my chart. While I was waiting my turn, I flicked open the chart to read it. There were lots of things written in it, but only one thing stood out. Large head! I asked the girl beside me if anything was in her chart about the baby's head. She had a look, and said no. I was frightened, but in my ignorance, was afraid to ask the doctor.

After the visit I went to my mother's. I cried and told her what I had read. My mother was so re-assuring, telling me not to worry that maybe they were thinking of a c-section on account of the baby being breach.

That made sense to me, so I felt relieved going home.

I decided not to tell Lar, as he was in good form again and I didn't want to rock the boat. Besides, what my mam said was probably right.

I did not put on a lot of weight during the pregnancy, just a "bump" which I thought was beautiful. I wondered about Lar. Did he think I looked dreadful, or was he just shy about the whole thing? I remember sitting in the bath the night before I went into hospital. Our toilet was in the bathroom, so we always left the door unlocked, in case anyone needed to use it. He came in, did his business, and walked out backwards, without looking at me. I felt sad.

I did not feel much kicking in my tummy, for reasons that will become obvious later.... but I did feel a bit of movement. I would grab his hand in bed and ask him if he felt it. He would only touch me for a second, pull his hand away, and say no. I put it down to his shyness, refusing to let myself think of anything else.

Meanwhile, mam was right, the doctor told me that it had to be a c-section, and that he needed me in hospital two weeks before hand for tests. I still never suspected anything, and made arrangements for the children to be minded. Lar decided to take his holidays after the baby was born, so for now he continued to work, making sure he saw the children every day. Pamela was sixteen months old now, and Valerie was six years. Pamela was too young to know what was going on, but I explained to Valerie that I was going into hospital for a new baby. She was delighted as she loved

babies. I went into hospital on a Monday, looking forward to the task ahead. I even asked Dr. Greene if I could try having the baby normally, after all, I was now over ten years married, and I didn't want to miss a thing. The c-sections in those days was a full operation, not like it is today.

Anyway, he told me that it was out of the question. I had a couple of scans during the weeks that followed, and on the Friday before the birth, I had an amniocentesis. If anything showed, they never told me. The night before the birth, Lar stayed late with me. He was very worried, but I kept re-assuring him that I would be fine. I reminded him that I was not the first woman to have a c-section, and wouldn't be the l last. He gave me a kiss, told me he loved me, then left.

Chapter Eleven
OUR THIRD BABY

I slept through the night but woke early. I was prepared by the nurse for the theatre and I was given a paper gown and hat. The other girls in the ward who were also awaiting births, were making me laugh to keep my mind off the operation.

They armed me with relics of all the saints in heaven, even putting one under my hat!

A lovely nurse called Ann Marie, came with me to the theatre, chatting all the way. She held my hand as I was given the anaesthetic, and Dr. Greene told me not to worry, I was in good hands.

A few hours later I was in the recovery room trying to speak. I could see Lar through a haze, but my mouth wouldn't move. However, I did manage to say "baby". Lar whispered, ' It's a girl, she's fine'.

The next thing I remember was being wheeled back to the same ward. I still couldn't speak, and I could see two of the girls crying. I remember thinking that they must be feeling sad because I am over it, and they still have to face it. It never occurred to me that their tears were for me!. I must have slept for a few hours, because the next thing I remember was Lar, a lady doctor and two nurses coming over to my bed. They pulled the curtains around us looking very serious, and solemn.

Then the doctor got straight to the point. 'Your baby is very sick', she said. I kept thinking, am I dreaming? Lar had told me that she was fine. 'What's wrong', I asked.She asked me if I had ever heard of spina bifida. Ironically, I had met that woman at the school, when I was six months pregnant, who told me all about her daughter with it. I said I had. 'Well', she said, 'Your baby is one of the worse cases, and we don't expect her to live'. I looked at Lar's face. His eyes filled up, but he was trying to be brave for me. The doctor left us and the nurse asked would I like a sedative, to help me cope. By this time I was wide awake and I knew that no sedative would make my baby better, so I refused.

When we were alone, we shed our tears behind the curtains. Lar had seen the baby and told me that she looked perfect, except for a hole in her back. Oh! How I longed to hold her. I was in a lot of pain and attached to tubes, but it was nothing compared to the ache in my heart.

When Lar left, the girls in the ward, were so kind to me. Before the birth , I had told them that I would have the biggest bouquet in the ward, as I had waited ten years for this. Alas, there were no flowers, just tears. Through my tears I remarked that I got no flowers. One of the girls took a rose from her vase, and put it in a lemonade bottle for me. It looked as sad as I felt.

The next day I was told that the baby was going to Our Lady's Hospital in Crumlin to be assessed. When Lar came in, they put me in a wheelchair to bring me to the Holy Angels ward to see her. When we got there we had to put on a paper mask and gown. A nurse brought her out, but she couldn't let me hold her because of the big hole in her back. I cried so much that the mask turned into shreds on my face. She did indeed look perfect, and I thought she looked like my sister Joan. We only saw her for a few brief minutes, then she was taken away to Our Lady's Hospital. I thought to myself, that I will never get over this. But I was concerned for my two other children, so I knew that I had to be strong. Besides, would this throw Lar into a deeper depression? I hoped not, I needed him right now.

When I was well enough, the nurses helped me into a bath. After helping me wash, they left me alone for a few minutes. I remember looking down at my stitched up belly. It felt like my soul had been ripped out. The memory of that empty feeling will stay with me forever. I wondered about God. Why would he do this to me? I was a good girl who never missed mass and said my morning and night prayers. Why would he give me a baby, then take her away? 'Oh God' I prayed, it doesn't matter about the 'imperfection' we will love her anyway, please don't take her back. I had to stay in hospital for two weeks after the birth. On the day I returned home, Lar decided to bring me home first before collecting the children. When I walked into the empty house, I wept uncontrollably. I didn't know how I could face this day, never mind the weeks ahead. Because of Lar's depression, I felt that I couldn't talk about my true feelings. How I longed to talk about how I truly felt. But I had to smile now, my children were coming home. I hugged them so tightly that they had to wriggle away! I looked at them and realised that mammy better get her act together!

Before I left the hospital I had to give them a name for the baby. As she was born on midsummer's day in June, I insisted that it should be June. This time Lar didn't argue. In fact when he went on his own to register the birth I asked him was he sure he said June. I couldn't believe it when he said he registered June Elizabeth. I was so happy that he gave her my name as well.

Now I had to tell Valerie why I came home with no baby. We sat down together and I told her that she and Pamela had a baby sister called June, but she was very sick in hospital. 'But when can we see her mam' she said. She was too young to explain the seriousness of the situation, so I told her that when she got a bit better, that I would bring them up to the hospital.

June was now in Our Lady's hospital for sick children in Crumlin. We arranged to see the surgeon and expert on spina bifida, Professor Guiney. He explained that up to now, all babies with spina bifida, were operated on within a week, to close in there back. But the bad cases only survived for a year or two, so they had introduced selective surgery. And in his opinion, June was a bad case. She was paralysed from the waist down, which meant problems with her kidneys, bowel, etc.

We were heartbroken. We couldn't even take her home because there was a big mound of raw flesh growing out of the hole in her back, causing her a lot of pain. How cruel was this God. What is he thinking of? Or worse still , is there a god? I am afraid that I fell out with him at that moment. Black out!. I refused to say any more prayers.

But we had an obligation to our other children to bring them up as Catholics So, we continued to bring them to mass every Sunday, and teach them their morning and night prayers.

June was sent to a home for terminal care, when she was four weeks old. We did bring Valerie and Pamela to see her every Sunday, but they had to look through a glass window. Lar and I were allowed in but we couldn't hold her because of the hole. She lay on her her tummy all the time.

When I went out shopping with Lar, I would frequently wander over to prams, and look in at the babies. Lar was fed up with me doing this, and told me off many times. I felt hurt, as before June was born, it was something I always did. In fact, even today, as a grandmother, I still do it! Also, I didn't think that he liked me visiting June too often, in case I got too attached.

But, as mothers do, I found a way around it. I told him that I was visiting my sister Joan, every time. In fact sometimes, Joan came with me on the visits.

At Christmas, when June was six months old, she was doing almost everything that all babies do at that age. I kept saying 'Da Da' in her ear, until eventually she began to say it. The nun in charge of the home was Sr. Gertrude, a lovely woman. Lar and I went to her and asked if we could have June re-assessed. She agreed, and told us that she was thinking the same thing. So she promised, to follow it up as soon as Christmas was gone. I remember Connie bought June a red babygro for Christmas. She had found one that opened down the back so it did not hurt her. I will always remember that babygro on her with her blonde hair, she looked so pretty. I thought the Christmas holiday would never go, it seemed to drag in. Finally in January, Sr. Gertrude called us in to her office. She told us that Prof. Guiney was away on holiday, but that she had contacted another expert, a Mr. Lanigan in the Richmond hospital, and would we agree to it. She didn't have to ask us twice, as we jumped at the opportunity. Two weeks later, we brought a carry cot to the home to collect June. I wasn't allowed lift her so the nun carefully lay her on her tummy in the cot.

We drove over to the Richmond hospital with June screaming all the way. The nun told us later that it was from the noise of the traffic as well as the pain as she had never been out before, however even in the hospital she screamed.

She must have been in awful pain. When a mother knows her child is in pain, she can feel it too, and I wished I could take it away from her.

After examining her, Mr. Lanigan, unfazed by the screaming, spoke to us. I will never forget his words. He said 'There is no operation that will make your baby walk, because of the damage to her spine, however we can close in her back, and see if we can minimize the damage'

I wanted to give him a big kiss! At last, there was a spark of hope. But before we got too excited he went on to tell us the risks involved. He told us that when he closes the back, that the fluid may go to the brain, and she could die. Lar asked what were the chances of that happening. He told us 50/50.

Well, we thought, up until now we had no chance at all, so 50/50 seemed like pretty good odds to us.

And so it was arranged, she was admitted to the Richmond Hospital with the promise that they would operate the following Friday. Lar couldn't take time off work, so on Friday morning, when the hospital rang, to sign the consent forms, I had to go on my own. Evelyn next door took Pamela, (Valerie was in school) and Evelyn's husband Peter drove me in. The rain that day was non-stop and very heavy. So Peter said that he would wait for me. I was two hours in the hospital, poor Peter! He was so good, and I will never forget him for it. He sat in his car for the duration of my visit. I went up early to collect Valerie from school, which was beside the church. As I was early, I decided to go in and have one last word with God.

I remember sitting there not being able to pray. No prayer came to me. So I just said almost out loud 'If there is a god, I want a sign today!' I walked home chatting to Valerie asking all about her day. But June wasn't far from my mind. I told Valerie the truth, that if this operation worked, we could take June home. She was so excited, almost as if she knew it was going to work! Pamela was by now, not quite two. She didn't understand what was going on, so was her usual funny self. At that time she wasn't talking much and we used to say that Valerie was such a chatterbox that she did all the talking for her!

The hospital had told me that it was a three or four hour operation and that she would be in intensive care for a while. So they said not to visit that evening. I rang continuously but the answer was 'still in theatre'. Eventually, they told me things went well, and she was in recovery. At about seven thirty that evening Lar came home. I was dying to tell him the news. But before I could speak, he said ' You're not going to believe this'. He said that he called into the hospital, and June was in an ordinary ward lying on her back, smiling up at him!.

I suddenly announced, 'There IS a god. I asked for a sign and this is it'. Then Lar said 'Ask Evelyn to mind the children and we will go back in'. Evelyn was so happy for us, and gladly minded them.

When I saw June for the first time the 'right' way up, I got a lump in my throat. But the best was to come. For the first time since mid summers day 1976 I was able to hold and cuddle my baby. I can truthfully say, that I felt the same bonding that I felt with my other two children. This feeling was beautiful, how did I doubt that there was a God. He was just testing me to see if I was capable. Yes God, I AM capable, I can face anything now that you throw at me. I got a new strength that day. June needed post operative care, so I went in as often as I could, to help the nurses.

Chapter Twelve

WELCOME HOME JUNE

Two weeks later they told us that we could take her home. The nurse explained to me that because of her paralysis, her bladder and bowels didn't work like ours. I had to learn to remove her motions by hand, and to press on her stomach to empty her bladder. At first I was afraid that I was hurting her, but the nurse reassured me that she couldn't feel a thing. The nurse was great. She took my hand in hers and put it on the big scar on her back. She made me feel it, press on it and rub it 'Now', she said, Don't be afraid of it, because it's part of June.

So, armed with a load of instructions from the hospital, we brought our third baby home, in early February 1977. The excitement was like before, with our friends and neighbours in to wish us luck, and bringing lots of presents. Everyone was so kind, especially our immediate neighbours Peter and Evelyn, and Angela and Michael O'Keeffe.

We settled in to normal family life. I tried to work out a routine to keep the house running and everyone happy. I was doing well, and ever so proud of myself. But it was short lived, the rheumatoid arthritis came back with a bang. I woke up one morning, and had to crawl to the bathroom. I sat on the toilet and couldn't get up. I called Lar to help me. He was as shocked as I was. He lifted me up and tried to get me walking again. I was lucky that it was a weekend when Lar was at home. The pain was unbelievable, but I could manage to move after a couple of hours. But the pain wouldn't go away. I thought to myself, if I can struggle through the day looking after the children, Lar could do the housework.

So that's what I did. I did everything from a sitting position, and only stood when I had to. I took strong pain killers every four hours. Sunday was the same, so on Monday morning, Lar said to me 'What am I going to do, I have to go to work'? I looked at him, and I knew that this had all the hallmarks of another depression spell. So I told him to go to work that I would be fine. I knew that I was far from fine, but I had no choice. I got Valerie ready for school as best as I could, and Evelyn brought her up. So, now the two little ones had to be changed and fed. I took more pain killers than I should to cope. But I did cope, and another neighbour collected Valerie. When Lar came home I tried to smile for his sake but I was in so much pain that even my face hurt. He brought me back to the G.P. lifting me in and out of the car in the process. The doctor gave me stronger pain killers, plus an urgent letter back to the specialist.

A week later I went back to Dr. Casey, the rheumatologist in St. James Hospital. He wanted to keep me in, but I refused. So he started me on the gold again, but warned that if I broke out in a rash again, that I would have to come off it. It was sixteen weeks before it happened. I woke up with spots that looked like the measles They weren't itchy or sore, just there. I was doing so well on the gold that I contemplated not telling the doctor. But Mammy told me that the spots were a warning that they were affecting my blood.

So I had to stop the gold, and I was put on another drug that helped for a while. The pain was still bad but bearable. I developed a knack for getting through the day in my own awkward way. I went upstairs on my hands and knees, and came down on my bottom. To change the babies, I sat on the floor. We bought lots of gadgets for opening bottles etc., and generally tried to carry on as normal as possible.

Lar still liked to go out to the music sessions every Saturday night. With great difficulty I went with him. If I hadn't, I knew he would get in a mood that might last days. Many nights I sat at some cabaret show, with tears in my eyes from the pain. However, I was determined to continue on as normal. as best as I could. I even managed to sew when the children were in bed. I made all their clothes, including coats, hats, dresses, etc. I bought a knitting machine, so that I could knit their cardigans. In fact, the only things I had to buy were shoes and underwear.

So, financially we were comfortable. But health wise, things weren't good. I was struggling, and he was struggling with the depression, but in between, he was great. Life had to go on, and we were lucky to have three beautiful children. Valerie, the sensible one, Pamela, the funny one, and June the cautious one!

This is what kept us going, enjoying them and taking care of them. How lucky we were to have these precious children. Lar was a good dad, and very dutiful. He encouraged them to get involved in all sorts of activities. He had Valerie swimming at about five years old. We had to laugh at Pamela. She was such a happy child, and brought many a smile to our face. When she eventually started to talk, she did it back ways! 'A piece of bread give us!' she would say. Or 'daddy work gone' when Lar went to work, or singing 'Little star twinkle where you are!'

June was not able to get up to mischief like Pamela, but she told Pam what to do! One day I was knitting, but only half listening to them chatting. Next thing I heard June say 'Now Pam, jump on them'. I looked around and the floor was covered in cornflakes and Pamela dancing on them! I let a roar, 'What are you doing?' Of course Pamela laughed and said that June told her what to do. I knew then that June could get up to as much mischief as Pamela, from her chair!.

Valerie loved her teddies and dolls, while Pam loved motor cars and guns! June was more into puzzles and games. Playing a game with Pamela was trying, to say the least. She just had to win, even if it meant cheating! Many a game of snakes and ladders ended in tears. We would have to play again until she won, otherwise she was so sad. When Pamela cried, her tears were like a tap turned on full, so we all ran to cuddle her. Lar and I couldn't bear to see her cry, as normally she was so happy and funny, when she was winning!

She was very competitive from very young, so we knew we would have to steer her in the right direction. She started pre-school when she was three and a half, with Mrs. Kavanagh on St. James Road in Walkinstown. She loved it and listened to every word the teacher said. One day she came home from school, and she related the story of Snow White and the Seven Dwarfs. She was very concerned about the poisoned red apple.

After that, she never ate a red apple! No matter what I said to her, there was no way she would eat one. To this day a red apple would not be her favourite! Years later, I met Mrs. Kavanagh, and told her the story. She had a good laugh but after that, changed the wording for future reference.

Lar built an extension on to our house on St. Bridget's Drive. He spent months at it as he did most of it on his own. When it was finished, we moved the kitchen into it, giving us a bigger sitting room. Together, we decorated it, bit by bit. I was determined to do it up without borrowing money. So every penny I earned sewing, would go into the house, while we lived on Lar's wages.

Soon we had it comfortable, and looking good. We could now afford to save for a holiday every year. We fell in love with Co. Kerry. Our first year there, we went to Abbeydorney. Granda Swords came with us, and our accommodation was over the local pub! There was traditional music, story telling, and dancing at the crossroads. It was great fun but I found the stairs very difficult. On the other hand, Granda would crawl up every night, after drinking quite a few pints, saying 'This is what I've been looking for all my life, a few drinks, then up to bed!!!'

One night we were sitting watching set dancing, when Granda went missing. We thought he had gone to the toilet, but he was gone very long. He was a small thin man, but very strong as he had been a champion gymnast in his day. Next thing we spotted him! He was up on the floor with a partner doing the set dancing! His partner was a BIG woman, head and shoulders above him. He was an excellent dancer and tripped around like a young fella! We couldn't believe it! He had often mentioned that he was a good dancer in his day, along with Lar's mother. We just never realised how true it was. We laughed in amazement at him, taking the floor with such expertise!

That was the first of many fun holidays with granda. The children adored him, and he loved them. Many a time he would roll around the floor with them, trying to teach them gymnastics. He was very supple, and indeed I have a clear memory of him walking around on his hands in his sixties! Oh how I envied his energy! I still struggled to get through the day. But I loved when he came over and stayed the night.

We would have long chats when the children went to bed. He would constantly tell me what a great girl I was. It meant so much to hear him saying that to me. One night we were chatting about June, and that she would be in a wheelchair for life. He spoke lovingly about his wife also in a wheelchair for years before she died. Her name was Kathleen, but he affectionately called her Shally. He said to me ' If only I had Shally back, sitting in her wheelchair, I would be so happy, it wouldn't matter if she couldn't do any thing else, just sit and talk to me'.

He said to me, 'You know Betty, it's not nice when you lose your partner in life' It would be many years later, that these words would mean something to me..........

Granda, like many of his generation, only had a basic education. But he had a wisdom, and experience of life that you couldn't get in a book! I loved talking to him. Many nights I would stay up late while he related to me how life was for him during the war. He also loved to tell the story of how he met Shally. They met at a train station dance in Lucan. Apparently, in those days, there were dances held at many train stations. She was a good dancer, as was he, so they got on great. Every week after that, he cycled from Inchicore to Lucan to see her.

Any time we asked him what year they got married, he would scratch his head and say 'The year that there was no potatoes!' Many years after he died, I found out that there were no potatoes in 1942. That seemed right as Lar was the oldest and he was born in1943.

When June was two and a half years old, she was fitted with her first pair of callipers. Although she was paralysed from the waist down, these would enable her get into an upright position, thereby helping the kidneys. The day we brought her for them, I had her in the prettiest frilly dress. Alas, when she was strapped into them, the frills were in an uncomfortable lump underneath her arms! The fitter told me gently that callipers and frills don't work! I soon learned that little dungarees and plain pinafores worked best.

Although Lar was happy to see June standing, I don't know if he liked the callipers much. He never said anything to me, but I always knew when he stayed quiet, that wasn't good. Anyway, I was happy, June was happy, and her sisters thought that this was the greatest thing ever! They played 'Ring a Roses' with her in a standing position, Every time they 'all fall down' the squeals of delight from the three of them! Even though we had to lift her back up with great difficulty, it was worth it. She had a standing table that she was locked into, so that she could remain standing for thirty minutes at a time. To sit her down, there were two hinges at the sides of the callipers that we opened. It was hard on my painful hands when Lar was at work, but once June was happy, I worked through the pain. She also had a shasba trolley that she used, to get around quickly. This was a trolley with four wheels, the back two bigger than the front, that she could wheel herself. She loved it, following Valerie and Pamela around the house. Ah yes these were happy days.

Pamela started "big" school when she was four and a half. By that time, June had started a special play school in Clondalkin, run by the Spina Bifida Association. They had everything there including a physiotherapist. She loved the company of the other children, making friends almost immediately. She made special friends with Nicola Dredge. They were the same age, both had spina bifida to the same degree. I now had a few hours to myself when they were in school, so I took in extra sewing. At first I was making patchwork quilts, but found them too heavy for my hands after a while, as they were stuffed with Dacron, a type of wadding. I loved the creativity of the patchwork, but I had to be realistic. So I kept making them until I found something better. That was when I began making First Holy Communion dresses for the John's Street Manufacturing company. They were much lighter on my hands, and just as creative. In 1979, Pope John Paul came to Ireland. I would have loved to go to the Phoenix Park to see him. But the buses were only going so far , and it was a long walk. Cars were restricted, so driving was out the question. Besides, June and Pam were only three and four years old.

So, I togged up Lar, Valerie, and Granda Swords, to make the journey, giving them packed lunches, stools etc. tied on there back, while I watched the whole lot on television with the two little ones. They came home tired but hugely impressed. It was a great time for all of us. Granda kept saying, 'I never thought that I would get to see the Pope'. When anything was beyond words, Granda would turn his head from side to side as if to say 'no, I don't believe it!' So, he went around for a long time after that in disbelief.

Meanwhile, the Saturday nights out with Lar continued, some times with friends, sometimes with Granda, or some times on our own. We enjoyed each others company, still talking all night. We used play a game watching other couples. We could tell that they were a long time married if they didn't talk much. We thought that this was funny, because we had so much to say, and would often miss the top act while we were deep in conversation. The only thing that marred our nights out was that I thought Lar was drinking too much. I hated what he became when he was drunk. Some times he would just talk foolishly, other times he would get aggressive.

I soon learned to say nothing until he was sober again. No matter what I said, he denied drinking too much, so rather than come across as a nagging wife, I tried to put up with it.

Every year, we went to the oil company dress dance. My friend Áine and I would spend weeks before hand planning and making the dresses. Áine was a drinker, but we still enjoyed each other's company, with me stone cold sober, and her 'well on'. At one of the dances, Lar got really drunk, as did Áine. They spent the whole night dancing with each other, while I was left sitting, except when Áine's husband Sean invited me to dance. As the night went on, they were now "slobbering" over each other, in the middle of the dance floor. I was fuming. I could not believe that he would make a show of himself in front of his workmates, not to mention embarrassing me. I somehow got through the night, and with a forced smile on my face, said goodnight to all our friends. I drove home in silence. There was no point in saying anything to this drunken fool beside me until morning.

Next morning I brought him fresh orange juice and two headache tablets. When he was sufficiently awake I hit the roof. He asked me to keep my voice down as it was hurting his head! I related the night to him as I saw it. He told me that I was imagining things, that no way would he carry on like that. I would not accept that and wanted an apology for embarrassing me. It would be a few days before I got my apology, although it came without admitting liability!

His first day back at work after the dance he came home sheepishly. He said that when he was talking about the dance with his colleagues, they said to him 'I hear Sean nearly lost his wife at the dance'!

He was now under strict orders to keep away from Áine at the next dance. In fact I told Áine too, to keep her hands off my husband! Remember this is a man who is quite shy in every day life, but full of jollifications when drunk. We were now getting to the stage when he always got drunk on our nights out. Any time I tried to talk to him about it, he would say that he worked hard all the week, and deserved it.

He did work hard, both in the home and at work, and he was a good father. But I felt that I worked just as hard, and with constant pain. So I turned a blind eye to the drunken Saturday nights and got on with things. It was about this time that Lar, much to my disappointment, took up smoking. I know it wasn't the end of the world, but I I hated the smell with a passion. At first it was only when he was drinking, then it was every night to relax. I never related my disappointment to him, however I thought he knew how I felt about smoking, although thankfully he gave them up again five years later. In the meantime I had to put up with it. In October that year I began to lose weight for no reason at all. My normal weight was 8 stone.

Even when I was nine months pregnant on June, I only weighed 9 stone, but returned to my normal weight quite quickly. But now I was losing weight for no reason. My G.P. had many tests carried out but everything else seemed all right. He put me on a high calorie diet to try to improve things. It didn't work. I felt fine and could continue as normal so I expected that it would right itself in time. But Lar got very angry with me and said that I looked dreadful. Almost every day he would get annoyed with me. I could not believe his reaction, after all I did nothing wrong, and said so every time he raised his voice. I took Complan and all kinds of nutritious food to try and improve things. But I stayed at seven and a half stone. I had to put it out of my mind and get on with things as I had three children to take care of, one of them with special needs.

Chapter Thirteen
ON THE MOVE AGAIN

It was coming up to Christmas 1979, and we were wallpapering the hall together. We always did it together in those days, as we were a great team. We were talking about what the future held for us with June in a wheelchair, and my arthritis getting worse.

He was up the ladder with a length of wallpaper in his hands, with me holding the other end, when I said, 'You know maybe we should look for a bungalow now while we are young enough to get a new mortgage.' 'Ah for Gods sake,' he yelled laughing. 'Will you make up your mind before I do any more of this!' We put down tools, and had a serious talk. We decided that it was the right thing to do, but we couldn't leave the hall unfinished so we continued the decorating. The next day, we drove around looking at bungalows for sale. Most of them were lovely, but I didn't like thelocations. The following Saturday morning I was driving to the supermarket on Walkinstown Road, when I saw a bungalow for sale. I loved where it was, but it was wreck! I went home to tell Lar. He hopped in the car with me, and we went back down and parked outside. Lar wouldn't get out of the car when he saw it. 'It's a heap of junk' he said, 'No way am I leaving my lovely house for that!'

I had to admit our house was beautifully decorated, plus Lar had built on a kitchen extension himself. Also we had a back entrance where he had built a garage. We had a big back garden, where I grew vegetables, and a lawn where we had a swing for the children.

Lar refused to discuss it any further, end of story, the answer was no. One week later, I went down again to do my weekly shop. When I was driving home, I stopped outside the bungalow again. I looked at the garden, it was so over grown that you couldn't see the pathway up to the door. But I still liked where it was, close to the supermarket, church, and school. There was a sign up stating that it was now on view, so I went home and begged Lar to at least look at it. Finally he agreed, more out of curiosity, than interest.

So down we went and had a look. We discovered that inside was clean and newly painted, but clearly, it was an old house, and needed a lot of work. It was built in 1938, whereas our house was relatively new. Besides, there wasn't one press in the kitchen except for the one that held the sink up, and even that was old. There were no built in wardrobes, and the windows looked like they were the originals. We had every comfort in our house, including wardrobes that Lar built with me as the helper! But the bungalow had potential. I kept telling Lar that he was great at D.I.Y, and would get it up to scratch in a couple of years. He was starting to like the idea, now seeing it as a challenge.

Lar loved a challenge, especially when it came to D.I.Y. So we made a decision there and then to put in an offer for the bungalow.

While we waited for a decision from the auctioneer, we brought Granda Swords to see it. He was not impressed, and said so. 'You are selling your lovely house for this?'

Followed by the nodding of his head when something was beyond words.

But we were determined to look at our move as a great adventure. Besides, I had faith in Lar. I knew that if I earned the extra money, that he could do it.

Our offer was the only one and so, was accepted. The following day we put our house up for sale. Within twenty four hours it was sold! I suppose it's fair to say that the people that bought it only had to plug in their television!

On leap year day, February 29th 1980 we moved to Walkinstown Road. It was a brave decision because there was nothing in the bungalow. I went down with the children first while Lar and a neighbour moved the furniture. Because there were no presses in the kitchen, I put as much food as I could in the fridge. The rest I had to leave in cardboard boxes on the table. I had to fold the children's clothes on the bedroom floor. It was only when we moved in that I realised what we had taken on. I worried about the children leaving all the comforts behind. There was no heating in the house only a few old fashioned fireplaces. Our other house had central heating and I could heat the house with the flick of a switch. Here it would be a couple of months of lighting fires before we could afford central heating. On the first morning that I woke up after moving, I looked out at the back garden. I nearly died when I saw rats! Apparently there had been a bin strike in recent weeks, and because this was an empty house with a back entrance and lane way at the back, everyone used it as a dump! I was getting more and more worried about the children.

We rang pest control in Dublin Corporation that day and in fairness they came out immediately. They put down traps and poison and it cleared them out. So our priority was to get the back garden in order, for the children to play safely.

We got Valerie and Pamela into the local school, while June continued going to the special play school as she was only three and a half. The first few weeks were hectic trying to do everything at once. I had to do some serious sewing to keep the money coming in. At first I did couture work because that was were the big money was, but the fittings were time consuming and I didn't want to miss out on my children. So I tried to be a full time mother, sewing only while they were in bed or in school. I then met Mr. Hamill who had a shop in Parnell street Dublin specialising in First Communion dresses. He employed me to design and make the dresses for him. This turned out to be freelance dress designing at its best.

Mr. Hamill and his manageress a lovely girl called Keelin called every Monday night with fabric and trimmings, leaving the designs up to me.I loved every thing about the arrangements and besides, he paid very generously.

Within a few weeks we had enough saved to get the central heating in. That was our first priority because the bedrooms were freezing. When the fitters were finished installing the heating I was delighted and went around putting all the children's little knickers on the radiators to dry! Lar said 'Ah for God's sake the men are only at the gate and you're covering the rads!' But I didn't care, I had a lot of wet clothes lying around, so I did what any mother would do.

In the beginning I kept one of the bedrooms for my sewing leaving the three girls sharing a bedroom with bunk beds. It worked okay when they were small, but I knew eventually I would have to make changes. I hated making the beds because of my hands as they were quite sore and there were no duvets around at the time. Each bed had two sheets, two blankets, and a quilt. Even with Valerie standing at the other side, it still hurt me lifting the blankets. Anyway, I didn't dwell on it once they were made, besides, we had lots of work to do before we get this house up to the standard of our last house.'

Lar was now on shift work, but it worked out better for us because every second week he was here all morning to work on the house. Every other week he was home at two o' clock in the afternoon, and after a rest he would get back into the work in the house. I still loved him dearly and my heart would miss a beat when he came in the door. But I was still not putting on any weight, which made him angry. He kept telling me that everyone was talking about me and that I looked awful. I was so upset when he said those things to me because I couldn't make it right. He insisted he came with me to our G.P. again.

He spoke to Dr. Walsh and said ' Look at her she is so thin' he was pointing to my boobs. I was shocked as I had never heard Lar talk like that before. I know he always admired my boobs, but I thought he loved all off me! Dr. Walsh asked him was it just my boobs that he was worried about, to which he replied sheepishly 'well yes and the rest of her!' He reassured him that there was nothing wrong with me and if I continued with the Complan, plus high calorie drinks that it will get better. We continued to have heated arguments about it at home. Yet our sex life was wonderful and at those times he made me feel special. So all I could do was stuff my face with food praying that I would put on a few pounds.

One day when the children were at school, I went for my hospital appointment for the arthritis. On the way home I went into an underwear shop and bought the sexiest black bra that

I could find. When I got home I put it on, and admired myself in the mirror. I thought that it would be a nice surprise for Lar, remember I was still only 35 years old.

He came home at 2.30 in the afternoon. As usual my heart skipped a beat, and the children danced all over him like they always did. When the children went into another room I teasingly lifted up my top to show off the bra. He took one look and said 'Oh could you get one small enough?' It was such a hurtful thing to say to me and I walked in to where the children were, forcing myself to smile with them. I looked at my three wonderful children, who loved me unconditionally, I hugged them so tightly that they couldn't understand what it was all about. I was already feeling bad about myself because he told me over and over again that I looked awful, but this was unforgivable.

I never felt the same about my body again. It had taken me a long time when we first got married to undress in front of him, but now I was ashamed of my body.

That night we made love as we always did, (we never had to worry about contraception) but I no longer felt beautiful when he told me that he loved me. Instead I felt that this was just sex, a wifely duty.

On Lar's early shift, he usually came home at 2pm. One day I was washing the dishes in the kitchen when I heard his key in the door. Our bedroom was beside the hall door, so I heard him go in to hang up his coat, then march down the hall to where I was in the kitchen. 'You're disgusting' he said, with a horrible look on his face.

Immediately I thought maybe I left dirty underwear lying around in the bedroom.

'Why? What did I do?' He said 'You left the radio on in the bedroom and I'd swear it has been on all day!' I couldn't figure out how this made me a disgusting person, but yes, I had been listening to Gay Byrne earlier, when I was making the bed and yes it was on since 11am! I apologised like a bold child, and never left it on again.

I concentrated on the children and my work for Mr. Hamill. Up to now I was still managing the money. But shortly after we moved to Walkinstown Road, the oil company began to pay the wages into the bank. It was getting harder for me to walk to the bank when Lar wasn't home with the car. So he took over the finances. I had never realised how mean he was with money, until he started managing it. It never occurred to me until then, that in the nineteen months that we dated he bought me only two presents, and none since.

The first one was the watch that he nearly didn't give me, the second was the hairdryer, for my twenty first birthday. He broke a bracelet that my Dad bought for my eighteenth birthday, but he did replace it.

Since we got married, there was nothing. I dropped hints regularly telling him about the lovely presents that Brian bought Connie. All he would say was 'If you want something, get the money out of the bank!' So I never did take anything out of the bank, but with money I earned from a wedding dress, I bought myself an eternity ring.

I told everyone that Lar bought it for me. Many years later when Valerie was an adult, I could no longer wear it on my crooked fingers, so I gave it to her, which she still treasures. I told her at the time that Daddy bought it for me, but I eventually told her the truth because of events that followed later..........

We worked hard trying to get the house comfortable, only buying things as soon as we saved for it. Mr. Hamill was so kind to me. He gave me extra money every year for the dresses. He kept telling me that business was good, and my dresses were in great demand. I loved being appreciated like that and did everything I could for him. Sometimes he would ring for a certain size that he needed urgently. I would just say certainly, and have that dress ready that evening. No matter how much pain I was in, I would still sew.

We were both working hard, enjoying the children, and doing up the house during the first year on Walkinstown Road. June was coming up to her fourth birthday, and the next big thing in her life was her first wheelchair. We had asked the principal of the special school, her opinion on June going to main stream school. She thought that she would do very well, so she gave us a reference.

We approached the local school that Valerie and Pamela attended. Sister Hilary was in charge, a lovely young nun. She was delighted to take her, and as she would be the only child there with a disability, wanted to know what would make life easier for her.Apart from a ramp, and a special desk, every thing else was fine. We offered to pay, but she wouldn't hear of it. She got a new desk right away, and within a couple of months had the ramp in. So, as soon as she got her wheelchair, she started school. I don't think Lar wanted her in a wheelchair just yet, because he said, she was fine in the buggy. But I knew that he was thinking back to his childhood, with his mother in a wheelchair. I refused to leave her in the buggy any longer as she now wanted to move around herself. Besides, all her disabled friends her age, now had wheelchairs. Also, starting school, she needed to be as independent as possible. So, rather than argue with him, I pretended that I didn't hear him, and kept making arrangements. June loved the new school and soon made friends. At lunch time she was with Pamela in the yard, while Valerie came down to her every day to check that she was okay.

Now with the three of them in school, I was able to get into some sort of routine, with my sewing. Lar acknowledged that I was working hard and earning the money to make our house more comfortable. But I was still not putting on weight, so he regularly hurt my feelings, sometimes with words, more times with a look of disgust. Oh how I hated that look, I would rather have heard the words.I could not tell anyone, after all in every ones eyes, Lar was a wonderful husband, always working in the house, and a great father. When any visitors came, he would be in great form, always dominating the conversation. Sometimes it was hard for me to get a word in so I kept quiet except when he looked for my approval like 'Isn't that right Betty?'

I still loved this man with all my heart and soul, no matter how much he hurt me. In between times we would have a reasonably good relationship. We would make love every night, and he would always tell me that he loved me before he went asleep. We had so much in common, and we loved arguing about politics, current affairs, etc.By the end of our first year in the bungalow, we had our central heating, fitted wardrobes, fitted kitchen, and tidy gardens. We stuck to our promise of never buying on hire purchase, and even though some of our furniture needed replacing, we did it gradually when we saved enough money.

Our bungalow was only a ten minute walk away from my mother, but about twenty minutes for me! By now she was crippled with the rheumatoid arthritis, and permanently in a wheelchair. My sister Marie, sold her house to move back home and look after her, because daddy still worked and she couldn't be left alone. It was nice to have my family so near, whereby I could call in regularly and they called into me.

Meanwhile Lar's dad became ill and had to go into hospital. We were very worried about him as he waited for the results of tests. One of the days that Lar and I were visiting, a nurse came in and asked if he was a son. Lar replied that he was the eldest son, so she asked him to accompany her to the doctor to have a word with him. I knew this wasn't good news, but worse still, I also knew that Lar had no tact. I tried to chat and have a laugh with granda while he was gone, but my heart was in my mouth. Finally after about twenty minutes Lar came back. The look on his face was enough! He was no good at hiding his feelings, and he was white in the face. Next thing he blurted out ' Daddy why didn't you go sooner about this?' His dad replied 'Well I thought it was me varicous veins' But why? Lar kept shouting at him. I tried to calm down the situation by saying, 'Well look, at least you're in the right place now, so when they start the treatment, you will feel much better.'

I had no idea what the doctor told Lar, but I spent the rest of the visit talking my head off to cover up for Lar's awkwardness. He was staring at his dad in disbelief, just not able to hide his feelings.

After the visit, before Lar told me what the doctor said, I got angry with him for reacting like he did in front of his dad. 'I couldn't help it' he said 'I'm still in shock'. The doctor told him that his dad had prostate cancer, that had now spread into the bone. He said that if he had came about it earlier, they could have removed it before it spread. This indeed shocked me too. I found it hard to come to terms with the fact that we might lose him. I loved him dearly, as did the children.

Lar had to break the news to his sisters and brothers. In fairness, I think they had already guessed the news was not good. Even so, it saddened all of us.

Meanwhile after he was diagnosed, my own Mam became very ill. A couple of vertebrae collapsed at the back of her neck due to complications of the rheumatoid arthritis. She was now paralysed from the neck down. We were heartbroken. She was sent out from St. James' hospital to the Rehabilitation Hospital in Dun Laoire, were she was put into traction to see if it would help to reset her spine. After weeks of therapy she was sent back to St. James' as it didn't work. She never came home again from hospital. In March 1983, three months after Granda Swords died, Mam too passed away. This was a sad time for all of us and the children missed their nanny and granddad.

It was at about this time that I really started to notice a few different sides to Lar. He never missed an opportunity to be disrespectful to me. He started to get paranoid about the house. It had to be spotless at all times. I would get it cleaned early in the morning after I brought the children to school, but when he came home, it wasn't good enough. He would go over everything that I cleaned, and do it again! Now I was really feeling inadequate, between him not being impressed with my body any more, and not good enough as a housewife.

In the beginning I got mad at him for redoing everything that I did, then I learned to keep my mouth shut, and let him do what made him happy. One day he went to the cutlery drawer for a knife and fork. He looked at me and said crossly ' You have no respect for your home at all have you?' I asked him what was wrong. He replied ' It is just as easy to put the spoons in the right section as the wrong one' I said 'Did I put them in wrong?' 'Yes' he said, 'There's a spoon in the fork drawer'. I said nothing, but thought to myself, what is wrong with this man!

The worse the pain of the arthritis got, the worse Lar got about the house. I was struggling to keep body and soul together, but still couldn't tell anyone. I could no longer wear fashionable shoes, only sensible laced ones. I had arthritis lumps on the soles of my feet that felt like I was walking on marbles. So I had to buy shoes a size bigger so that I could put insoles in to cushion them. Even with that, I was in agony walking.

Meanwhile, I enrolled Pamela in the local gymnastic club, because Granda Swords had introduced it to her, and besides, it was a way to channel her endless energy!

June was involved in the wheelchair sports, and Valerie loved her girl guides. Within a year of joining the gymnastics it became clear that Pamela had talent in that direction. So we took her out of the local club, and sent her to one that was affiliated to the Gymnastic Association of Ireland. It turned out to be the right thing to do, as in later years she went on to represent Ireland, as a valued member of the Irish team. But right now it was difficult getting her over to Dundrum in Dublin, about twenty minutes by car from where we lived. If the traffic was bad, it could take forty minutes or more.

On Lar's late shift, I had to drive him into work a few days a week so that I would have the car to bring Pam to gym. I don't know how I managed to drive the car in those years, with the lumps on my feet, but it had to be done, besides if I said anything to Lar, he would just go into one of his moods. So I learned to avoid this at all costs.

I continued to sew for Mr. Hamill, as I was okay sitting down, but still in pain. I felt that I had to sew, not only for my own sanity, but also to keep my joints moving, however painful it was. As well as that, Mr. Hamill depended on me and appreciated the work that I did. It was he who made me feel good about myself.

On the face of it, to outsiders Lar was the perfect husband. He even built me a double workroom at the back of our house, which was great because it gave us back a bedroom in the house that we now needed for our growing family. He was continually doing up the house, one room after another. He became obsessed with housework, polishing and shining every spare minute he had. Many people would say to me 'Oh I'd love to be married to him!'

The frustrating part was that no matter how hard I tried, it was never good enough, he went over everything I did. I remember many times standing up to get a painkiller to take with my last mouthful of tea, when I turned back, the cup was emptied, washed and put away!

One day when Lar was in work, I turned on the television while having my lunch. Oprah Winfrey was on and the subject was obsessive compulsive disorder. I then thought that this was what Lar must have as the symptoms seemed the very same.

In a way I was relieved, because it meant that I wasn't such a bad wife. When Lar came home, I discussed it with him, but he refused to talk about it except to say that someone had to keep the house clean!

But every thing had to be right, and put in their proper place. I got the children to tidy up their toys when I knew he was on the way home from work. The children were happy and they didn't notice any insults that he threw at me. I would always laugh with them, so like all children, when mammy was happy, they were happy.

I tried to hide the pain I was in as much as I could. When I couldn't, Lar got into one of his moods, making a bad situation worse. The pain in my joints was so bad that even the bed clothes were hurting. Also it was getting harder for me to put on and take off my clothes. I got Valerie to help me most of the time. She was such a kind helpful child from very young. When June was ill with frequent kidney infections, she would vomit day and night until the infection cleared up. I regularly had to get up during the night to wash her and change the bedclothes. One morning when I was making breakfast, June said 'I got sick during the night mam'. Then Valerie told me that she cleaned up the sick, washed June, put on clean pyjamas, and changed the bedclothes! She was only twelve years old! I never heard a thing! I gave her the biggest hug ever.

It happened many times after that, and she would not wake me. I kept telling her to call me but she didn't. Pamela was a deep sleeper, nothing would wake her!

I had to get out of bed at 6 o'clock every morning. I was so stiff and sore that it gave me time to take painkillers and walk around to loosen out before I woke the children. I know it's hard to believe, but no matter how much pain I was in, I liked to wake them up with a song! I would walk into their room singing in an operatic voice 'Love is all I have to give'. Truthfully, I hadn't a note in my head, but it made the kids smile, even if they put their heads under the blankets first! June took the longest to get ready because of the incontinence as I had to give her a bed bath, remove her motions, and empty her bladder. So I gave the other two their breakfast first, and while they were eating, got June ready. When I got her callipers on I lifted her into her chair. It was getting harder for me but I would never let her know. When she was ready I could concentrate on the other two, although Valerie was able to do everything for herself at this stage. After breakfast I walked the children to school. I was able to hang on to the wheelchair to get over, but coming back I had to hold onto the wall. I could no longer carry shopping so I used a shopping trolley. June would wheel it in front of her and I would wheel June. We were like a train, until we got to the lolly pop lady, who very kindly held on to the trolley until I got back from the school.

I would then go into the supermarket to shop. When I got home, I would make the beds with great difficulty, sort out the washing, tidy up and leave the dinner prepared, before going out to my workroom to sew. In the afternoon, I collected the children from school and gave them their dinner. After dinner I helped them with their homework, sometimes ironing at the same time. I had to sit down while ironing, because my knees were so sore. I could not peg the clothes out on the line, so I waited for a light breeze and put them over unpegged.

On Lar's late shift, he would do the cleaning and polishing, while I continued to shop, cook, wash and iron, and generally do all the mammy things. I always took Tuesdays off from sewing, and the two of us, on his late shift would have dinner out. These were great fun, trying different places every week.

At these times he was his old self and great company, chatting through the meal laughing and arguing about current affairs, politics etc. We differed over many political figures and this was one thing that I wouldn't give in on. When he realised that he could not win the argument he would say ' Ah you cannot see anything bad in anyone'!

Chapter Fourteen

A DISAPPEARING RAINBOW

Lar was energetic and adventurous. I was well aware that my illness was holding him back, and he continued to tell me so. Although June was disabled, I do not believe that it was a big problem at that time. We just had to check when we were going anywhere, that it was wheelchair friendly. Also, I took full responsibility for everything that had to be done for her, including hospital visits etc. It was my way of trying to make life easier for Lar.

Every Monday night Mr. Hamill paid me by cheque. The amount I earned was equal to Lar's wages. He was now managing the money so I left the cheque on top of the television every week for him to lodge in our joint account.

I never felt that I could touch that money, even for the children. He gave me an allowance every Friday for food etc. I continually ran out of money especially when paying for extra activities for the children. I felt that I had to account for every penny so I seldom asked for extra money. Instead I tried doing extra sewing like alterationsthe odd wedding dress, to get cash, that I could hide on Lar. Out of this, I could buy the material to make the children's clothes, uniforms etc. I seldom bought anything for my self, except that if I had any fabric over from other people's work, with their permission I would keep it.

From time to time, I ran out of cash especially when the communion season was in full swing. This was because Mr. Hamill paid me by cheque, and I was far too busy to take on other cash paying work. So, I robbed a cheque from the back of the cheque book, stub as well, and cashed it in our local supermarket. Either one of us could sign on our joint account cheque book.

Lar was meticulous at checking the figures on our account, and every penny was logged in a list that he kept. One morning he was going through the figures, and missed £50. He asked me if I had written a cheque, and out of fear, I said no. He was like a mad man, giving out about the bank, so it was no time for me to confess. I managed to convince him that maybe it was our mistake, hoping he would let it go.

He did but he wasn't happy. In those days all cheques cashed against you were returned, so now I had to watch the postman! The bank statements were addressed to both of us, so it wouldn't be unusual for me to open it. I removed it before he came home, so I got away with it for now.

Alas, I had to do it a few more times, but it was getting harder. He said to me one day that we should change banks as this guy in our present bank was working some kind of scam! I decided after that not to do it any more if I could help it. When I got paid in cash from my 'little' jobs, I kept it secretly from him. It was the only way that I could manage. He did not realise how valuable it was to us, for me to make the children's clothes, and I felt that he expected me to work miracles with the allowance he gave me.

In fairness though, I never discussed it with him, I just struggled on. Maybe I wanted him to think that I was a good manager. But I think the real truth was, I was afraid of confrontation. I knew he didn't rate me as a housewife, so I didn't want to be a failure at managing the money.

We had many holidays in Blackpool with the children. There was so much to do there, that the children loved it and wanted to go back year after year. We made sure that they had fun filled days, so that they were exhausted by bedtime. Their favourite was Pleasure Beach, with all the rides and fun stalls. Lar brought Valerie and Pamela on everything, including the 'White knuckle rides'. June was a bit nervous, so we didn't push her. I was the one standing by, holding the cardigans!

Pamela wanted to get on everything, no matter how scary it was, in fact, the scarier the better. Lar loved that about her, I suppose because it brought out the kid in him.I have fond memories of Blackpool, but sad ones as well. One year I was in so much pain that I never slept for the whole holiday. I remember lying in bed during the night and not being able to wipe the tears from my eyes because I couldn't lift my hands. Lar liked to go out every night on holiday, so he got frustrated when I was limping along. He also liked to 'pub crawl' to see what was going on in all the pubs. I would just get comfortable sitting somewhere, and he would say 'Come on, let's try that pub across the road'. Sometimes the entertainment would be so good that we would stay, and I would be delighted. I used to hate the walk back to the hotel. Lar never walked beside me, instead, he would be ten yards ahead. He said it was a strain for him to walk slow, so every few yards he would look back and let out a frustrated sigh.

In the mornings, I got up an hour earlier to loosen up. I tried my very best not to let the children know how much pain I was in. I wanted them to remember the fun they had on our holidays, and looking back on the photographs, I think they do.

The only shoes that I could wear on holidays were trainers. The thick rubber soles cushioned the lumps on the soles of my feet. One night in Blackpool, we booked a cabaret show in a club. I was looking forward to it because it meant that we would be staying in the one place for the night. When we were getting ready to go out, Lar looked at me and said 'You're not going out to a club in those shoes are you?' But I told him that I didn't have a choice, I couldn't walk without them. 'Well' he said, 'Be prepared to be turned away, because they have a man on the door and a dress code'. It took the good out of the evening, even though the man welcomed us to the club, I had a heavy heart all night, knowing that Lar was ashamed of me.

Coming home I remarked how we were welcomed into the club and nobody said a word about my shoes, and he just said 'Yes, I'm surprised at that!'

Some times I wished I had the strength to give him a good shake, but most times I just adored him, no matter how he insulted me. We could have great laughs together because he had a great sense of humour. Also we enjoyed the same kind of music. Lar had a good record collection, ranging from Woody Gutherie and Jack Elliot to Leon Radburn. We read the life story of Woody Gutherie, and would spend long hours talking about the life he had. Lar would sing many of his songs accompanying himself on the guitar regularly. I loved to hear him sing, but he didn't realise how good he was, so he seldom sang for anyone else, except when he was in the ballad group with the other guys, or if he had a few drinks. As the children got older, he sang to them before bedtime, teaching them the songs. Of course they thought he was great, and he was. He loved the guitar. Anytime he was worried, or had a big decision to make, he would play it and go into another world.

It was hard to believe that he would get so aggressive towards me if the housework wasn't up to scratch. I kept trying harder and harder to get it right, but it would be many years before I was to realise that it would never be right.

When we had visitors he was full of fun, laughing and telling jokes. In fact I remember a relative saying to me one time 'It must be hilarious being married to Lar!' And of course I was the envy of everyone with all the work done in the house. Valerie and June, learned to appreciate nice things and kept their rooms clean. But Pamela's was a disaster area! Even so, Lar couldn't bring himself to say anything to her. She was Cuddles, so every now and then he would try to tidy it for her.

In fairness, when the children were small, he never got cross with them. I remember one time Pamela kicked the door off the sideboard in a tantrum. When Lar came home, he said 'Ah its ok, I can cut a piece of of the door and move the hinges!'

Pamela was so full of fun that it was hard to get cross with her, even when she got up to mischief. She loved to be ahead of everyone else in school, so she always learned the next page in her reading, to keep on top. One day she came home from school and said ' Mammy I'm the best in the class'. Oh I said, 'Did the teacher tell you?' 'No Mammy' she said " I noticed it myself!"

Another time I bought her and June a new pen each for school. I overheard her saying to June 'These pens are no good'. 'Well mine writes lovely', said June in reply. 'Oh yes', said Pam, 'So does mine, but they are no good for chewing!'.

The pubs in the early eighties closed at eleven o 'clock on weekdays, so Lar began calling in on the way home for a quick pint. Sometimes if he finished early enough, he would have a few more. I would stay up late with his supper ready for when he came home. I hated when he came home on the late shift after a few pints, and I told him so, but he said that I was ridiculous, as he was just having a drink after a hard days work.

On the early shift he would not drink on Monday, Tuesday, Wednesday or Thursday because he had to get up at 5.30am for a six o'clock start. But all the other nights he would have a few.

I got tired waiting up late for him but I still made his supper and left it on the pot.On Saturday nights we still got a babysitter and went out. He did the drinking, and I did the driving. I got to hate our nights out now. Every week it was the same, as soon as he started drinking he insulted me all night. He made it clear that the arthritis ruined HIS life. He reminded me of all the things we couldn't do because of the arthritis, and June.

When he was finished hurting me because of my illness, he would then tell me how hopeless I was at housework. Every week I drove home in floods of tears, while he sat in silence beside me. I would try to compose myself when I got to the house, in case the children were still up. I would still make a supper for him, then go to bed. In spite of my illness and Junes disability, I never asked him to stay home from work on our behalf for all the years he worked for the oil company.

In fact the only time he missed work up until he retired, was when he had the flu' or on a few occasions a bad hangover on Monday mornings. Regularly he would wake up the next morning full of the joys of spring, chatting away as if nothing was said the night before. So I too continued on as if nothing happened. I would be so glad for the children's sake that he was in a good mood, that I felt there was nothing to gain by prolonging it.

Financially, we were doing well, with Lar's good wages, and my sewing for Mr. Hamill. We were able to open a deposit account and put Mr. Hamill's cheque in it every week, at the same time we were now able to change our car every two years without borrowing. I also encouraged Lar to put a small amount in the credit union every week. We had a book each, and put the same amount in regularly.

All this time he was controlling the joint current account and giving me an allowance each week. I never questioned him as I would never argue over money, and we never did. He was a fanatic about paying the bills on time. I used to joke with him saying that the postman was only at the gate, and you're running up to the bank!

Chapter Fifteen
THAT BLASTED ARTHRITIS!

The arthritis was taking it's toll on me by the mid eighties, and I knew that I didn't look my best. I was unable to either dress or strip without help, so Valerie helped me into bed every night. She was so gentle with me and nothing was too much trouble.

Still, I did all the "mammy" things, and never missed any parent teacher meeting. I would always turn up, leaving home early to hobble over. Lar was usually in work or if he wasn't, left it to me as that was "woman's" work.

He never gave me much sympathy for my pain and expected everything to be done in the house, if he wasn't there. I still got up at six o'clock every morning and tried to exercise and meditate to get going. He would get up at ten if he was on the late shift and look around at the house. Shouting at me he would say' You're up since six so what were you doing all this time? After listening to this day after day,I yelled back at him 'Where were you until ten o'clock?' 'Bed' he roared back. 'Yes' I said, 'And I rest my case!'

I was now getting fed up going out on Saturday nights and coming home in tears, so I gave it a miss for a while. He went out to the local pub on his own so he would not have to drive. I enjoyed sitting in with the children and they were delighted to have me there. I did not wait up for him but made his supper as usual and left it on the pot. Next morning he would tell me who he met and we would chat about the interesting people he was with all night.

He was a very dutiful man and did not tolerate infidelity in marriage. He always took the high moral ground, no matter who it was that was cheating.......

I began keeping a diary because I couldn't tell anyone the way he was treating me, so a diary was the next best thing. Not one of my lovely sisters suspected a thing, nor my Mam and Dad. I still went out with my sister Joan every Tuesday night.

Sometimes we did a course together like cookery and flower arranging, other times we went swimming or for a drink. Neither of us drank, so we would just have a
mineral or coffee

One night she told me how she envied me with how great Lar was. I had a bad time that day with Lar throwing insults at me. I said to Joan, 'Everything is not as it seems'. So I told her a few things about my real life. She could not believe it, because everyone loved Lar, even my parents thought he was great! I was amazed that my mother didn't figure it out as she was great at seeing through people. I was glad that I confided in Joan, as when things got bad I could talk to her. Besides, she never once told another soul about my situation.

Strangely enough, on the face of it we were a normal married couple. We still made love every night of the week although I hated the ' drunken nights'. I have to say that he did make allowances for the pain I was in when he was sober, and he was gentle.

He still said 'I love you' before he went to sleep, so I believed he did.

I still loved him with all my heart and soul, and thought that someday he would realise how much he was hurting me, then he would be full of remorse, and we would live happy ever after.

There were lots of meetings and get togethers in the Spina Bifida association for June. Lar came to a few of them at first but then he refused to go. I asked him why and he said that he didn't want to be in a room full of people where the only common denominator was a disabled child. I put it down to his shyness and just went on my own. One year there was a party on for them and I asked him to go but he said no.

I knew he didn't want to go but I thought he'd help me with the wheelchair.

However Valerie said that she would love to go, so she did and we had a great time. When we came home we were having trouble turning the key in the hall door as it
kept sticking. Our bedroom is right beside the hall door and I knew Lar was in bed. But we had no choice but to call him to

open the door. He jumped out of bed aggressively and began shouting at us. June was terrified, while Valerie and I tried to reason with him. It was clear to me that he was drunk, for no amount of talking worked. 'You're trying to make me feel guilty for not going' he roared. Nothing could be further from the truth. I knew he was uncomfortable in those situations, so once I had Valerie to help me I didn't mind. The shouting went on for quite some time so I explained to the children in a whisper that daddy had too much to drink and didn't realise what he was saying.

Never the less they were still frightened, and still remember to this day. Next morning I got cross with him over frightening the children, and all he said was 'I don't know what you're talking about'.

By now Pamela was doing well at the gymnastics, and we all took a great interest, especially Lar. We got involved with the club and fund raised so the team could go to America. In fairness Lar spend long hours organising poker classics, sales of work etc. which for him was unusual as he always said to me' Never volunteer for anything, I learnt that in the army'. But then, this was for 'Cuddles' the apple of his eye! Valerie was allowed to accompany Pamela to America. They were there for a month and although they had a ball, we missed them terribly. June was lonely too without them. We counted the days until they returned. Pamela represented Ireland many times with the national team, and we were so proud of her. One time she was going to Manchester with the team, and we were getting ready to go out to the airport with her. Lar looked at me in my jeans and runners and said ' Don't tell me you are going to the airport like that in those runners'. I was so hurt in front of the children that I struggled to hold back the tears. I said 'Lar if I could wear stiletto heels, I would wear them'. 'But' he roared 'You can't go out like that'. By now we were both raising our voices and Pamela started to cry. 'I'm not going' she said through her tears. I gave her a big cuddle and said, 'Come on Pam, you sit with me in the back seat'. So we all poured into the car and headed for the airport. When we got there and met up with the other mothers, I had to laugh! All of them were in track suits and runners! Lar laughed too when I pointed it out, but it was too late now, the damage was done. Once again my feelings were hurt, and in front of the children.

I loved when Lar would have a few months of good moods, and he did. Life was great even though he never lost an opportunity to remark on my clothes or my household skills. I buried my head in the sand most times, especially for the children, and for peace. I began to go out with him again on Saturday nights. Sometimes they ended like before, with me in tears coming home, other times it was good if we were with friends.

I never told Connie for years how Lar was at home, about the house work. But one day I said it in joke about him always going over everything I did. She told me that when they were small, they all had to share the housework from very young on account of their mothers illness. They were told by their dad that they would be put into a home if they didn't keep the house clean. She recalled that when she and Lar had to scrub the kitchen floor, that his side was always cleaner than hers!

That chat with Connie made a lot of sense to me. I then tried to excuse his obsession with the housework, but I couldn't excuse the insults and criticisms.

She also told me that whenever he spoke about me to her, that he praised me constantly. Although I believed Connie, I could not even imagine him praising me!

Anyway, I convinced myself that he loved me as much as I loved him.

In 1986, Pamela got a bad injury in gymnastics. It was a terrible time for her as she was beginning to peak at the game. We worried about her but she was very brave. She had her knee operated on and would remain eight weeks in plaster.

We spent every day in the hospital, sometimes taking turns if we couldn't go together. One night we were there together, when her coach Frank came to visit. He was the best coach in the country and looked after the national team. We were chatting all night, when I said to him 'Frank, what made you get involved in gymnastics?' He went on to tell me about how he got involved many years ago.

On the way home, Lar said' I nearly died when you asked him that, it was a stupid thing to ask!' In my own mind I did not think that there was anything wrong with the question, but then all night in bed it kept going round and round in my brain. For a brief moment I worried in case I embarrassed Frank, or Lar, but then I decided that this was another put down. Normally, Lar dominated every conversation, so it wasn't very often, that I got to talk. I wanted to pick him up on it the next day, but as usual for peace I let it go.

Pamela went back to school on crutches after two weeks at home. She loved school and hated to miss out on anything. But we were a sorry sight walking to school. I was hobbling and hanging on to the wheelchair, while Pamela hobbled beside me with her crutches! However we battled on together and very soon Pam was back at the gym in training again.

After my mam died in 1983 I became very close to my dad. I was a daddy's girl throughout my childhood. I suppose because there were no boys in our family, Daddy brought me to football matches. So from very young I developed a love of soccer which in those days was unusual for a girl. I had good knowledge of the teams and the players, and when television came into our lives, I watched every match that I could. Dad and I would have long conversations about players and teams. I remember shortly after I married, I was visiting mam and dad while dad was watching a match.

He said to me ' Look at this young lad, he is magic on the ball'. I had to agree, I never saw anything like his skill. He went on to become one of the best players ever. He was George Best!

Dad came to visit me every day after mam died. Our house was only a ten minute walk from his. I loved seeing him every day, especially when Lar was on the late shift. I could have normal conversation with him without watching every word. And I knew he loved me warts and all. He had nursed Mammy for years with her rheumatoid arthritis, so he knew better than most, the pain that I was in. He came up with all sorts of suggestions to make life easier for me. He gave me a cutlery set belonging to Mammy that was specially for people with rheumatoid arthritis. They were an odd shape but comfortable to use. Lar made a laugh of them, so I put them away and never used them. I did not tell Daddy, as he thought the world of Lar.

I was in the worse pain ever during the eighties. Never, at any time did I ask Lar to stay out of work on my behalf, and he never offered. He was continually annoyed that the arthritis ruined his life, and kept telling me so. At times I used think that if I ever got better, that I would never talk to him again.

One day on one of my visits to the rheumatic clinic, Dr. Casey was giving me instructions about resting my joints. I broke down and told him about the home situation. He kindly listened and let me talk for as long as it took. He said to me 'Your husband needs help'. I agreed, and explained to him about the depression. Dr. Casey said that he would refer him to an excellent psychologist in Dun Laoire. But my next problem was getting him to go. So I went home and told him the truth, and what Dr. Casey said. Amazingly, he agreed to go. Even though his behaviour was getting me down at times, I thought it was brave of him to go.

He went for six sessions, and I was invited to attend the sixth one with him. We couldn't pronounce the psychologist name as it was foreign, so we called him Migallo So for the last session, I met Migallo for the first time. He said to Lar, 'You have a beautiful wife and you should be proud of her'. I got a fright as no one ever described me as beautiful! It made me feel good, but Lar just shrugged.

Things improved slightly after that making it easier to get through the day. Alas, it only lasted a short time and the hurtful remarks were never far from the surface. But the children were a big part of our lives, so life went on. As I said earlier, Pamela (Cuddles) and Lar were very close. He would often come home early from work and take her out to Seapoint for a swim. I was delighted for Pam as I knew how much she loved swimming, but I was beginning to notice that June felt left out. Pam was like Lar, full of adventure, were as June was nervous and had to be encouraged out of her comfort zone. She was a happy child, but shy, and only told me her real feelings. I tried to get her involved in extra activities including swimming, wheelchair sports, and the Order of Malta. One day she came home from school announcing that her friends Nessa and Laura were joining the tap dancing class. She asked if she could go too. I explained as gently as I could that she would not be able to dance. 'Oh I know that' she said, 'I only want to learn the songs!'. I had to laugh, but then realised that she loved singing and had a nice voice, so much to her delight I let her go.

I liked to let the children join as many activities as they could manage. The only problem was getting to and from the venues if Lar was working. When he was at home we were able to share the journeys. Valerie was getting old enough to walk to the Girl Guides herself with her friends to the local school.

One day June and Pamela got their eyes tested in school. June came home with a form for glasses. I was surprised and questioned her about the reading test. She said that she could not read the last four lines. So I asked Pamela could she read them.

'No' she said, 'Then why did you not get a form too?' I asked. 'Because, I learned them off before it was my turn!' I did not let her see me laughing, but I explained to her that you have to tell the truth for an eye test. It would be a few months before she got a new test and glasses. Lar tried to stop me from getting them, refusing to believe there was anything wrong with her eyes. ' Besides,' he said ' gymnasts don't wear glasses'. This was in the days before contact lenses, However I insisted that she wear them, and she admitted that it was better.

Life was indeed hectic at that time. I was on a lot of medication to cope with the pain. I often didn't sleep for weeks. I remember trying to sleep with my arm in the air to try to relieve the throbbing. I would listen to Lar snoring beside me, and thank God that he was getting a good nights sleep. I did novenas to every saint in heaven, praying for help. I bought every book that was ever written about rheumatoid arthritis. I tried every diet, every alternative medicine, every quack in the country, all to no avail. I took cod liver oil every morning for years. No matter what anyone told me to try, I gave it a go. I spent a lot of money on acupuncture, and herbal medicine, but I soon realised that the small amount of relief came from conventional medicine.

One day my next door neighbour, who is a deeply religious lady, told me about a healing priest from America who was visiting the Priory in Tallaght Dublin that night. She suggested I go along and I would find some comfort. Valerie was about fifteen at the time so she took care of the younger ones while another neighbour kept in touch with her. I had bought an old car a few months before so I painfully got in it and away I went. When I got there, it was a charismatic meeting and everyone was greeting new members with a hug and kiss. I felt very uncomfortable, both physically and mentally. I'm not a touchy feely person, and the only people I ever kissed were my husband and children! However, this was desperation time and I'd have kissed anybody who would make me better!

The priest was very nice, placed his hands on my head and prayed. He told me he would ask God to relieve me of my pain. He then gave me rosary beads and prayer sheets. I got into my car and headed home feeling very spiritual but in a lot of pain. I remember sitting in the driveway at my house working up the courage to open the door of the car. It was an old Renault 4L and the door handle was in a "slit" in the door. I had to use my hairbrush to open it, as my fingers wouldn't bend to put in the slit. Anyway with great difficulty I opened it and went into the house, still feeling holy and peaceful. Valerie was waiting up to help me into bed. Lar was on the late shift so Val helped me make his supper and left it on the pot. (No microwaves then). I sat on the side of the bed with my arms out while Valerie took off my clothes. She was so gentle, putting on my nightdress then easing me into bed.

We talked for a while and I told her all about the evening with the healing priest. Just then Lar burst in the door in a panic. 'Quick' he said 'Get up!, someone tried to

rob my car from outside of the pub and all the wires are stripped! I need to tow it home with your car'. Valerie said 'Daddy, mam is in terrible pain, and I've just helped her into bed'. He yelled back, 'Ah for jaysus sake, I only want her to sit behind the wheel while I tow it'. Valerie tried telling him how hard it would be to get dressed again but he was shouting now and getting aggressive.

I asked Valerie to help me back into my clothes and he drove my car down to the Long Mile Inn. When we got there, he jumped out and checked the car again. I sat in my car and he came running back to me shouting 'Are you not getting out to look at the damage?' I called out through the window 'I forgot my hairbrush to open the door!' He yanked the door open and yelled 'For jaysus sake'........and rolled his eyes to heaven!

I got out and he showed me the wires pulled out, ready for a hot wire robbery. I was in so much pain that for a brief moment I wished it had been robbed so that I could have stayed in bed.

He tied a rope to the cars and I sat in his, steering it while he drove mine. Halfway up the Long Mile Road I thought he was going too fast, and I felt that I didn't have control of his car. Stupidly I gently hit the brake, and the rope broke!.

He jumped out of the car again and gave me an earful. I was too exhausted to answer him, so I hoped he would just get on with re-tying the rope and go home. Somehow we made it home, and poor Val was still waiting up for to help me back into bed. Next day, he talked non stop about the near robbery. I just listened, but in my mind I was saying that he should not be drinking on his way home from work. I could have

said it to him, but it was easier to say nothing.

The whole episode upset Valerie, so I played it down in the days that followed for her sake. But deep down I was angry for the way he spoke to me that night with no regard for my feelings, or my pain.

Early in 1987, my body was in a mess from the Rheumatoid Arthritis. My feet looked dreadful with my toes on top of each other and the lumps on the soles getting worse. My two knees were enormous with fluid making walking more difficult. I now weighed eight stone but looked out of proportion with my swollen knees.

Lar would tell me from time to time how bad they looked, as if I didn't know myself! In front of the children he would tell me that my toes were in a mess. But I would make a joke out of it and say, 'Ah I saw the days when you used to kiss them!'And he did! 'Well,' he would say smartly 'I wouldn't kiss them now'. I dreamed of getting them straightened, and walking barefoot in the sand. But for now I was in too much pain to worry about how I looked.

On my next visit to the clinic, Dr. Casey made an appointment to remove the fluid from my knees, and inject them with steroids. I was delighted and thought the day would never come. I remember going alone to have it done. On arrival, I was walking from the car park to the main door of the hospital, when I looked down at my knees. They were so big that they wobbled from side to side as I walked down an incline. Lar was right, I truly was in a mess!

The procedure was painful as my joints felt as if they were on fire. However as I slowly hobbled back to the car, I thought my knees looked beautiful, as they removed fluid from them before injecting the cortisone. When Lar came in from work he didn't think they looked much different, but I could feel the fluid goneand some relief from the pain.

Every year, we still went on holidays with the children, and we had an occasional weekend away on our own. I never really liked being on our own, because he would spend the weekend telling me what life would be like if I didn't have rheumatoid arthritis. Usually I was in too much pain to re-act, but what was the point? He was convinced that it had ruined HIS life.

I was still an independent woman financially, so many times I told him that if he couldn't cope, I wouldn't blame him if he left me. I had hoped that he would say that he loved me too much to leave, instead he said that he couldn't live with the guilt if he did leave. Sadly, that was not what I wanted to hear.

Amazingly I could still sew but while I could get comfortable sitting at the sewing machine, cutting out the dresses was painful. Mostly because I couldn't stand for long periods. I bought myself a high stool which helped, but to cut dozens of dresses at a time, I used an electric cutting machine, and therefore needed to stand, for full safe control. Mornings were my best time of day for this, so I got up at six to exercise and get going. I would cut for an hour, then get the children up and ready for school. Valerie was a teenager now and needed no help, but was a great help to me!

I had difficulty getting up from a sitting position, so if I was expecting anyone to call for a fitting, I kept walking around until they came. Monday nights Mr. Hamill camepunctually at 10pm. He was like clockwork so I stayed on my feet from 9.30 and gently walked around the workroom. Neither he or Keelin ever knew the pain I was in as I greeted them every week, but after they left, I fell in to bed with pain, leaving Lar to lock up.

By now I was fed up with a life of pain, and wished I could just enjoy my family and get on with my life. In September of that year (1987) Dr. Casey told me of a new drug that was having amazing results in America. He had just returned from there so he was interested in trying it out on a few patients. He explained that it was a serious drug and it did have side effects, but the results would hopefully outweigh the side effects. It was Methotrexate and it was a chemotherapy drug but it was discovered that it helped rheumatoid arthritis in small doses.

Without hesitation I agreed to try it. I told myself that I had nothing to lose. He said that I would have to get a liver function test every month for as long as I was on it.So he gave me the first dose, it was one 10mg tablet every week. I looked at the tablet in disbelief. I was used to taking fistfuls of tablets every day to keep going. How could one tiny tablet a week be of any help to me? Dr. Casey assured me that I should get relief in about a month.

It did make me feel a bit sick but only on Sundays, the day I took it. Three weeks later, I woke up with no pain for the first time in years. I was still stiff and my lumpy feet were sore, but that throbbing pain was gone.

I went to mass that Sunday and although I still couldn't kneel down, I thanked God with all my heart, and prayed for Dr.

Casey. In private, I cried with relief, although I held my breath for a while in case it didn't last. But it did.

I still had sore joints, but that severe throbbing pain was gone. I had hoped that it would make a difference to Lar's moods, but it was the same as ever. Sometimes they were good, and I would be full of plans, But then he wouldn't talk for days.

Most times I pretended that I didn't notice, and continued to ask how his day went in work. He usually went into detail about his day because he knew that I was really interested in where he went and who he met.

Chapter Sixteen

THE PERFECT FAMILY

It was about this time that I realised he frequently mentioned Maura who worked in the office. Her job was to allot the work for the day to each driver. Allegedly, according to Lar, Maura could make or break your day, depending on what trips she gave you. He alleged that she had her favourites, and if you weren't one of them you got a bad day. So Lar told me that he had to keep on the good side of her to get a handy day.

But I worried when he told me about other lads who stood up to her, got lots of bad days. I hate unfairness, so I had many an argument with him over this. I couldn't understand how he had no bother shouting at me, and yet he would not say a word to her. In my opinion he sat on the fence and let the other lads fight with her.

One of the other lads told him one day that Maura said 'I wouldn't throw Lar out of the bed for eating crisps!' I asked him what was going on here, and he dismissed it saying Maura just liked him. I put it out of my mind, telling myself that Lar had a good sense of duty like his father before him, so he wouldn't do any thing wrong.The yearly dances in work had not been mentioned in a few years, and we had lost touch with Sean and Áine , so I never thought too much about it. But then one day at the supermarket I met one of the other 'work' wives. She asked why I hadn't been at any of the dances in a few years. I had no idea that they were still on so I was embarrassed and didn't know what to say. I confronted Lar when I got home and a row broke out. His defence was that he thought I wouldn't want to go because I wasn't well and couldn't wear the right shoes! I was hurt and sad. True, I was in pain, but he knew I would have made a real effort to look decent in front of his colleagues. I now knew that he was ashamed to be seen with me for sure.

There was another 'do' for the company staff every Christmas. He never failed to tell me about that one, because it was staff only. He never missed going to any of them. He sometimes drove, but with the new drink driving laws I drove him and often got out of bed to collect him if he couldn't get a taxi. The majority of the staff were men but there was a few female office staff including Maura. One year the party was being held in Killarney and there was free drink for everyone on the train the whole way down to Kerry. I knew that he would take full advantage of it down and back.

The night before, he was in great form , all talk about what was ahead. He said to me almost casually, 'Maura said she would wake me up on Sunday, so that I don't miss the train back'. 'What' I said, 'I hope nothing is going on here'. 'Ah don't be silly' he said 'She was only messing'. Nevertheless, I went out early next morning and bought a small travel alarm clock, I was leaving nothing to chance.

I was such an innocent soul, as if a little clock could do anything. But deep down I kept thinking of his sense of duty, and anytime he heard of infidelity he always took the high moral ground. Besides, in my mind he loved me deeply, and couldn't live without me...........

Meanwhile life went on as normal, the children were getting older, and to everyone we knew, we were the perfect family. Most days I acted like we WERE the perfect family. I think a lot of people envied us, because we had no financial problems at a time when the recession, during the eighties, was gripping the country. We could still go on holidays without touching our joint bank account. I never ceased to thank god for the gift of sewing. Indeed to this day I still thank him, and I never took it for granted.

When Valerie was about fifteen, she also took an interest in fashion. I was delighted and taught her how to make some of her own clothes. She picked it up very quickly, in spite of me being right handed and her left handed! We had many a laugh over this, especially when she would do something 'upside down' but with the right result!

I then taught her how to make the handbags to match the holy communion dresses for Mr. Hamill. She was great and in no time at all, she was earning her own pocket money. She had a talent not only for dress design but for interior design as well. She always had her opinion of what way we would decorate the house. I remember one day she came home from school while Lar was halfway through tiling the kitchen wall. She took one look at it and said, 'That colour doesn't work, it looks awful'. Before she came home, we were standing back after every tile, admiring it, convincing ourselves that it looked good. Now with Valerie home, everything came to a standstill. It was a bit like 'The King's New Clothes'. I had to admit the bright red tiles looked better in the kitchen showrooms!

We took back down every one of the tiles and abandoned them, but next time we bought tiles, it was with Valerie's approval!

Pamela's day was full. She was very bright in school without effort. Although she studied hard, it seemed to come natural to her. After school and homework, she went to her gymnastic classes. She was also a strong swimmer, and in later years became the Leinster spring board diving champion. She and Lar were extremely close, and he would talk about her for hours to anyone who would listen.

One day when June was in her early teens, she said to me, 'Mam, I don't think Daddy like's me'. I was shocked. I had no idea that she felt like this. I reassured her that indeed he did love her as much as her sisters. But her words haunted me. Was I so caught up in other things that I hadn't noticed something? I did realise that Lar and Pamela were like pals. But I knew it was because her sense of adventure, was exactly like his. Pam's life was full of fun and games, and at that age she didn't notice that Daddy was spending more time with her than the other two. But Valerie was older now and well able to fight her corner for attention.

That night when Lar came home I told him what she said. He laughed and said 'that's silly'. Well to June it was a big thing so now that I was aware of how she felt, I made sure she wasn't left out. June was by nature nervous and had no confidence. I madea real effort to bring her school friends home to our house because her friends houses weren't suitable for wheelchairs.

I encouraged her to join anything she was able for, including wheelchair sports. I made friends with lovely neighbours called Sonny and Ida Kelly. Although they had seven children of their own, they loved June and she loved them. They cared for her so much that they dug up their garden and built a ramp so that June could go in and out on her own! This made a big difference to her as the Kelly's house was four houses away from ours, so she felt all grown up visiting on her own. And no matter what time of the day and night she called, they made a big fuss of her. They treated her like one of the family and she always came home laughing and full of chat.

They were the only people that could get June talking as she was very shy. One day Ida took June on the summer project to the Japanese Gardens with some of her own children. June was terrified going through the tunnel, so Ida lifted her up in her arms, callipers and all, and carried her all the way through! I worried about Ida when I heard about it later as June was getting older and heavier, but Ida just laughed and said it was good exercise! When June related to me later about the tunnel, she said 'I'm never ever EVER going to the Japanese Gardens again'……. and she didn't! I loved being a mother, and Lar was a good father except when he left June out of some things. He had very little interest in any of her achievements. Anytime she won medals at the wheelchair sports, he would whisper to me that they probably gave a medal to all the kids. I would be furious when he said that because nothing could be further from the truth. I know, because I was there at many of the meets. But the difference when she brought her medals up to Ida and Sonny. They made a big fuss of her and told her she was great. No matter what the children won I too made a big fuss. Pam won some great awards for her gymnastics and diving, while Valerie's claim to fame was the Miss Shiny Shoes in the girl guides!

In 1989 Lar's youngest sister Ann died. She was 42 years old. It came fairly quickly after she was diagnosed with cancer, probably about eight weeks. We were all shocked, as it didn't seem like she was sick for long. On one of the times I visited her in hospital, my knees got locked from sitting in the one position.

I went to stand up but couldn't, then Ann got out of bed and lifted me up out of the chair! Three weeks later, she died.

I remember standing at her grave, thinking of her two young children, and realising how short life is. Ann and I had been good friends as well as sisters-in-law, and shared many a night out together. We had gone to swimming lessons, whereby she could swim after the second lesson, and I was still hanging on to the bar at the end of the course! She was a great cook and loved children. My girls loved visiting her and so were very upset when she died, especially Pamela, as she was her godmother.

Lar too took her death badly. They had there arguments like all siblings do but I know he loved her dearly. Death of a family member especially so young put a new meaning on life. I came home from the funeral, vowing to appreciate my family while I was still able to.

I was now making a super human effort to be a good wife, doing everything to take the pressure off Lar. In no time at all we were back in the old routine. Me, pretending to the outside world that everything was wonderful, while Lar lost no opportunity to point out my failings.

In 1990, June had a serious operation in the Mater hospital. She had a set back after it, and ended up in intensive care. Things weren't looking good. We were at her bedside night and day sick with worry. But thankfully she pulled through it, although she spent almost three months in hospital. By this time, Lar had taught Valerie how to drive, so it was great that she passed her driving test, and could help with the visits.June was in a ward with five other people. One of them had a remarkable effect on me. Her name was Kate, and I guessed that she was in her late sixties. She was suffering from Altzheimers disease. The nurse told me that it was a sudden onset of the disease, and that six weeks ago she was driving her own car, and playing golf.

She wasn't married, and she lived alone. I wondered to myself, how do we know that she didn't have symptoms for months before, if she lived alone? It was clear that she was a gentle soul, a real lady. One day she asked me to buy her oranges the next time I was coming in, giving me a pound for them. I didn't want the money but she was getting upset because I offered to pay. So to keep her happy, I took the pound. Next day I arrived with the bag of oranges. She looked at me vacantly as I handed her the bag. She just kept saying, 'no thank you'. She had no recollection of asking for them, or who I was. I left them on her locker, but she just kept bringing them back over to me. Finally I gave them to the nurse who said that she would keep them and give her one at a time.

For two months I made friends with her, helping in any way I could, as she had no visitors. We would be good friends all day, but next day she would have no idea who I was. In those two months I learned a lot about this disease, and I realised how sad it was. Sitting there one day with June, while Kate was sleeping, I wrote this:

The old woman in St. Teresa's ward sits looking into space
No sign of recognition on her lonely worried face
She will not move until a nurse might take her to the loo
And back again to sit and stare with nothing much to do.

Yet still she whispers thank you to a kindly act or deed
The old woman in St. Teresa's ward of whom visitors take no heed
The sadness in her vacant eyes that no one ever sees
Her now redundant gentle hands rest idle on her knees.

I bet behind those big blue eyes a story could be told
Of love and life's ambitions long before she grew old
I bet behind that wrinkled face a beauty she has been
I bet she broke some young men's hearts when she was just sixteen.

Perhaps you had a hectic life with boyfriends by the score
Perhaps you had a special one who passed on long before
I'd love to get inside your head and chat with you awhile
'Cause every time I pass your bed I'm haunted by your smile

I guess you loved the great outdoors, your skin is golden
brown
I'm sure you walked with head held high when shopping in
the town
I'd say you danced the night away in those happy days of
yore
And many friends from everywhere came knocking on your
door.

Where are these friends from yester-year with whom you
shared your past?
There must be one who still believes true friendships always
last
So friends of Kate I say to you please call awhile and see
Although her mind is now confused it could be you or me.

The old woman in St. Teresa's ward just sits alone to pray
But she drove her car and played her golf eight weeks ago
today!

I never forgot Kate. She gave me a new insight into what can
happen in life. There is nothing like a hospital ward to bring
you down to earth. It is the one place where you cannot 'keep
up with the joneses'.

My dad called in to me every day at four o'clock. He was now
retired, but he went into town every day with his bus pass.
He loved to go to the courts and watch the different cases up
before the judge, telling me all about them when he came. We
would have long discussions about the guilt or innocence of
individuals. Other times we would chat about football, but we
always watched 'Countdown' on channel four. This was a word
game show that we both loved.

The children enjoyed his visits as he made them laugh. He had a
great sense of humour that never failed to cheer us up. He was
also a very generous man, who donated thousands of pounds
to his favourite charity, (Council for the Blind) He never spoke
about it but I found out by accident.

Daddy loved Lar. He thought I was so lucky to have the perfect husband. I never let him know the difficult time I was having. When Dad was visiting, Lar was on his best behaviour, always laughing and joking with him. In fact, he was great company, no matter who visited us. He would dominate the conversation, and make everyone laugh, or talk about the children's achievements.

When we were alone, I began to wonder if perhaps it was me. He didn't have much respect for me, so I didn't feel like a worthwhile person. I never felt good enough.I remember having a discussion with him about male and female. He told me that in his opinion woman were not on the same par as men! He agreed that he was a male chauvinist. I couldn't believe it! Here he was in a house with four females, and none of us were on a par with him!

Needless to say, he wasn't getting away with that! Every female that crossed our door, both relatives and friends were told in front of him! It was great to see him trying to talk his way out of it.

Valerie went to the Grafton Academy to study dress designing, after doing well in her leaving cert. She was excellent at it and with me giving her tips at home, she passed all her exams. On Saturdays she worked with Mr. Hamill, to get as much experience as she could in fashion, and also for extra pocket money. It was here she met her future husband Wayne, a real nice lad from Blanchardstown. When we eventually got to meet him, Lar and I liked him instantly. It was clear that he was a good lad who cared deeply for Valerie. June and Pam loved him as well and looked forward to his visits. Many a day when June was in hospital, he would sit with her on his day's off work. Consequently, he and June became very close.

Valerie and Wayne sat in on Saturday nights to let Lar and I go out again together. By now I did not have that throbbing pain any more, although some of my joints would be sore from time to time. If I sat for long, my knees would lock so getting up would require a big effort. But I learned to laugh at my limitations. I knew what I was able for, and what I couldn't do. Dancing on my sore feet was out, so when we were at family weddings etc. I sat and enjoyed the music while everyone else danced. I remember my niece's wedding at the last dance everyone was up on the floor including Lar and all my sisters. There was cheering and laughing and I was sitting down cheering and laughing too. Then I looked around me to see the empty tables and seats. I realised that I was alone, sitting there clapping with my crooked hands.

For the first time ever I was filled with self pity. I looked over at Lar who by now had a lot to drink. He was full of jollifications swinging around with anyone and everyone. My sisters too were having a ball. No one noticed that I was sitting there on my own. However, when the dance was over and everyone came back to the tables I joined in again, refusing to wallow in self pity. I wouldn't mind but I was used to opting out when it came to dancing at every wedding, so what was different about this? I truthfully don't know. Perhaps it was because that now the real bad pain was gone, I was paying more attention to other feelings.

At the rheumatic clinic the physiotherapist made splints for my hands. She explained that if I wore them each night in bed, and an hour during the day, that it would stop my hands getting worse. If they got any worse she said that I would not be able to grip things in the future. This worried me, as I loved my sewing.

The splints were awkward ugly looking things, that took some skill to strap on to my hands with crooked fingers. However I mastered it after a few days. Every night that I wore them to bed Lar made a laugh of them. I got very hurt when he laughed so after a while I stopped wearing them. I'm not blaming him, I should have been stronger, less 'touchy'. But the truth was, I was still a young woman, and strapped up hands weren't very sexy!

So I abandoned them at night, but wore them for an hour during the day when Lar was at work. I have to say, when my wrists were sore, they gave great relief.

Chapter Seventeen

BACK TO SCHOOL

I always had a liking for writing and verse, but I realised that without the proper education, I was limited. Still it didn't stop me writing funny verses for the children. Many times if I had a complaint to make about some product, I would do it in verse, and subsequently would receive a gift from the manufacturer. It became a fun thing with the children, and they thought that I was great!

So at age 47, I went back to night school to study for Leaving Cert English. Pam was studying for her Leaving cert too, so we had great fun swapping notes. Lar never commented one way or the other, so I've no idea how he felt about it. And as it was at night, it didn't interfere with my household duties. However, my dad encouraged me as did my sisters, especially my youngest sister Rita, who was now a teacher. Just like years earlier, I was an eager student, reading up on Hamlet, Yeates etc. I looked forward to my classes, and studied late into the night. It gave me a new confidence even though I was the oldest in the class! The other pupils were mostly young boys and girls, the same age as my children, repeating the Leaving Cert. Halfway through the course, I was visiting the rheumatology clinic with Lar. Out of the blue he said to the doctor 'Can you do something with her feet?' I was not expecting this and didn't know what to say. But before I could say anything, the doctor said that he would send me to an orthopaedic surgeon for his opinion.

I was glad in a way but nervous of surgery. In any event, an appointment was made, and I went along, accompanied by my husband. Lar has suffered on and off with lower back pain. So, there I was sitting in this special chair with my two feet up on a platform as the doctor examined them. Lar struck up a conversation about lower back pain. 'What could it be?' he said to the doctor. 'Look' he said' I am very supple' bending down showing the doctor how he could touch his toes! Meanwhile, the doctor is trying to assess my feet while looking over at Lar doing his exercise! I was feeling embarrassed with the state of my feet as it was, without him going on about his back and delaying things! The doctor stopped looking at my feet and looked over at Lar, out of courtesy. 'Well', he said, 'I don't know, it would have to be investigated'

'Could we get back to my feet?' I asked, wishing Lar would shut up! My knees were starting to hurt with my feet in the air. Thankfully the doctor got on with it, telling me that he could indeed remove the lumps from the soles of my feet and straighten my toes. I was delighted but nervous. We had a good laugh on the way home at the way the visit went.

Two weeks later, I went in to St. James's hospital for surgery. When I woke after the operation, my dad was sitting beside me. I was very sleepy and thought I was dreaming. I must have went back asleep, because when I woke the next time Lar and the girls were there. We pulled back the bedclothes and looked at my feet. Although they were well bandaged up, I could see that the toes were straight. I was in a good bit of pain but it was worth it. I was now glad that Lar nagged me about them for years, and that he eventually asked the doctor about them.

I was told not to walk for a couple of weeks, until the soles of my feet healed. That will be the hardest part I thought to myself, not least because I needed to exercise my joints to stop them getting stiff.

But for now I was behaving myself in hospital, armed with lots of books to continue with my studies. My Dad came into me every afternoon, and I looked forward to his visits. One day, he was sitting in the chair beside the bed, and we were chatting away. Suddenly without warning, he fell forward and seemed to go into a kind of faint. I let a shout 'Dad, Dad, what's wrong?' A nurse heard the commotion and ran over to us. I tried getting out of the bed with my bandaged feet. The nurse got a wheelchair and put him in it. She said that he will have to go to casualty as she didn't like the look of him. I kept talking to him but he wasn't making any sense. Just then as luck would have it, Lar walked in. The nurse instructed him to run to casualty with him.

He was gone a long time and I was sick with worry. There were no mobile phones then and I had to contact my sister Marie as he lived with her and she would be expecting him home. I got out of bed and walked on my heels to the nearest public phone. Within an hour Marie was at the hospital and took over from Lar. Lar came back to me to break the news that dad had a stroke. My heart sank. The joy I felt with my 'new' feet was gone. I only wanted to see my dad. Later that night when Dad was settled in a bed, Marie came in to reassure me that he was recovering well, that it was a mild stroke. Nevertheless, it took the wind out of my sails, and brought me back to the real world.

Next day Lar brought me in a wheelchair to see Dad in a ward on the next floor. He certainly looked better than I expected, but had no recollection of what happened the day before. He could not or would not talk about it. Marie spoke to a doctor who told her that the following 24 hours after a stroke were crucial, but the signs with Dad were good.

We both left hospital around the same time, each of us recovering in our own way. But now it was a worry every time dad went out, especially for Marie. He began going off into town again and coming in to me at 4 o'clock as before, but if he was a few minutes late going home, Marie checked with me to make sure he was okay.But in time, we all got back to normal. I was delighted with my feet and for the first time in years could wear fashionable shoes. Not high heels, but comfortable fashionable ones. And the best part was, I was now a size smaller, so I now went from size six (sometimes seven to accommodate insoles) to a five! I made myself lots of 'flowing' skirts, and for the most part, felt like Cinderella before midnight!

I continued with my studies, and in the following June, sat the leaving cert English, with Pam. My children thought it was great fun, that Mammy was doing the leaving cert. But I took it seriously, and like all the young people doing theirs, I was nervous on the day. I did the pass paper, while Pam did the honours. Nevertheless, I thought it was difficult enough, although maybe it was because of my age.

When the results came out in the summer, I got an honour, so I was dancing around the kitchen with Pam and her eight honours! I was so excited, that I promised myself that I would go back the following year to study a couple more subjects. Alas, so many things were happening in my life, that much to my regret, I never did go back. But I still have my certificate hanging up with pride!

Later that year, Daddy had another stroke, but this time he didn't do so good. He got senile dementia following the stroke, and went into a nursing home. It was so sad visiting him when he was so confused. I collected Marie every night and we went together to the home. He knew we were familiar but he was unsure of who we were.

In fact, one night when we arrived there, he was throwing pillows at the nurse. We were shocked, as this was the gentlest man in the world. When he saw Marie, he said ' Here's Mammy now, she will sort you out!' He became gentle again when Marie spoke to him, and helped him back to bed. He thought Marie was our mother who had died nine years before. It was heartbreaking to sit with him, looking at a man that was so full of life, wisdom, and humour, now only a shell of his former self.

At home I lay awake thinking of him every night. I wondered if perhaps he understood all we were saying, but his brain couldn't communicate with his mouth. It set me thinking about strokes, how do we know it's not like I said? Doctors can only give their educated opinion, but they are not God. So I made up my mind that I would talk to him as if he knew everything I said. He loved the poetry of Robert W. Service. His favourite was 'The Shooting Of Dan Magrew'.

So I read it out to him regularly, and convinced myself that he was smiling at me each time. Marie was the practical one and would organise his personal things. She made sure that he always had his clean pyjamas etc. and she regularly moisturised his skin. My other sisters sat with him during the day and weekends. It was sad when we all met up with one another. Five sisters, who felt helpless, looking at our devoted Dad. It was hard for me to say how I was feeling. I talked to Lar a lot as he had also lost his dad. Although he was very fond of my Dad, he never went to see him much in the home. In the early days when dad got sick first, he visited him a few times with me in the hospital, but that was it. Lar liked to go to the pub Friday, Saturday and Sunday nights. At this stage, Valerie and Pam were out these nights, so I would ask him to wait until I got home, as I didn't want June in the house on her own.

Even though she was now sixteen, and in spite of her disability, was very independent, I got anxious when she was alone in the house.

Most times I was home in time, but occasionally I was delayed. Lar would be standing with his coat on waiting for me. Sometimes he didn't wait, he'd just go. If I got mad at him he'd tell me that I was ridiculous. Perhaps I was. In any event I continued on as usual at home. Getting up at six, bringing Lar in a cup of tea every morning, sewing for an hour before I helped June get ready. She still needed help with the double incontinence, so there were major wash ups, and bed baths every day.

Val was now working in the design room of Hickeys clothing factory, Pam was in her final year at secondary school, and June in fifth year in Ballinteer Community school. When all had left the house after breakfast, I did the housework, shopped, and sewed before making the dinner. I tried to get as much sewing done as I could during the day because I visited dad every night. One night I was with him on my own. I kept talking to him, telling him all the news but as usual, there was no reaction. I wandered on home that night thinking about my memories of childhood, and how cruel life is, so I stayed up late and wrote this:

Dad

I looked at your face, to see could I find
A little bit more than a feeble old mind
For you are the dad that helped me to grow
That taught me the lessons, I needed to know

You are the dad that showed me back then
To ride on a bicycle, to write with a pen
You never knew, but maybe you did
That you were my hero, when I was a kid

You could move mountains, build a brick wall
Solve any problems, no matter how small
You were the dad, that lifted me high
When I tumbled over, and started to cry

Good fun could be had, you often told
Without any money, or silver or gold
The best things in life, you always told me
Were the things the good God has given for free

Your silly tap dance, and funny old song
Brought many a wedding and 'hooley' along
The laughter from childhood, still rings in my ears
When your corny old jokes reduced us to tears

Alas, nothing is forever, you used to say
But it's not very easy to see you this way
If its true the good God is gentle and kind
Why then did he leave you with a feeble old mind?

Early in 1993 I went to St James's hospital for tests, following
recurring chest infections. It was discovered that I had an
enlarged heart and high blood pressure. Lar wasn't too pleased
that there was something else 'wrong' with me, and went
around feeling sorry for himself. I ignored him, took the tablets,

and got on with life. I still never asked him to stay home from work, as I was able to do all the 'mammy' things as well as sew. I also brought June to all her hospital appointments, which by now had become more frequent. I was determined to take the pressure off him by doing everything myself.

June and Lar, in my opinion, were never that close no matter how hard I tried to encourage it. They would 'joke' with each other but there was no serious conversation. Consequently she was closer to me, and her sisters. They loved her. But he did a master piece on the house for her, building ramps front and back and adapting the interior to meet her needs. But he never brought her out on her own, or seldom had much of a conversation with her, except to joke with her occasionally. So I made sure that she didn't feel left out by taking her out myself. She continued to tell me that Dad didn't like her, while I reassured her he did. I convinced myself that he did care about her because the alternative was too hard to comprehend. There was a lot of hard work in caring for June, but I never asked for help. Maybe it was because I felt a certain amount of guilt, as many mothers of disabled children do.

In February 1993 Dad was taken back to St. James's hospital with a bad infection. He was very ill from then on. A few weeks later, we got an urgent call from the hospital that he had another set back. Marie and I went up immediately, followed by my other sisters. We were there until 2 am, then the nurse assured us that he was now stable and that we should go home. It was a freezing cold night. I drove Marie home as we lived near each other. As I expected, my house was in darkness with everyone in bed when I got home. I was too tired and cold to make a cup of tea so I went to bed. I quietly got undressed so as not to wake Lar, because he was on the early shift and would be getting up at 5.30. I carefully lifted the duvet and got in. Next thing he roared ' You're bleedin' freezing keep away from me!'. I jumped with fright! Then I rolled myself up in a ball and moved out to the edge of the bed, and cried myself to sleep. I cried for my lovely Dad, who never raised his voice to my Mam in his life. I cried for the fact that Lar never asked how he was, even though he knew we were sent for urgently. I knew now that I was married to a selfish man.

And yet I loved him with all my heart, no matter what he said or did. I had great admiration for him driving those big long oil tankers. He was an expert driver, and excellent at his work. His knowledge of every road in Ireland never ceased to amaze me. He brought us to almost every county, without looking at a map! This was the man I loved, not the aggressive moody one who could insult me at the drop of a hat. Daddy died three weeks later aged 79, two months before his eightieth birthday. It was on a Sunday evening and all his five daughters were with him when he passed. I came home very sad and broke the news to Lar and the children. The children were upset, so I explained to them that granda had been so sick it was better now that he wouldn't suffer any more. Lar was standing with his coat on ready to go to the pub.

'Ah that's terrible, I'm sorry, he said. Then he looked at his watch and said ' I'm going up for a couple of pints, I won't be long, talk later', then he was gone. I felt annoyed with him, for leaving me to console the children, but in truth, I was glad, because when the children were in bed, I wanted to be alone. My thoughts wandered back in time to my childhood, remembering with great affection, the wonderful dad I had. So instead of feeling sad, I felt proud, happy, and grateful for the man that was my Dad. After the funeral I had an emptiness that lasted for quite some time. But inevitably life goes on without our loved ones and we cope because we have to. Dad left each of his five daughters a few hundred pounds in his will. Marie handed me mine in an envelope, and I showed it to Lar. I hadn't decided what to do with it, but Lar took it and said ' I will put it in our savings account for Pam's education, your dad would like that'. I was disappointed as I was given no choice, he just took it. There was enough money in the savings account for Pam's education, so I wanted to use it for other things. I wanted to buy a new overlock machine for my business.

Why was I afraid to speak my mind to him? I don't know. Sometimes I couldn't understand how I could be a good business woman, a good mother, a good sister, giving excellent advice to others, and yet acted like a child when it came to my husband! There were times when I did the most childish things, rather than stand up to him. Like when we run out of washing up liquid, I would pour water in it so he wouldn't tell me that I had forgotten to buy it again! Another time when we had red carpet in our sitting room, there was a part of it worn whereby you could see the sacking. I use to get one of the children's red felt tipped pens and colour it in so Lar wouldn't see it! June saw me do it one day and I said to her 'This is our little secret'.

I wouldn't mind but it was in a place beside the settee where Lar sat, so HE probably wore it out! This wasn't the journey I'd planned when we started out on the road that had a rainbow around the moon.

Chapter Eighteen
OUR FIRST SUN HOLIDAY

Having holidayed all over Ireland, much of England, and once to France, we thought we would give Spain a try. Valerie was delighted to look after June and Pam who were now teenagers. We booked about six weeks before hand, giving us time to make sure all would be well at home.

A few days before we left Lar came home from work and said 'You won't believe this!'. I told Maura a few weeks ago that we were going to Spain, and she booked for the same apartments for the same time!' I asked him how could she possibly have known where we were staying, and he admitted that he told her.

I wasn't happy at all, but at this late stage I felt that there was nothing I could do about it. In any event, off we went on our first sun holiday. We arrived in the evening, and I was glad that I couldn't see Maura anywhere.

We booked a ground floor apartment on account of my arthritis, so the swimming pool was only a few feet away. Next morning, out we came with the sun cream and the towels under our oxters and our books as we are both avid readers, From overhead we heard 'Howya Larry'. We waved, then made ourselves comfortable under our umbrella. After a while, Lar who is a strong swimmer hopped into the pool. I continued relaxing and reading. When I looked up later, he was nowhere to be seen. I shaded my eyes and scanned the pool, then I saw him. He was over the other side leaning on the edge, talking to Maura and her friend. They were both topless, and I could see that Maura was well endowed! At first I thought to myself how embarrassing it must be for him, because the Lar that I knew was very shy. Over an hour went by and he was still laughing and joking while I was left on my own. Now I was embarrassed, sitting there, totally ignored by all three of them. I stood up, put on my shoes, and went for a walk. I walked around the back of the apartments on to a lonely road. I know it was foolish of me but I just had to get away from the situation. I didn't know where I was for a while, but when I decided to go back, I retraced my steps. It was now near lunch time, and when I got back Lar was finally walking back to our chairs. 'Where did you go' he asked 'I went for a long walk because I got fed up waiting for you. He yelled at me 'Ah you're carrying on ridiculous'. 'They called me over, so what could I do?' 'Well you could have called me over and introduce me' I said, 'after all, up to now Maura was just a name to me'.

'Well you will meet her tonight as I said we would meet in the pub after dinner'. I was fuming that he made arrangements, without consulting me. Even when we went out to dinner, it was to a restaurant that Maura recommended. I was having a bad feeling about this holiday, and I was glad that we were only there for a week.That night we met in the pub as arranged and Lar introduced me to Maura. She was a big girl, probably in her late thirties while I was in my late forties at the time.

She briefly acknowledged me, then chatted away to Lar as if I wasn't there. Her friend was a quiet girl who didn't say much, but kept smiling. We took our seats in the pub that by now was full to capacity of holiday makers. There was a sing song, much like any pub in Dublin with many Irish and English people there. It was difficult to hold a conversation with the noise, but Maura made a good attempt at it. I was sitting with Lar on my left, she was on my right and her friend sat beside her. She continued to chat away to Lar, leaning over me as if I wasn't there. Then coming near the end of the night, with the whole place heaving and everyone singing at the top of their voices, she joined hands with Lar, waving them over my head. The band was singing 'Sweet Caroline' and it was at the line 'touching hands reaching out, touching me touching you'............that she grabbed his hand. I was between the two of them, feeling very much like an invisible wall flower. She just didn't see me at all! On the way back to our apartment, She walked with Lar ten yards ahead of her friend and I. I watched her linking him and felt sick. Lar knew that I couldn't walk as quick as him, but he never even looked back. Only for Maura's friend being so kind to wait for me, I would've got lost. I thought to myself as I tried to keep up, that this is not the holiday I planned.

I spoke to Lar about it the next day when he was sober. But I got nowhere with him, just the same old words 'You're being ridiculous'.

I did my best to steer him away from Maura for the duration of the week, but at night it was difficult. During the day we either went to the beach, or walked around town. It wasn't my best holiday. I tried not to embarrass Lar in front of a work colleague but I felt that she disrespected me as his wife, so the only way I could handle it was to avoid her as much as possible. Somehow I got through the week, but I was glad to get home. The children were excitedly asking us questions about the holiday and of course I said we had a wonderful time. I wanted to yell at Lar when we were alone and tell him how I truly felt, but like a coward, I let it go.

Any time after that when he mentioned Maura in the course of his work, I closed my ears. Even her name made me feel angry, especially as he was still trying to stay in her good books, to get a 'handy' day's work. I had more admiration for the lads who stood up to her, regardless of the consequences.

However, life goes on and when I was with the children I was happy, and could forget all else. The best thing about the children getting older was that now they wouldn't tolerate Lar insulting me any more. If he said anything derogative, they would yell back and tell HIM to look in the mirror at himself. It wasn't long before he realised that with four females in the house, he was outnumbered, and in fact laughed about it. I was enjoying the children as much as adults as I did when they were children. I loved listening to their stories about boyfriends etc. and encouraged them to bring them home. Pam had a huge amount of male friends. When they were younger they would congregate at our front door, laughing and talking. But as the years went on, and the lads voices broke, you would think that there was a row at the front door!

I kept asking her to bring them in so as not to annoy the neighbours, but they loved hanging out at the door. They were all lovely lads who went on to finish their education like Pam.
I was very protective of the girls, and when they brought home boyfriends, much to their embarrassment, I lectured them. Lar too was protective towards them, although he never said a word, he constantly instructed me to warn them to behave themselves.I remember continually saying to Wayne, now Val's husband, ' Anytime bad thoughts come into your head, just you remember my face!' He must have been sick listening to me, but even though he laughed, I hoped he got the message!
I often wonder did I spoil that beautiful moment when the time was right, did he remember my face? In any event, Val chose a wonderful lad who is a credit to his parents Monica and Robert.
When Pam first went to Maynooth university, she stayed with my sister Rita from Monday to Friday as she lived beside the railway station. After a while, she missed all her friends so she came home. She commuted to Maynooth by bus, losing her bus pass on a regular basis. Every morning I would say 'Pam, glasses, bus pass, keys It got to the stage that June would say it with me and in unison! But to Pam, life was just fun and not to be taken seriously. In spite of Lar's moods, I was of the opinion that my marriage was a happy one. Yes, we had a lot of 'hard knocks' but I thought we were talking our way through them. Every morning I brought him a cup of tea before he got up. At the weekend, I would sit on the bed chatting. I liked to hear about who he met in the pub the night before because he always seemed to meet such interesting people when I wasn't with him. It would be many years before I copped on that he seemed to socialise with separated people. He would tell me the intimate stories of different couples break-up, ranging from an alcoholic wife to a husband coming home to find his wife in bed with the local priest! We had a laugh about how individuals were caught out.
In spite of the hard time he gave me, I was in awe of this man. Yet in some ways he frightened me, especially when he shouted

at me. I remember one night we were having cross words as we often did, about how the arthritis had ruined everything, in fact he blamed it on his depression. In fairness it seemed to start around the time that I was diagnosed, so perhaps it had some bearing on it. Anyway during a heated argument, I yelled at him ' Your sister Ann was right, you ran away from trouble'.

I was referring to something that Ann told me years before, that his dad said when he went off to England before his seventeenth birthday, and eventually joined the British Army. She and Connie were only fourteen and fifteen years old, and so had to help in looking after the two younger ones. Ann missed a lot of school, while Connie had to work from very young. This is why his Dad said that he ran away from trouble.

Perhaps it was an unfair thing to say but he was yelling worse things at me, so I tried to hurt him as much as he was hurting me. After all, I was in a situation not of my own choosing, and in severe pain as well.

He went to the pub, but when he came back, he stormed into the bedroom. He woke me by yelling into my face, and pointing his finger aggressively at me. I was so frightened that I cannot remember what he said. I froze and held my breath hoping he wouldn't hit me, as he is very strong. I think he left the room quickly, afraid himself of what he might do. I never said one word, not even sorry. For a long time after that I could not get the image of his wild face out of my mind. I kept asking myself over and over again, how could I love this man? And, as time went on I found lots of reasons to love him. The times that he was nice to me, I thought he was wonderful, and I was lucky to have him. Unfortunately, those times were fewer than the bad times. But the children and my sewing kept me busy. My sisters envied my great husband. Any time they called, he had some project on the go, either building on extra rooms or redecorating the house. He was a perfectionist, no matter what task he did. All his spare time was spent on the upkeep of the house. I still did the general housekeeping, but if he wasn't happy with it he would do it himself. The only sister that he didn't fool was Joan.

I continued to confide in her, as I was finding it hard to keep up appearances.

Meanwhile, other things were happening in my life that kept my mind busy. Pam wasn't happy getting the bus to Maynooth every day, and was hinting at her Dad and I to buy her a car. We talked about it, and I agreed with Lar to get it as Valerie had the use of the family car.

Within a few weeks Lar had her driving, and she passed her test first time. We took the money out of our savings in the credit union for the car. She was delighted to have her own car, but it was a nightmare for us! She was driving everyone everywhere day and night coming home in the early hours. Lar was loosing the head, and insisted that I talk to her. He could never fight with Pam, but expected me to sort it out. I tried talking to her and thought I was getting through, but it never lasted long. Finally she decided to move in to an apartment in Maynooth with her friend from college. We worried about her leaving home, but in fairness, she got a part time job at night, and studied hard. She continued to bring home her washing at the weekend and I would give her a few pounds for her rent, and to run her car. One day I was washing her jeans when I saw that the whole knee was all frayed and torn. Being a dab hand at sewing, I put a patch on them, a master piece of work. I was looking forward to surprising her but when she saw them she nearly broke down in tears!. 'Mam,' she said, 'I spent ages trying to get that frayed look, and you've ruined them'. This was my first introduction to the 'raggy' look! I laugh at the memory now, but it was oh so serious at the time.

On the home front I got some bad news.

Alas my dear friend Mr. Hamill died. He was a wonderful man who was very kind to me, so I was sad at his passing. He gave me the confidence to believe in my ability, never failing to praise me for everything I made for him.

I wasn't sure what to do after Mr. Hamill. I knew that I would always sew, but what next? I wondered if I should continue making communion dresses and sell them.

SALLY'S ALLEY

Valerie decided to start her own business and asked me to go into partnership with her. I liked the idea she had, so decided to go for it. She rented a stall in the Liberty market in Thomas Street to make and sell children's communion and day dresses. Lar helped her set it up and fitted it with shelves etc. We would sew all week, then Val would sell at the weekend. Business was good and we were learning a lot about retail. We also learned about shoplifting! June would often keep Valerie company, and frequently caught shoplifters shoving dresses up their jumpers!

One day I was delivering a car load of communion dresses. I parked the car at the back of the market and left it for five minutes (locked). I went back out to get them but my back window was smashed, and the dresses gone. That was a dear lesson, we never left anything in the car again.

After a few months, we were getting ambitious so we decided to look for a regular shop to rent. We found a nice one on Sundrive Road in Kimmage Dublin. Once again Lar did a master piece on it with shelves, rails etc.

Valerie was great at window dressing, buying and meeting customers, while I stayed at home to sew. We called the shop 'Sally's Alley' on account of Lar's pet name for Valerie. It came from an incident when she was three years old, her friend next door Helena O'Keeffe could not say Valerie. When she called for her she would say ' Is Salerie coming out'? We laughed at the time at her little face, so innocent! Anyway over the years it became Sally to Lar. He had a nick name for everyone, he called me 'Beb' in the early years.

We built up a trade of regular customers selling children's clothes of every description, making what we could, and buying what we couldn't. Our best sellers were the communion dresses, because they were different from everywhere else. Val and I designed our own and seldom repeated a style except if asked, for twins.

But the rent for the shop was high, eating a good bit into our profit. During the communion season we didn't notice so much, but for the rest of the year after we took a wage and paid our bills, taxes, etc. the profits were small. We also had to employ an assistant because it was all too much on Val to do everything.

We had a few bad cheques plus a couple of break-ins. On one occasion the thieves robbed the alarm as well! Another morning we arrived and the shop door was wide open, with steel door bashed down and the lock broken on the second door behind it. I couldn't understand why someone would go to all that trouble for a few children's clothes! And of course we did not claim on the insurance because in our ignorance, we thought that the fact that our premium would go up, it wouldn't be worth it.

We really had no business sense at all, as we were paying a high premium and never claimed once.

June did her Leaving Certificate in 1994. She did well considering that she lost a lot of schooling with hospital stays, and infections. Her kidneys were not good on account of the paralysis from her waist down. She had double incontinence and so still needed help with her personal care. Pressure sores were now also becoming a problem. I would no sooner get one cleared up after months of care and dressings, when another one would start. In spite of this we encouraged her to be as independent as possible, and when she asked at eighteen years old could she learn how to drive like her sisters, we agreed.

But for her to drive, it meant a car with hand controls. We had two cars, the 'good' family car, and my 'banger'. Lar was always at me to get rid of the second car, telling me over and over again that we didn't need it. I refused, because I had a lot of hospital appointments for June and I, and very often Lar would have the family car in work. But now I was in a situation were I would consider trading it in for one with hand controls for June. So that is what I did. A car for a disabled person here in Ireland is free of all taxes, so it meant that we could get a new car at a good price. We got a Nissan Micra automatic complete with hand controls, that could be driven with or without, which meant that either Lar or I could also drive it.

As I said earlier, Lar was an expert driver, so after he drove it around for a while to familiarise himself with the hand controls, he started teaching June. Within a few weeks she was driving on her own, much to the delight of us all. When she passed her driving test five months later, we had real cause to celebrate!

I was so nervous when she started going out on her own but Lar kept telling me to 'let go' and she would be fine, and of course he was right. To watch her get in and out of the car on her own had to be seen to believe. As I said, she had no movement below the waist so she depended on her upper body to do all the work. First she would 'bum' in on the passenger side and put on the seat belt as she had limited balance. Then she took the wheels off the wheel chair and put them behind the seat. The next part was the most strenuous. It involved 'bumming' over to the drivers side while dragging in the main body of the wheelchair to park on the passenger seat. I put a long strap on the inside of the passenger door so that she could pull it closed it when she was in position. When she arrived at her destination, she did the whole lot in reverse. Needless to say, we always helped when she was going and coming, but when she got to her destination, she was on her own. I was so proud of her independence and her perseverance to be like her sisters. Truly, she was a remarkable young lady from day one. After she finished her Leaving Certificate, she went to secretarial college, so she was able to drive to it herself every day. She was on disability benefit from age sixteen, so I encouraged her to open a bank account and save half of it every week. So now at eighteen, she insisted on paying for her own collage fees, another example of her fierce independence.

When she finished college, getting work proved difficult with the wheelchair. Most buildings were not wheelchair friendly and a high percentage of businesses were not interested in a person with a disability. They never actually said so, but we proved it by omitting the facts in her C. V. She got no interview when she mentioned the wheelchair, but did if she omitted it.

But the excuse over and over again was the premises was not suitable. I went with her to some of the interviews and in truth they were a bit awkward for the wheelchair, but many of them were fine. But June could see that they were uncomfortable with a wheelchair, as they made all kinds of excuses.

One day she got an interview with South Dublin County Council. She did not mention the wheelchair. The morning of the interview, she insisted on going alone. I had no expectation of success because of all the interviews she went to before.

She came home pleased with herself, and a few days later got a letter to commence work. She told me that when she wheeled into the interview room, she said to the panel of three, 'I'm sorry I didn't mention my wheelchair in my application, but usually when I do, I don't get an interview'. They were very understanding, and took a chance on June, thereby breaking new ground in South Dublin County Council.I can truthfully say that since then she proved her worth, and became somewhat of an expert on all matters concerning the local authorities!

Pamela was a year and a half older than June. She was studying hard for her degree in Maynooth university in between partying! I was a bit worried about her as she had no clear direction of what she wanted to do in life. We spent long hours going over the options but came up with no answers. Her subjects were Maths and Biology. I suggested teaching, as my sister Rita was a teacher and she could point her in the right direction, but after considering it for a while, she decided against it. Then she thought she might do marine biology but that too couldn't hold her interest.On her summer holidays, she went to the Isle of Man to work as a waitress so that she could save money for the following college term. I hated her going, as I thought like most mothers do, that she was at an age when she needed me, even if she didn't think so.

Lar said let her go, the experience would do her good, but I still wasn't happy. Reluctantly, I gave her my blessing, but with bucket loads of warnings and advice! She got work in one of the big hotels and from what she told me, did very well. She loved the island and the people, so went back again the following year.

After graduation, she decided to look for work in the Isle of Man. But here she was , armed with a degree in Maths and Biology still not knowing what she wanted to do.As luck would have it, she made a decision during the course of her first job with Ernst and Young. She loved maths, so with the help of her employers she studied accountancy. She qualified in what seemed like record time, and settled in to what would be a career that she loved, on an island she loved, and would eventually marry a young man that we all loved!

Back in our shop, we were wondering if we should keep going, with the rent so high. We considered our options as Valerie wanted to continue to be self employed, and, although we weren't making big money, we were making a living. Besides, her relationship with Wayne was now serious, and they were talking about marriage.When they told us of their plans, we were happy and gave them our blessing. If I was to 'hand pick' my two sons-in –law I would have chosen the same two! They are hard working young men who are family orientated and they have great respect and love for my 'good' girls!

Lar got on well with both of them and he too was happy with their choice. Valerie and Wayne bought a lovely house about twenty minutes drive away from us. It was still under construction when they paid their deposit, so we were able to photograph almost every brick that went up! It was an exciting time for all of us, making plans for the wedding, and buying ' bits and bobs' for the house. When they were setting the date for the wedding, Valerie had to take into consideration our busiest time in the shop. She decided that ideally the best time would be at the end of the communion season, which was the end of May. So she told me that the last Saturday in May was about the best. I was looking at the calendar with her as she pencilled in May 27th, (1995). I kept staring at the date, and said to Val, 'Would you believe that on that day twenty five years ago, you came into our lives?' Now her dad would be giving her away on the anniversary of when we got her!. It would be a bitter sweet moment for all of us!

Connie and Lar had a falling out a few months before Val's wedding. They had many a falling out in the past as siblings do, but would make up again, with a gentle push from me. But this time it was lasting longer than I had hoped, and despite talking to Lar about it for hours on end, he still wouldn't talk to her. I felt like banging their heads together, as I knew they loved the bones of each other.

Unfortunately, Lar was one for holding a grudge for a very long time, and if you crossed him, he never forgot it. I tried the usual ' life is too short etc.' but to no avail, he was adamant that he wouldn't talk to her.

We were now in an awkward situation when Valerie was making out her wedding list, as there was no way she was getting married without Aunt Connie there. We discussed it for hours with Lar but his solution was not to invite them. My heart was breaking for Valerie, as she only wanted a happy wedding day surrounded by her family, extended family and friends.

Finally, I made the decision. 'Ok Val' I said, 'Let's invite Aunty Connie, Uncle Brian, and all the cousins, because this is what you and I want and your sisters (they loved aunty Connie too) so your dad is outnumbered.' We won't tell him yet. Valerie was happy with that but worried about going against Dad. I re-assured her that I would talk him around eventually. Truthfully, I wasn't sure that I could, but I needed Valerie to stop worrying and enjoy the excitement of planning her wedding. So, without his knowledge, the invitations went out. Now and again he would bring up the subject and feel sorry for himself, saying that it's very sad that so few of his family were coming to the wedding. I would point out to him that his family was small enough without leaving out Connie. I was still hoping that I was getting through to him, and I prayed to all the saints in heaven to help me.

Meanwhile Valerie went shopping for the fabric for her wedding dress. I really wanted to make it for her but she insisted on making it herself. There was a lot of work on the one she designed, but she still wouldn't let me help her. She chose an ivory dress, a gold jacket with a drape at the back, and the whole lot hand embroidered with Celtic designs. It took weeks of hand sewing, and I was frustrated that she wouldn't let me help because I love hand sewing. But this was Valerie's project, so I had to be contented to take a back seat.

It turned out absolutely beautiful, so I was glad I let her get on with it. Pamela was bridesmaid, and we were lucky to have her, as she was still in college and leading a very busy life! Trying to get her for a dress fitting was difficult to say the least, besides, Pamela wasn't a 'dressy' person, more a 'ripped jeans' type. But in fairness, when we did finally get her to a dress rehearsal, she looked so pretty, that I had tears in my eyes.

I made a suit for myself that looked respectable, but the shoes were another story. There was no chance of wearing fancy high heels, when I was lucky to be able to walk! In any event, I bought shoes that were more sensible than fashionable, but they looked ok. I'm not sure what Lar thought about my outfit as he passed no comment.He on the other hand, was wearing a tux like all the men in the bridal party, and beautiful tartan waistcoats that Valerie made as Wayne's father is from Scotland, so the whole look was colourful.

Two weeks before the wedding I dropped the bombshell. I told him that I instructed Valerie to send Connie and family the invitations. As I expected, he wasn't happy and hit the roof. 'This is going to be very awkward for me!' he said. 'What am I going to do?' He continued 'I feel sick in my stomach, I hate weddings anyway, now this!'

I couldn't understand why he wouldn't make up with Connie in the meantime, after all this had gone on long enough. But no matter what I said, he refused to talk to her. So I made up my mind that this was Valerie's special day, and I would do all I could to make it so.

Chapter Twenty

THE WEDDING

On the morning of the wedding, I was feeling very excited for Valerie, but anxious that every thing would go according to plan. I got up at six o'clock as usual to 'loosen up' my joints and do a bit of relaxation, and breathing exercises to give me the best possible start to the day. Valerie got up after me, and seemed in great form, or if she was nervous, she never said so. We had a nice relaxing breakfast before the fuss began. Then there were showers, hairdo's, dresses, flowers, a visit from her cousins, a few neighbours, etc.

Lar got up last, but it was mostly because he knew that there was no chance of getting to the bathroom early with all the women in the house! He scrubbed up well, and looked quite handsome in his tux! But he was more nervous than Valerie. He hated being the centre of attention, so I tried re-assuring him that all eyes would be on the bride.

June looked lovely too in a beige trouser suit that I made for her. Valerie invited June's best friend Nicola, who was also a wheelchair user, to the wedding. She made sure that she chose a hotel that was 'wheelchair' friendly, so that June would feel comfortable. Valerie was always sensitive to June's needs, and included her in every thing. In fact she wanted to have both June and Pam as her bridesmaids, but June refused. I'm afraid she is very like her Dad in so far as the 'centre of attention' is concerned! But Valerie, while she was disappointed, respected her wishes.

The marriage ceremony should have been in our local church, the very one that her dad and I got married in but Valerie thought it was too big and cold, so opted for Kimmage Manor, a small intimate church, about five minutes away from our house. Our local priest Fr. Ryan officiated. He had only recently been transferred to a country parish, but was delighted when Valerie asked him if he would come back to conduct the ceremony.

June and I arrived at the church first where everyone had gathered. When I got out of the car I looked for Connie, and gave her a hug. I asked her did she remember this day twenty five years ago, when she got two buses from Ballymun with two babies, to see our 'new baby'. She hadn't remembered the date of course, but was delighted to be reminded. I was so glad that she was there in spite of the 'falling out' with Lar. It was a beautiful ceremony, and I got a lump in my throat as I watched Valerie walk down the aisle with her dad. I spent the whole time re-living the last twenty five years, remembering the joy that she brought into our lives. I looked at Pam, my beautiful tomboy looking like a lady now, so pretty. I thought to myself, how lucky I was to be blessed with three wonderful children. Motherhood is indeed a great gift, and three times in my life I was given that gift.

The reception went well, and I think a good time was had by all. But of course, Lar still wouldn't talk to Connie. During the night as tradition has it, we sat with and got to know Waynes extended family. But coming near the end of the night when Lar had a good few drinks on him, I said 'Come on, this has gone far enough!'. I marched him over to where Connie was sitting with the family, and of course Connie put her arms around him and gave him a hug. After the 'ice' was broken, we had a great time laughing and joking for the rest of the time. When we came home after the long day, Lar was happy again to be talking to Connie, as I knew he would.

I missed Valerie terribly from the house after the wedding. Although they had their house six months before the wedding, she never left home until the day of her marriage. Luckily we still were involved in the business so I saw her almost every day. We were starting to have second thoughts about the shop, as Valerie now had a mortgage to pay and the rent on the shop was increased.

We had become friendly with one of the 'reps' who sold us the communion accessories, headdresses, gloves etc. George had a great knowledge of the communion trade and knew almost every shop in the republic of Ireland!

We had a talk with him, and he agreed that if we were to give up the shop, that he could sell our dresses nationwide. So with a little bit of sadness, we closed the shop a few months after Valerie's wedding. George introduced us to more 'reps' who supplied fabric and trimmings. Very quickly we got a good range together, and George took them around. We were amazed at the reaction we got and the orders that came in. In the meantime we made samples of children's summer and winter dresses, and showed them to a wholesaler that we befriended in the shop. As a result we were very busy and had to enlist not only more staff, but relations, and friends. Lar did great work on the workrooms and we invested in more machinery. Good machinery is expensive so we had to start off with an overdraft with help from the bank and advice from our accountant. Thankfully we never got into 'real debt' so within a year, we turned it in to a profit. All in all, the business was going good, and we met some lovely people in the trade.

Pam graduated from university in 1996, and we were all out there watching the proceedings with pride. It was a great day, and we took lots of photos and went for a meal afterwards.

She took time out after that, still undecided on what she wanted to do. Finally, she decided to go back to the Isle of Man, to look for work. Valerie travelled with her to make sure that she got safe digs. Val came home then when she was fixed up, and in no time at all, she got work in one of the big financial houses over there. It was then that, realizing her love of figures, that she studied accountancy.

She came home almost monthly at first as the plane trip is only 35 minutes, in fact it took longer to get to our house from the airport, than the plane journey!

In what seemed like no time, she qualified as an accountant. We helped her with a deposit for a house, and shortly after , she met Robert, her husband.

Meanwhile June was still working away in South Dublin County Council, driving in on her own every day.

In 1996, there were rumours in the oil company of a takeover. Within weeks of the rumours, many workers were made redundant, with a 'last in first out' rule. The redundancy package offered was generous, but even so, Lar was holding his breath, after all he was not quite 54 years old. But he was one of the lucky ones and so was safe for another while.

By 1997 he decided to take the redundancy offer, and retire. His retirement made a big change in our lives, not to mention more mood swings, and more aggression towards me.

I tried to stay calm, and take it in my stride, and most of the time encouraged him to take up other work. It was just before the property boom when houses were at an affordable price, that we decided that we could afford to buy a second house with the redundancy money, and rent it out. We could do it because we now had no mortgage on the family home since 1995. And, because of my dressmaking business we were able to buy our car, pay for holidays etc. without borrowing money.

So we had no outstanding bills when Lar got the money. We bought the house, in Old Bawn, near the new Tallaght hospital. We did a lot of work on it to get it nice before renting it but we would soon learn that it was a waste of money judging by the way the tenants treated it! We changed our car so that Lar could use it as a hackney cab, to do some part time work. He also had a good pension from the oil company. Also, in 1997, Valerie and Wayne announced they were expecting their first baby. We were overjoyed beyond words with excitement. Our first grandchild! I was so happy that I didn't know how I was going to wait until next May! This was the best news ever and I rang all my sisters with a smile on my face!

Unfortunately Valerie was very sick throughout her pregnancy. She regularly had to be hospitalised as she kept getting de-hydrated. But in her good spells she worked hard in Sally's Alley. Wayne loved cooking, and he was very good at it. One Sunday he was cooking duck with all the trimmings and invited the three of us up for dinner. I was looking forward to it as I had never tasted duck before, and besides, it would be a real treat to get my dinner handed to me! On the Sunday morning, after helping June with her personal care, Lar and I were busy cleaning the house. I was in the kitchen, and he was in our bedroom, polishing and shining as usual. About an hour before we were due to leave, I went into our bedroom to see why he was so long. I could not believe it when I saw him pulling everything out of my wardrobe! I said 'What are you doing?' He said 'I am going to wash the inside of your wardrobe'. 'But,' I said, 'The inside of the wardrobe is spotless!' 'Yes', he answered, 'But it hasn't been washed on the inside since we got them'. I was annoyed with him taking my clothes out of the wardrobe, and told him to put them back, and I didn't want the insides washed out. There was an almighty row, which unfortunately June witnessed, but I got so angry. Finally he threw out the basin of water and told me to put my clothes back, and that I was a disgusting person. I told HIM to put the clothes back as HE pulled them out. He refused, and kept ordering me in front of June to put them back. When I continued to refuse, he said 'Right, if you don't put them back, I'm not going to Valerie's'. That stopped me in my tracks, as I thought about Wayne cooking all morning for us and Valerie looking forward to us coming. So sheepishly, I put them all back. There was silence in the car all the way to Valerie's. I felt sorry that June had to see this, so I made a big effort to engage him in conversation, but it was strained. When we arrived, Val was very sick again and Wayne was doing his best to cook and take care of her. When I saw her I quickly forgot about my own problems as I was so worried. We had a beautiful meal, but poor Val could eat nothing. I knew she had to go to the hospital again, so Wayne and I went with her, while Lar took June home. Thankfully she recovered after a few days, and was back working within the week. But to this day, I cannot look at duck without thinking of my first taste of it that day!

The dressmaking business was very busy, so I didn't have much time but we found the time to look together for the house. It was a strange feeling, shopping for a house, with the full price in the bank. I look back now and wonder, was I far too smug then?

We looked like the perfect family that everyone would like to be. I had three great children, all now earning good money, in jobs that they loved. Yes, in later years I would accuse myself of smugness. We put the new house in both our names, as was our family home. Well, after all we were a couple, but this decision would have a major effect on our lives at a later date.................

Lar then threw himself into work in the house, while Valerie moved house again to a bungalow near us, but it was a wreck. Within a few months they had it decent enough to move into it with great help from Lar. When he was busy he was in better humour, and easier to live with. He also helped us in Sally's Alley with deliveries. But all was not as it seemed. It was clear to me that Lar didn't 'fancy' me as a woman. I felt a failure, but continued trying to be a good wife. No matter how much he insulted me, I still loved him with all my heart. Yet I knew deep down that if someone continues to hurt you, then they don't like you. But I buried my head in the sand. I suppose when the children felt that we were a family, I was happy.

I would find out in later years that I never fooled Valerie. Being the oldest, she saw and heard a lot more than I thought! Even though we seldom had 'words' in front of the children, clearly she knew something wasn't right. Pam noticed nothing, thank God, living in her own fun filled world of gymnastics, swimming and school.

June would tell me many years later that she knew we weren't the same as other mammy's and daddy's. She felt that other dads treated the mammy differently. We had many weekends together away, while June stayed with Valerie, but I always came home in tears. One such weekend we went to Kilkenny Never during the whole time did he walk beside me. Sometimes I would lose him if he went too far ahead. He constantly looked behind rolling his eyes to heaven with a frustrated look on his face. When I caught up with him he would state the obvious 'God you really can't walk!' He refused to walk with me, telling me it was a strain to do so.

On the last night there, when we got back to the hotel, there was a private party in full swing, but no seats. They were a jolly lot and quickly made room for us at the table, insisting that we help ourselves to their food. After about ten minutes, Lar was feeling uncomfortable, and whispered to me. 'You stay here, I'm finishing the night at the bar!' I felt lost and alone when he left, so just went up to our room to bed. I was disappointed that he couldn't share the last bit of the weekend with me. But this was how it was now, I felt like I was only a burden on him.

I was glad to get home to my children, who were delighted to see me, even with my crooked walk! Deep down I longed to be loved and cherished by Lar, but it was never to be. The one thing that kept me going was the love of my children, and the memories of when love was young. When I was feeling sad I would doodle in my diary, before I went to bed. One such entry dated May 17th 1990, was:

> One half of a pair,
> Reaching out reaching, reaching
> Never getting there
>
> Coping, hoping, hoping
> And yet,
> I've been there, long ago,
>
> I know,
> Nothing on this earth lasts forever
>
> Except, Perhaps?
> But no, not even that
> Let go, let go...............

I was increasingly fed up with the criticism and the insults day after day. I kept out of Lar's way as much as possible unless his mood was good. But he followed me around asking why I wasn't doing housework. I did as much housework as any other wife, as well as sew every day, but it was never good enough. He would go over most things I did saying, 'Ah you're like your father'(a reference to his easy going nature)Sometimes when he decided to decorate the house again, we would discuss colours.

Half way through the conversation he would say, 'Ah you don't have a clue, I'll wait 'til Val comes and ask her'. I hated being dismissed like that, but I would leave it and go with Val's choice. Many times Val would choose the same colour as me, and I was glad. Besides I did value Val's opinion.

Chapter Twenty one
A NEW BABY

Valerie worked very hard throughout her pregnancy, both in the business and in her home. We were all looking forward to the baby's birth. On May 28th 1998 she started labour early in the morning so headed for the Coombe hospital. By the afternoon I was in the waiting room with a packed lunch! Wayne was with her in the labour ward so every 20 minutes he came out to tell me how it was going. Coming near the time I was outside the labour ward listening to the last stages, with tears in my eyes and my heart in my mouth. O how I wished I could go through it for her. Every time I heard the midwife shout PUSH I was standing there PUSHING! I could imagine Wayne too mentally pushing with her, so we were all pushing!!!!!!

Then I heard the whimper of a baby. Shortly after, Wayne came out to give me the good news, 'It's a girl and all is well'. We had a little cry, but they were tears of joy. A few minutes later, I was allowed in and not only did I hold my grandchild for the first time, this was the first time I held a new born baby! Remember Val and Pam were three months when I first held them, and June was eight months before they closed in her back so we couldn't hold her until then.

I was very emotional looking at this little miracle in my arms, and yes I did indeed 'live to see my children's children' Lar came to the hospital later with June and Pam. We were all so excited and proud as were the other grandparents Monica and Robert. This was there first grandchild too, so we all went to the pub later to celebrate. Lar loves babies so he was in great form and the humour was good. Val and Wayne chose the name Ciara, which we all agreed was nice.

Val and I continued with our dressmaking business as it was doing well. During the day, because now he was retired, Lar did some of the housework himself. The house was always clean, as there were only the three of us now at home, Lar, me and June.

He would wash the floors, put the dishes in the dishwasher, and make our bed. When it was needed he cleaned the windows. I continued to shop, cook, wash and iron, as well as sew full time now. My hands were getting more and more twisted from the rheumatoid arthritis, but I could still do almost everything with them, even the most detailed bead work on our communion dresses. I could not manage the hoover so Lar did it. We had an upright one that I could manage but when it needed replacing, Lar insisted on getting a cylinder one that I couldn't manage. I kept asking him to get an upright one but he refused, saying smartly 'I'm the only one who does the work in this house anyway'.

He never lost an opportunity to put me down. I tried agreeing with everything he said, to avoid confrontation, but it only made things worse. If he got no reaction from me, he would shout at June over something trivial, as he knew that would bring a reaction from me. Then if June ignored him he would shout at her little dog and throw it out the back, making June very upset.

I couldn't take it when he upset June. I yelled at him one night 'What would your drinking buddies think if they knew you were taking out your anger on your disabled daughter?' I thought that got through to him, but it didn't last long.

June's pet dog was a little Tibeten spaniel. She loved her and 'Charlie' loved June. Every evening I knew when June drove into the driveway as Charlie would sit looking at the hall door wagging her tail. She would jump all over her when she wheeled in. Then when she was eating her dinner, Charlie would sit faithfully beside her wheel. Of course no matter how many times I told June not to, she still gave her tit bits from the table. No wonder Charlie had no time for me when June came home!

My heart problem started to give me trouble, and I ended up in hospital a few times, but only for a couple of days at a time, until they got it back ticking regular again. What I had was Atrial Fibrilation, and it meant that I would get a rapid heartbeat for days on end. It is very frightening, and any time I get it I think it's never going to be right again. Some times when it was bad I would try to stick it out for days rather than tell Lar, but then they told me in the hospital to go in straight away because while the heart is beating faster it is throwing out clots. Any time I had to go in, Lar felt sorry for himself, even though Val took care of June, so he only had to care for himself. He continued to say 'We can go nowhere with your health and Junes'. It always made me feel worse to hear him say it even though I knew he felt it.

But I was never in hospital for longer than two or three days, so he had nothing to do at home except the cleaning and polishing, and he did! When I came home I just got back in to my daily routine, and continued on as normal.

Like I mentioned earlier Lar talked in his sleep every night. For all the years that I know him, he never said a curse word in front of me or the children. The worse he would say was 'Ah for Jaysus sake!'. But when he was asleep, I learned all the curse words ever known!!!!! And the worse part was, he would roar them! His sister Connie told me that she and Ann would stand outside his bedroom door before we were married and laugh at the words coming out of his mouth.

Sometimes I couldn't sleep if my rheumatoid was acting up, and I would have to listen to him all night. I suppose I got used to it and marvelled at the fact that he was in such a deep sleep, when I couldn't close my eyes.

But then, according to him I began snoring. I don't know if I always snored or if everything about me now was irritating him. Night after night he would yell in my ear ' AH for Jaysus sake I can't sleep with your snoring!' Many times I jumped with fright and my heart went into A-Fib. One night I grabbed my pillow and went in to the settee. It was peaceful there but he followed me and ordered me back to bed!

Like a lamb, I did what I was told. Other nights he would grab HIS pillow and go up to the attic bedroom. It became an ongoing problem after that, so I slept very little at night for fear of waking him.

I was still trying my best to please him and to be a better wife. But he was always angry at the hand he was dealt in life. He told me that all our friends and relations were having a great time while he couldn't go anywhere, because of June and I. I began feeling sorry for him and told him I was booking a holiday for the two of us to New York. He looked at me 'stony faced' and said 'We can't afford it'.

'Yes we can' I said, 'I have the money'. He knew at the end of the communion season that I always had extra money. Even if I hadn't, we could still afford it, but he hated spending money. He didn't mind if I spent it, as he looked on my earnings as extra. And to be truthful so did I.

We set off for New York in May 2000. It was very exciting, and Lar's mood was never better. We stayed at a posh hotel on 'Lexington Avenue' beside Fitzpatricks hotel, and across the road from the Waldorf. It was amazing looking out of our window, watching crowds of people rushing everywhere, many of them drinking cups of coffee as they ran along. Next day after a good night's sleep, we ventured out to enjoy our holiday. We did all the tourist things visiting Central Park one day, went upThe Empire State Building another, then the Twin Towers, (it was before 9 11). I remember talking to a black lady there when I bought a gadget for opening bottles. She was so jolly, and told us that she loved our Irish accent. I thought of her on 9 11, and have thought about her since. I pray that she didn't go into work that day, or if she did, got out safe.

We went into Chinatown and had a 'real' Chinese meal. It was delicious but I didn't like looking at the fish swimming around a tank, killed only when someone ordered it! Lar still tended to walk away from me as we strolled along, but I hung on to him when the crowds got bad. One day as we walked along, he stood and said 'Look at the height of that building'. I stood looking at the way it rose up into the sky, it was amazing. Seeing it on television would not do it justice, I was like a child as I marvelled at the building. But when I lowered my head, Lar was gone! I stood there terrified wondering what to do. We had no mobile phones at the time, so I thought I would have to ask a policeman, of which there were loads. I did not move for a few minutes, and luckily Lar retraced his steps and found me.

There's so many people in New York that it would be easy to get lost on your own, but I made sure that I held on to Lar, after that!

The trip went too quickly, and it seemed no time before we were heading home. Lar loves flying, but I don't, even though I've flown many times with him. Like I mentioned before, Lar has no tact, and we were no sooner up in the air when he started explaining to me in detail why planes crash! I only wanted to go asleep and wake up in Dublin! Thankfully I did go asleep and woke up as we were approaching the west coast.

Lar was in a good mood for a few weeks after the American trip, and when we got the photographs, we relived the whole thing again! But it wasn't long before the insults started again. He would continue to tell me what wonderful wives his friends had, and clearly, I didn't come up to the mark. Also, every so often he would take out old photographs of when I was in my twenties and say, 'Look at how well you looked in this'. I did not need reminding of how well I looked when I was younger, I needed reassurance of how I felt now, and I hoped that my twisted body, still contained the real me. But to him I was a failure as a wife, and he said so many times in his own subtle way. I knew my appearance bothered him. Now, he never touched off my crooked hands or gave me a hug. Many times after a tough day, I ached for a hug but

sadly, never got one.

Sally's Alley, was now busier than ever. We were making communion dressesfor all the big stores in Dublin, and around the country. I was really enjoying it, but I had to battle with Lar every day. 'Look at the state of the kitchen' he would say when he got up in the morning.

By the time he got up, I would have helped June with her personal care, so that she could get to work on time, plus I would have cut a couple of dozen dresses, to have ready for the girls when they came in.

Also, he never went to bed without cleaning the kitchen, so there was very little to do. I tried to pretend that this wasn't happening, that deep down he really loved me and couldn't do without me, because that's the way I felt about him.

But the insults went from bad to worse, day after day telling me how useless I was. Every night my way of relaxing was to sit at the kitchen table with a glass of water and do the 'Herald' crossword. I always loved playing with words, in fact when we were married first, we would do the crosswords together.

Some time I would be falling asleep because I was so tired from working all day.Occasionally I would stand up, just say goodnight and go to bed. He would say aggressively ' I don't know any other woman who would stand up and go to bed, leaving the paper open, a glass on the table, and the chair not pushed back.

'You are a very untidy person'. I was so tired that I let him say what he liked, but June wouldn't let him away with it. Anytime he said anything insulting to me she shouted back at him. They would continue it for hours, as neither one would let the other have the last word! I often fell asleep to the sound of 'It is, it isn't'.

June's kidneys started to give trouble, in her twenties. They were never good to begin with as one of them only worked at about 25% and the 'Good' one at 75%. But apart from regular kidney infections, they were working to some degree. She had a few spells in hospital, but always recovered and went back to work. She hated fuss, and so never told anyone when she was in hospital. Even in hospital, she never stayed in bed, preferring to get dressed and into her wheelchair. An independent girl, who seldom complained although she had a lot to complain about.

I used look at her attitude to life, comparing it to her dad, and wonder what was going on that head of his! Here was a healthy man, who moaned from the time he got up in the morning 'til either he went to the pub, or went for walk. (I don't know if he really went for a walk) but that's what he told me.

For the children's sake I laughed at his 'moans'. I told him I was making him President of the Moan and Groan society!. At least that brought a smile to his face!

Chapter Twenty two

ANOTHER WEDDING IN THE FAMILY

In 2002, Pam and Robert set their wedding date. Pam wanted to come home to our local church to get married, so Robert was okay with that , as was his parents, and extended family. She asked Valerie to arrange it and to book a venue. The date set was December 23rd, two days before Christmas, and it was now only three months away. I knew it was short notice for the church, but as a family, we were well known to the parish priest, so I thought that would make a difference. But I was wrong. Because Robert was not catholic, he would have to spend at least six months studying Catholicism. It was a big let down to us all, as now the hotel was booked, and a deposit paid.

Robert accompanied Pam to a mass in the Isle of Man, in an effort to find out what it was all about. I was interested to know what he thought of it so I asked him. He smiled and said he was amused at the way everyone stood up, sat down, over and over again until the end! I must say, after his observations I was conscious of the same thing every week after that, and realised how pointless it was!

Anyway we tried every parish, every priest, anyone we knew in religion, but all to no avail. Lar was getting annoyed as he hated weddings anyway, and suggested that she get married abroad, like a lot of couples were now doing. But Pam and Val were determined to have the ceremony in her home town. Besides, Robert was happy to marry Pam anywhere. On the other hand Robert's father wasn't too keen on entering a Catholic Church, so that posed another problem.

After trying every parish in Dublin, we then looked at any church that would perform a mixed marriage. A friend of Valerie's recommended a lovely Presbyterian church in Lucan Co. Dublin. Pam and Robert went to see the vicar and were hugely impressed with him, so everything was arranged. But there was a new problem. Because Robert's father wouldn't go into a catholic church, Lar dug in his heels, and refused to go to the Presbyterian church. I was so annoyed with him, because he never cared about any religion, neither his or anyone else's. He was just being his awkward self, and determined that no one would 'get one up on him'.

Val and I never told Pam, we continued to make the arrangements, make the dresses, and send out the invitations. I was certain that Lar wouldn't say anything to Pam, after all this was 'Cuddles' and he would never hurt her! Even as an adult he still called her cuddles. He continued to argue with me about it, but I just kept repeating that this was Pam and Robert's special day.

Meanwhile Valerie was pregnant again with our second grandchild. I was so excited, with two things to look forward to now, the wedding, and a new baby.

Valerie was sick constantly throughout the pregnancy, but she never stopped working, and organised the wedding according to Pam's instructions. They were on the phone regularly updating the situation. Pam had no idea that her Dad was 'in my ear' every day about the church. I was now fed up listening to him and threatened to tell Pamela. Finally, he backed down, and started helping us.

Pamela's wedding dress turned out lovely. Because it was Christmas time, she chose an ivory dress, with a dark red velvet coat over it. We had to wait until the week before to try it on, as she wasn't coming home until then. But I was familiar with Pam's measurements, and there was only a small adjustment to the length. The bridesmaid was a new friend from the Isle of Man, and I didn't meet her until a few days before the wedding, but with the measurements they sent me, I did well!

Alas, the day before the wedding, her bridesmaid was very sick, and flew home! We quickly asked another friend, home for the wedding, would she stand in. Thankfully she did, but she was a completely different size to the first one so the night before the wedding, I made a new dress, with the new bridesmaid at my side! It didn't bother me at all as I had bought a roll of the material, and besides, sewing kept me relaxed for the evening.

The next day was the usual hustle and bustle of a wedding in the house! I was surprised at how calm Pamela was, getting ready for her big day. Lar seemed in good enough form, but then he got a phone call from Connie's husband Brian. He said that Connie was unwell and could not make the wedding. On top of that, his brother could not make the ceremony, as he had to work, but promised to make the reception. Next thing I saw that look on Lar's face, when I walked in to the sitting room. 'I feel sick' he said. Valerie overheard him, and thought his stomach was sick. She said 'Dad I have tablets for sick stomachs'. My heart broke for Valerie, she had morning sickness herself, but she was more concerned about her dad.

I knew what he meant. I told Val, that he wasn't 'sick' it was an expression he used when he wasn't in control. 'None of my family will be in the church' he said angrily.I could tell that he wasn't happy at all, especially as all my sisters would be there, and many of Robert's extended family. I tried to comfort him as Connie's husband and his brother Len would be at the reception.

Somehow we got him to smile walking down the aisle with 'Cuddles'. I know deep down he was happy for Pam, as he loved her very much.

The vicar gave a lovely sermon, reminding us what life was about, and how short it was. I was so moved by the ceremony, that I wrote to the vicar a week later to tell him and thank him. He spoke words that I know Pam and Robert will always remember. (At least I hope so!)

It was a fun reception, and I think everyone enjoyed it, I know I did.

Pam and Robert stayed in the hotel with Roberts family over night. Next day before they set off on honeymoon they called back to us. We talked for hours about her wedding day, which was indeed a day to remember.

The experience of the vicar and the Presbyterian church touched me. Because here was a man, who welcomed everyone of all religions and none, into his church, and besides, he was happily married (he said) with three children. To my mind he had a connection with the 'real' world, that our Catholic priests don't have.

I was born a Catholic and will always be Catholic but now I see all the things that's wrong with our church.

Our parish priest, who knew us as a family, in whose church my children made their First Communion and Confirmation, turned us away because of Pam's mixed marriage. And in the light of all that has been revealed since, my faith is weakened, but hopefully not gone.

After Pam's wedding, Junes health deteriorated and her kidneys failed. She had been getting weaker for some time and could no longer transfer unaided in to her car. She was hospitalised many times and had some serious infections.

In March 2003 she went on dialysis. At first it was two days a week, but she was unhappy about it and very frightened. I tried reassuring her and learned as much as I could about the procedure. It would be three hours twice weekly and she could continue working. The fact that she could continue to work cheered her up. One of her dialysis days was Saturday, so it was easy to work up her hours and clock out at 4 o'clock on Wednesday for 'late shift' dialysis.

She could not drive herself to the hospital for dialysis as she would have to park too far away from the main entrance, and, on those days she had no energy until she got dialysis. So on Wednesdays, Lar got up early (8.30am) and brought her to work. At 4pm he went back to pick her up from work, and bring her across to the hospital. Coming home the hospital provides transport for all patients so she came home in a 'wheelchair' taxi.

She did well at first except that Lar is not a morning person and moaned a few times getting up early on Wednesdays. But we ignored his grumpiness and got on with it. June never told anyone in work that she was on dialysis. In fact for years they had no idea why she got off work early some days.

I encouraged her to tell them, or even her best friends, but no, she refused. When she was on dialysis for a few months, her doctor told us at the outpatients clinic, that she would now have to do three days a week. She was very upset and on our journey home I pointed out the positives, like she would feel better for longer, and therefore would get back some energy to transfer into her car. But she was so worried and so was I. When we arrived home, June went into her room, and I went into the kitchen to break the news to Lar. 'What' he said when I told him 'that means I have to get up TWICE a week to bring her to work!'. I couldn't believe his reaction. Here was I looking for support to console June, and his biggest worry was getting out of bed twice a week at 8.30am.

I said 'Lar, I will do Mondays and you will still only have Wednesdays to do'. He sheepishly said 'No I'll do it'.

I am an early riser and had no problem bringing June any morning of the week, but I originally asked Lar to do the Wednesdays because he was not working now, and I thought it would be nice for June to have his company for half an hour once a week.

Even though I was working, I would abandon everything for June. She was so independent that she hated putting anyone out.

But I loved helping her, and no matter how sick she was, she always made me laugh. However, she settled in to her three days a week dialysis, and did indeed feel much better. After six months we were asked to see the transplant team in Beaumont Hospital, with a view to the suitability of a kidney transplant.

Her two sisters were the first to offer a kidney to her, as did Lar and myself, but at that time in Ireland they did not have the facilities for 'live' transplants.

The transplant team assessed June and after many tests, was placed on the list. Although its not really a 'list', more a pool, of suitable patients. June asked the team many questions, like for example, 'Is the transplant more difficult in patients like her who are paralysed from the waist?. The answer was yes, because the veins are narrower in the lower limbs, but they had done it a few times and they were successful. They were very reassuring, but made no false promises, telling her that she could be waiting from a few months to a few years.

It was important, they said to have a bag packed, and to be ready day or night for the call. Not everyone had a mobile phone at that time, at least I didn't, and neither did Lar. So the girls got together and bought one for Lar, so that if we got a call to the house, we could contact him immediately.

For weeks I noticed he didn't bring the phone with him when he was going out. I was disappointed after the children bought it for him. So I told him , and he replied 'Sure I would be no good to you if you rang as I cannot drink and drive'. 'But I can drive', I said, 'and I'd like you there for support'.

'Ah you'd be better off ringing Wayne', was his answer (Val's husband). I was so annoyed with him, and wondered if I was a nut case for still loving this man!

How could he put his pub nights before everything else? Like most parents I would have walked around the world to get a new kidney for June. But Lar never let anything interfere with Friday Saturday, and Sunday nights in the pub.

I had no doubt that I would only have to ask Wayne, and he would come immediately, but that wasn't the point.

I had many sleepless nights worrying if we would get a call during the night, but as it happened, the years went on, and there was no call.

The dialysis was working well for now' and June continued working. She had quite a few hospital stays, some serious, some routine, but like a bouncing ball, she recovered each time.

It was now 2003, and Sally's Alley was doing well. Ciara (our granddaughter) was getting bigger and so cute. Lar and I doted on her, and baby sat whenever we could. Lar loves children, so he spent many days with Ciara, bringing her to the park, and for a ride on the bus which she loved.

He would play endless games with her when we baby sat, often marching up and down the hall, playing school with her!. Sometimes I would look and wonder if it was me that brought out the worst in him. Because this was the man I loved, the man that could give his senses to a child. He brought her everywhere, as he did our children, when they were small.

Once, Val and Wayne stayed with us while they were getting an extension built. Val and I were in the workroom, as was Ciara, while Lar was in the house polishing and shining as usual. Next thing he called me into the house. Seemingly, he was cleaning Ciara's bird cage, (Ciara had two budgies, Mork and Mindy) when one of them got out. Our pet dog pounced on it and killed it instantly! Lar was in a state, worrying about what to say to Ciara. Before we could discuss it, in walks Ciara. 'Where's Mindy?' she asked. Immediately Lar said, 'He fell off his perch and broke his leg, but I brought him to the bird hospital, and they are fixing it'. She was sad, but accepted it in her own childish way. But that left us in a dilemma. Lar went everywhere looking for an identical coloured budgie. He came home delighted when he got one the exact same colour. Alas when we put it in the cage, it was smaller than Mindy! We thought that Ciara mightn't notice, but she did. 'Why has he got smaller granddad?' she said. Quick as a flash he said 'Well he was very sick so he wasn't eating his dinner, but now that he's well, I'll give him extra, to fatten him up!'. When we were on our own, we had a good laugh and we were glad that we could remedy the situation. She never found out the truth, but she will now when she reads this!!!

On June 27th that year, Valerie gave birth to our second grandchild, Emma Mary, as beautiful as her name. She was born during the night and we were minding Ciara, but she heard me on the phone so I told her the good news. She was so excited, that she hardly slept that night. Next day I brought her to see her new sister, stopping on the way to buy a little teddy. It was another happy day in my life, as I held her for the first time. Oh! How I love the smell of new babies! Holding this little miracle, is again beyond words

Settling back in to Sally's Alley was harder now with two children, but with everyone helping, we could keep going. We had our bad days, like if one of the children were sick, but either one of us kept the workroom up to date.

June would have a good run of health for a while, but then she could have some really bad infections that floored her, so she had to go into hospital many times. I worried about her so much that I spent most of my time in the hospital. I hoped and prayed for that phone call from Beaumont hospital, but alas it was in vain. But in between times, when she was well, we rejoiced. I learned to live for today, and just got on with things, coping with any problems one at a time, as they occurred. Lar was the dutiful loyal husband, doting on the grandchildren, cleaning, shining, and keeping our family home and our rented house up to date. He still lost no opportunity to put me down and insult me especially when we were alone. I tried to ignore it most of the time, because I loved him and thought he couldn't live without me......................

Chapter Twenty Three
STRANGE BEHAVIOUR

Lar had no confidence in himself, so I continually reassured him, and praised everything he did. Even when he was going out drinking, I told him how well he looked. I truly thought he couldn't live without me.

I could not sleep with worry when he was out late. Instead, I made his supper, and stood looking out of the window for hours on end. Sometimes it would be the early hours when he came home, telling me he was in 'Mick's' house, a work friend who was also retired. Every morning I still brought him in a cup of tea, and at weekends would chat about where he went the night before, as well as our usual political debates. Many times we would have to agree to disagree over current affairs, but most times it was light hearted stuff.

Then one morning I went in with the tea and cheerfully said 'Where did you go last night?' I was shocked when he shouted in an aggressive voice 'Why?'. I got a fright and walked out of the bedroom.

While I was making his breakfast, I felt that I had no right to ask him where he had been. But it was part of our 'Sunday morning' routine, along with a fry up, that I couldn't understand why he got so aggressive.

When he got up I asked him was it not normal for a wife to be interested in where he had been, after all I trusted him one hundred per cent. So in a grumpy voice he told me what pub he was in the night before. But after that I seldom asked where he was and he wouldn't volunteer the information.

I was now getting fed up the way he was treating me, but I was so worried about June, that I took it all, just for peace. I worried too about Pam. I knew she was happily married but I was now in a situation that I couldn't visit her, because June couldn't miss her dialysis. But she was so good, coming home almost monthly, to see us.

The plane journey from the Isle of Man is only 35 minutes, and, as I said before we were longer on the M50 back to our house. But I missed her so much. On her trips home, the two of us would get up early and have long chats about life in general. I looked forward to our chats each month to catch up on all the gossip!. Besides, sometimes Lar wouldn't talk to me for days if he was in a mood, so I depended on my children, more and more.

Also, now I hated bedtime. He never came to bed at the same time as me, he stayed up until 1 or 2am. The only time he watched television was when I was in bed. I was nearly always asleep when he came in, and he frequently woke me, but the sex now wasn't loving, just sex. At this time I never felt loved, like I did when there was a 'rainbow around the moon'. Instead I felt used and wished it was over, especially when he was drunk. He would never talk about it the next day, only returning to his usual 'shy' self. I knew that I couldn't talk to anyone about it, certainly not my children, and my sisters thought he was perfect! In fact Lar thought that he WAS perfect, and said so many times.

He told me I was very lucky to have him, and that every guy he knew didn't do half as much as what he did. He got more selfish as he got older, only suiting himself. When Pam was home, she often went to the pub with him, and he loved that. Pam was still his 'cuddles' and the fact that she enjoyed a drink with him was even better.I liked her going with him too, because I think they had good chats with each other, and he came home in great form. Valerie didn't take a drink, and he would never even consider going out with June.

June had her own nights out with her friends, sometimes she would drive, other times if she was going to be late, she ordered a wheelchair taxi. Wayne would often bring her to wherever she wanted to go, and would offer to collect her. Most times he did , but occasionally she came home in a taxi with her friends.

One such night she was out late, as was Lar. I was home alone anxiously looking out of the window for both of them. At last the taxi pulled up at about 1.30am. I was just about to go out to help June out of the taxi and up the ramp, when along came Lar. I was glad that I wouldn't have to go out as I had my coat on over my nightdress! Next thing, I couldn't believe my eyes. Lar walked straight passed June and the taxi, never said a word and came into the house. I ran to the door saying 'Why aren't you helping June?'.

'Ah' he said, The taxi man is helping her', then he marched into the kitchen and heated up the supper I made for him, in the microwave. I was angry with him, but ran out to push June up the ramp. I could not believe that he never looked at her, even to ask if she had a nice night.

June went straight into her room, and I followed her. I never mentioned her dad, I just spent half an hour chatting and listening to how her night went.

Next morning, when I brought him in his tea I told him how angry I felt, but he just repeated the words he always says if I question him 'Ah you're being ridiculous'. There were times I thought that maybe he was right, maybe all marriages were like ours. Maybe it was I who didn't live in the real world. I looked around at other couples and they seemed on the same wavelength as each other and certainly appeared happy. But then on the face of it, we looked like the perfect couple that had everything.

Lar liked to be in control of everything, and in a way I let him, partly for peace, but mostly out of fear. He would never physically hurt me, but mentally I crumbled inside with his hurtful remarks.

He now controlled our joint bank account, while I ran the household budget out of my wages from the business. The joint account paid electric, phone, gas and television cable, plus house insurance, and changing the car every two years.

Because of the rented house, and Lar's pension, we were liable for tax, so I paid all taxes. At the end of each year we claimed back medical expenses, from the tax office. I paid for all medical bills that the V.H.I. did not cover, but whenever we got a rebate from the tax office, the cheque was made out to Lar. Even if it was made out to me I would still lodge it in our joint account, but I could never figure out why they sent it to him.

When bills came in, he queried everything. He got angry if I left a light on, even though Sallys Alley paid half of the electric bill on account of our workrooms at the back of our house. We had a separate phone line for the business, but he blamed June for the house phone bills.

He moaned so much about the phone bill that June handed him the money for it. He saw me watching him to see if he would take it, after all, June handed up money every week out of her wages, and besides, she had a lot of friends who were wheelchair users, and the phone was her only way of contacting them.

As I expected, he got embarrassed and wouldn't take the money. So after that any time he moaned about the phone bill, I would remind him that June offered to pay.

In the summer of 2003, Pam decided to buy a house in Ireland. She already had a lovely house in the Isle of Man, but herself and Robert thought that now was the time to invest in a second house. They chose Ireland, because they thought somewhere down the line, if they decided to live here, they would have a house.

Lar went with them looking at houses all over the place. Eventually, they decided to settle for Mullingar. They bought a beautiful bungalow on its own grounds, only a few minutes away from the hustle and bustle of Mullingar town. It was a lovely spot, so peaceful, fresh air and lots of trees.

It wasn't long before she furnished it, and had it looking like a new pin. When she came home after that her and Robert spent a lot of time there.

We all went down regularly, in fact, Val would stay with the children frequently, while Lar kept the gardens in order while Pam was away. Lar was regularly on the phone to Pam, giving her an update on anything he did in the house. Between keeping the family home in order and watching our rented house, plus contributing to the upkeep of Pam's, he was kept busy. I was glad that he had a purpose to his day, as he is not one for sitting around.

I still thought that loving him, even in his bad moods, was enough to keep our marriage strong. I praised every bit of D.I.Y, that he did, and it boosted his self esteem. I also continued to tell him how well he looked when he 'scrubbed up', even though he continually insulted me regularly.

Pam was doing well in her job and was very career minded. I wondered if she thought about babies, or would she wait a few years.

Then in the summer of 2005, much to our delight, she announced that she was pregnant! Herself and Robert were so excited, in fact the whole extended family were thrilled.

For Robert's parents it was there first grandchild, and they too looked forward to the birth. I missed not being able to see Pam every day, but she was in regular contact by phone and came home as often as she could.

Each time I saw her she was putting on weight rapidly. I was convinced it was twins!

Then she came home with one of those new DVD scans whereby you could see the baby clearly in the womb. It was the most amazing thing ever, and I had to control my emotions looking at it.

I desperately wanted to be with her for the birth, or at least stand outside the labour ward like before, but I couldn't leave June, as she was now on dialysis three times a week, and got a lot of infections.

However Lar said that when the time came, he would go over, I was glad that at least one of us would be there for that special moment.

Also in the summer of 2005, Lar was talking a lot about his drinking buddies, according to him, a bunch of separated guys. He always seemed to drink with separated people. One Sunday morning he said to me, 'I was embarrassed last night in the pub by a woman'. 'Oh' I said 'What happened?'. 'Well', he said, 'I know these two women from drinking with the guys, and one of them was missing last night, so I asked her friend where she was. The woman said that she was in Spain for a week, but broke her ankle. 'Next thing' he said, she takes out her phone and said ' Would you like to talk to her?' She then called her friend and handed him the phone. I listened with interest to his story, even though it sounded odd.

He told me he was so embarrassed that he didn't know what to say to her. So I asked him, 'What DID you say?' He mumbled something about just asking how she was, but I had an uneasy feeling about this.

As the day went on, I put it out of my mind convincing myself that it was harmless, and eventually I forgot about it. Besides, Lar may be difficult to live with, but he disliked infidelity in marriage, so I was full sure of myself. Anyway, he was now 62 and a half years old, and I was 61, and coming up to our 40th wedding anniversary.

I was beginning to notice that he did not do as much around the house as before. A few times I caught him ironing, and got a shock, as he never ironed before in our 40 years together. But it was only his own clothes that he was ironing, nothing else. His explanation was that he was helping me.

Six months before, we had bought new wooden flooring for June's room and the hall. He was full of enthusiasm when we bought it, telling me that he would paint first, and then put down the new floor. Usually when we bought anything requiring DIY he would get stuck in straight away and have it done in no time. But now there was no talk of doing it and I almost forgot it was up in the attic. But Valerie kept telling him that the hall was gone 'shabby' and it needed paint and the new floor.

He would say 'Oh yes, I will start it soon', but soon never came...................

There were things I noticed that on reflection should have rang alarm bells, but I lived in a busy world, running the business, and taking care of June's needs. I had a full day and with the arthritis, was exhausted at night time. Anyway, for all his faults I knew Lar wasn't THAT kind of man.........

Christmas 2005, we spent in Valeries house enjoying the grandchildren, and looked forward with anticipation to the birth of Pam's baby in January. A week before the birth, Lar told me that he changed his mind, and wasn't going over to

Pam's for the birth. I was so disappointed as he knew that I couldn't go. It was upsetting telling Pam, as she and Lar were great pals, as well as father and daughter.

He couldn't give me a reason, just kept saying, he wasn't going. I know now why he didn't want to go, but at that time I had no clue. I tried reasoning with him but to no avail. He just stuck to his guns and said no, I'm not going, end of story. Valerie too was disgusted especially as he promised Pamela. So Wayne took a week off work to look after the two children, while Valerie went over. She waited until we got word that the baby was born, then she was on the first available flight over to the Isle of Man.

Our first grandson Aaron, was born on January 7th, 2006. Robert,Pam's husband was very good and was on the phone constantly to us during her labour.

Unfortunately, things didn't go well , so she had an emergency caesarean section. Oh how I wished that I could be with her at her most difficult time. It was heart breaking that neither her Dad or I was there.

Our only consolation was our beautiful new grandson. How I longed to hold him like I held the other two, but it would be six weeks before that happened. Robert sent us photographs immediately, and I proudly showed them to everyone. I instructed Valerie to take lots more when she was there, as I couldn't get enough of them! I studied everyone of them carefully, and convinced myself that he was the image of Pam! The other grandparents Rob and Doreen of course had a different opinion, and who would blame them? Aren't all grandparents the same?

Anyway, the joy of a new baby took my mind off other things. I was on the phone everyday talking to Pam, and like an eejit I asked her to let me hear him when he whimpered! I felt that I knew him already, and it kept me going until I could hold him in my arms.

Meanwhile, Lar's late nights got later, regularly coming home in the early hours. His excuse was always the same, he was in Mick's house, and I had no reason to disbelieve him, because they were good friends.

One night I was lying in bed awake wondering why Lar was still up, as he had come home at 1.30am. It was now 3am and not a sound in the house. I got up and saw the light on in our spare room where I kept the computer. I gently pushed open the door.

Immediately Lar jumped and threw his phone behind the computer and blocked me with his body from going in.

'Oh' he said, 'You gave me a fright!'. I got a shock and wondered what secret he was keeping from me but I didn't ask. Still it worried me and I lay awake wondering all night what it was. I knew he wouldn't cheat on me because he is not that kind of guy. No, there had to be a simple explanation and he would tell me in the morning. Next morning there was no mention of the incident and I never brought it up in case he would think bad of me. It was the late nights and the drinking that bothered me more. Our sex life was now reduced to a few drunken gropes which I hated, so most nights I pretended to be asleep. When he had no drink we would just cuddle up together, chat for hours about the children and grandchildren, then fall asleep. It was mostly on his drinking nights that he got annoyed with my snoring. I consoled myself by the fact that we were now in our sixties, and that its probably like this with most couples our age.

The arthritis acted up now and again, but it was bearable. Sometimes my knee would be very painful for days on end, then it would clear up and my ankle would flare up. I was used to the flare ups so just got on with things. But my heart condition was now acting up regularly. When it went into A-Fibrillation, I got a rapid heartbeat that I had no control over. I had to go into hospital, for intravenous medication until it went back to normal. Sometimes it took just 24 hours but other times I was in for two days before it would regularise.

I always made sure everything was okay at home before I headed in to the hospital. I did not want Lar to worry about anything only himself while I was out of action.

Anyway Pam and Robert came home with baby Aaron, when he was six weeks old. And yes, that old feeling came back when

I held him for the first time. Another little miracle in my life, so small, so precious. Oh! That lovely smell of new babies, everyone should have that experience! Even though my wrist was acting up and very painful, I didn't let that deter me from my cuddle!

How I wished I was younger again and back to the baby years. I told Pam and Val to treasure them because the years go by, in the blink of an eye.

Pam and Robert were home for six weeks, and so, wanted to spend time in their house in Mullingar. We visited regularly as it was only an hours drive away. Lar went down more often on his own during the week, and Pam was delighted to have him around.

Meanwhile June continued with her dialysis three times a week. Much to my disappointment she had a pressure sore on the bottom of her back that had got worse. I had been very careful of pressure sores, taking care of them for almost thirty years, but this was the first one that got out of control. I blamed myself, but the doctor told me that it was her general health that contributed to the deterioration of it. It got infected so she had to be taken off the transplant list for now. She was so disappointed as were we all. She had to have surgery on it which made it bigger and look worse, but the doctor told me it was necessary to get down to the healthy tissue. He said it would take quite some time for new tissue to grow, maybe years, so a

kidney transplant was out of the question at the moment.

But for now, major dressings had to be done every morning, so the tissue viability nurse taught me how to do them at home. June wasn't happy, I think she felt that a bit of her independence was taken away from her. But in no time it became part of our morning routine and as before, we just got on with it.

It was coming up to that time when we change our car (every two years). We had a look around at a few but couldn't agree on one. Lar wanted to buy a Skoda because it was cheaper, but I wanted a Toyota. Eventually, he gave in and we bought the Toyota. The trade in difference was 9000 euro, so we just wrote a cheque for the full amount. I never checked our current account, but I knew we could well afford the money, as this was our routine every two years.

I didn't use the car very much as my wrist was painful so I borrowed June's car when I had to, as hers is automatic. Many times June drove me anywhere I wanted to go, having fun in the process!

I loved Saturdays with June. She was on a special renal diet that she kept to rigorously, but she was allowed to 'cheat' three hours before dialysis. So, with June driving, off we went to the shopping centre, where we would shop and then have lunch, timing it precisely. She had a great sense of humour so we spent most of the time laughing. She preferred to wheel herself but if my knee was bad, she let me wheel her to hold on. It was difficult at times if my wrist was bad getting the wheelchair in and out of the car, but between the two of us we managed. Jokingly she would say, 'Ah Ma, between the two of us we make one good body! Lar filled the car with petrol, because we could not manage the pumps.

I do not think he liked me being out of the house for long on Saturdays. He never said so, but I knew he would prefer me to do housework. I did it all the week, so Saturdays with June I felt was allowed. I used to leave his dinner ready when I went out. Usually I put a casserole in the oven with instructions on when to turn on, and when to turn off.

He could do anything except cook, in fact he was capable of burning water!

He was starting to look very 'snazzy' going out, especially Saturday nights. He was also in great humour for the hour before he left, asking June if she wanted anything. One Saturday night about two hours after he left, my mobile phone rang. Up on the screen came Lar. I was surprised he was ringing, as he never rang before. I answered it in anticipation and delight, waiting to hear his voice. All I heard was loud traditional Irish music! I kept saying 'hello' but realised that he had hit his phone by mistake, and it dialled my number. I continued to listen to the music, I could hear muffled voices but I couldn't make out what they were saying. June and I listened together, for a few minutes, laughing at how stupid he was for ringing me.

Next morning when I brought in his tea, I asked where he was. The Village Inn in Crumlin he said 'Why' he said. So I related to him about the phone call, music etc. And he denied he was anywhere there was music. When he saw how adamant I was, and June also heard, he said, 'Oh yes, there was music in the next room, but I wasn't in there. It was clear that he was lying, but I let it go.

The following week he told me that he must have lost his glasses in the pub. I asked what pub, and again he said The Village Inn, in Crumlin. I knew he was very fussy about his reading glasses, as he had paid three hundred euro for them. He said that he would go down later to see if they were handed in.

Later that day he was sitting at the kitchen table cursing at an old pair of glasses that he was trying to fix. I went over and lifted our phone to ring the pub. 'Who are you ringing?' he said. I answered ' The pub to see if they were handed in'. 'DO NOT RING THE PUB' he roared agressively, so loud that I dropped the phone with fright! I walked out of the kitchen thinking what is wrong with this man? I was only trying to help, but it was clear that I could never please him. It was only when he was going out to his drinking buddies that he was in good form, even chatting to us before he left. I never mention them again.

Chapter Twenty Four

BETRAYED!

It was coming up to the end of Pam's six weeks home, and for most of the time my wrist was painful. I was careful holding Aaron making sure I was in a sitting position when I held him. Much to the amusement of everyone, he yelled each time! I was so disappointed as I loved holding him.

During Pam's last week, I was at the hospital for my usual visit, when I asked the doctor to look at my wrist. He agreed that the pain was lasting too long, so gave me a form to have it x rayed. The queue in x ray was out the door, but I didn't want to waste any more time as Pam was going back the next day. So I put the form in my bag promising myself that next week, when I'd more time, I would follow it up. Next day Pam came to spend the last day with us. I wanted to make the most of it because it would be some time before we would see the baby again. Oh how I wished he let me hold him without yelling!

Valerie had just announced that she and Wayne were expecting there third baby. Much to our delight, our family was growing and I was happy. On Good Friday 2006 my world would change forever. Pam was sitting breastfeeding Aaron on the settee, and I was beside her with a smile on my face, amazed at this miracle so contented in his mammy's arms. Lar was in the kitchen struggling to key in credit on his phone with broken glasses. The baby was finished feeding, so Pam called Lar to get the baby buggy from the car, so he could have a sleep. Lar said he would, but continued to 'play' with his phone. Fifteen minutes later, he was still at the phone and Pam said 'Give it to me and I'll fix it while you get the buggy'. Next thing he roared 'No!' in a cross voice to Pam. We all got a shock and looked at him he jumped up, grabbed his phone then went out and got the buggy.

Afterwards, he disappeared upstairs to our attic room that he built. Val and Wayne and the children were gone home, while Pam's husband was gone to the shops, leaving Pam, baby, June and I. Pam, was always a happy person but she turned to me and said 'Mam, I think dad has another woman!' I laughed out loud, as I thought Pam was smiling saying it. I said 'Ah will ye go way outa that, sure he's sixty two years old!' Mam, she said 'There is something going on because when he was in my house, every time his phone rang or text he ran into the bathroom'. Just then June said that she noticed he was hiding the phone lately. She said he put the charger for it upstairs. That got me thinking, because there was only me, June, and him living in the house. He knew June couldn't get up the stairs with the wheelchair, and because I had difficulty with the arthritis, I never went up the stairs at all.

When he came back in to the room, June asked him why he brought the charger upstairs. 'Ah its better upstairs' he said. 'Why is it better' she asked. 'Because I was tripping over it in the bedroom' he said. Now I got suspicious, because the plug in our bedroom was in a corner, far away from the bed.

I felt sick in my stomach, telling myself that no, it couldn't be true. Not Lar, he had no time for people who cheated in marriage, taking the high moral ground every time, besides we were forty years married now, that had to mean something.

I never said a word to him, for now I needed to think. We said our tearful goodbyes to Pam, Rob, and Aaron, later that day. It was Good Friday and there would be no pubs open that night, so I was in the car with Lar that evening as he took 150 euro from the pass machine. That night I went to bed at about eleven, while he stayed up 'til the early hours. I could not sleep and was still awake when he came to bed. He had been drinking cans from the fridge, and after another attempt at a drunken 'grope' I pushed him away, and he quickly fell asleep.

I lay awake wondering what I should do next. The truth was, I was afraid of him, and dreaded the thoughts of a row. Yet I knew that I had to find out for myself.

I was disgusted that the children figured it out, while I had no clue. I lay awake thinking that before I accuse him, I had to have proof. Should I follow him tomorrow night, or will I try to find his phone? I watched the clock on my bedside locker all night. I kept thinking of things that happened during the past few months, like the hours he spent upstairs when he came in from the pub, the night he threw his phone behind the computer when I walked in on him.

I was starting to see the clues now. I got up at six the next morning like I always do, and looked for his phone. It wasn't downstairs, so up I went on my hands and knees to search upstairs. About eight steps up there was the phone at my nose! Clearly he put his hand through the banisters putting it well out of sight and out of my reach, knowing I would never go up there, and that June couldn't.

Unfortunately, I knew nothing about mobile phones at the time. True, June had given me her old phone, so that I could text her when she was in dialysis, but that was all I could do with it. So I lifted his phone but couldn't do much with it. Then I found a list of phone numbers, more by accident than anything else. I looked down the list of numbers and recognised my children's and mine. The only other number there, was entered as Win. So I wrote down the number and put the phone back. Later that morning I went in cheerfully with his tea and talked about his drinking buddies in The Village Inn , trying to find out if he was going again that night. I was thinking that I might follow him, but inside I was shaking, annoyed with myself I tried to act normal but my mind was all over the place. I had mixed feelings, furious one minute, then hoping my suspicions were wrong the next.

I couldn't bring myself to say anything, as I still feared him and his aggressiveness. Besides you could never have an argument with him, as he had to get the last word. Sometimes I thought he was addicted to being right! But this situation was serious, so I had to do something.

Today was Saturday, and I went through the motions of my usual day with June. We went to the Square Shopping Centre, in Tallaght, and did our shopping as usual, before stopping for lunch. June and I talked about her dad, trying to make some sense of it. I decided that I would follow him that night, but June didn't like the idea of it, especially as I told her not to tell

Valerie or Pam. I didn't want to upset Val because she was in the first three months of pregnancy and very sick. Pam was back in The Isle of Man so it wouldn't be fair I thought, to have her worrying so far away.

While we were sitting there having our lunch, June asked me for the phone number that I found on his phone of 'Win'. She dialled it and asked to speak to Win. A man answered and said it was the wrong number. So we discussed it further, and I said 'Maybe it is the number of 'The Village Inn'. But she tried that, and it too was the wrong number. We were puzzled, so gave up.

I bought new clothes that day, because I did not want to be instantly recognisable, if I was following him. Also, I never wore my hair up, as it was difficult with my crooked hands, but I was going to make a real effort that night.

After I left June in to dialysis I went home and continued the day as normal. He was in great form, ironing his own clothes for that night. I was feeling frightened of what lay ahead. What if it was true that he had another woman? What would I say if I confronted them? One thing was clear, there was something going on, and no matter how much it hurt, I had to get to the end of it, as I couldn't live my life like this. By the time June came home from dialysis, I had my mind fixed firmly on what I was about to do. As Lar was getting ready to go out June pleaded with me to at least tell Valerie. She was more concerned for my safety, than of what I would find. I had everything ready to go the minute he would walk out the door. Just as he went, June asked me again to ring Valerie, and this time handed me the phone. Of course, I thought that he was going to The Village Inn in Crumlin, like he always told me, so I didn't mind being late for my 'grand' entrance.

But because June was so worried, I rang Val. I explained my plan and told her of the phone number of 'Win'. She said 'Call out that phone number to me', and I did. There was silence at the other end of the phone for a minute as she looked something up. 'Mam' she said 'That is the phone number of the window man that put in our new windows!' Well even in my sadness, I had to laugh!

I had a long talk with Valerie after that, and she succeeded in talking me out of following him. 'Even if you are right mam' she said, 'Don't bring yourself down to their level, you are better than that'. So I didn't follow him, but I was now more furious for not doing anything. But as Valerie said, the truth will come eventually. Next day was Easter Sunday and the three of us were invited to Val and Wayne's for dinner. We always went for dinner on Christmas and Easter. We brought easter eggs as usual for the children and enjoyed their excitement as they opened them. The dinner was lovely and Lar eat everything that was put in front of him. He had a great appetite and loved his food. After dinner we played with the children, and sat around chatting. About two hours after dinner (4.30pm) Lar started making eyes at me to go home. He always did this when he was tired or had enough. I looked at the clock and thought it was too early to leave, so I pretended that I didn't see him. After another few minutes, he sat beside me and gave me a nudge to go.

I felt a bit embarrassed because Val and Wayne went to a lot of trouble to make our day, and I knew I had to do what he said. Why didn't I stand up to him and refuse to leave? Because I didn't want to upset him, making life more unbearable when we went home.

I hated saying goodbye especially to the children, and I was annoyed with myself for doing so. But home we went, stopping at the shop on the way so that I could buy the Sunday newspaper. When we got home, Lar went straight in to bed with the paper. June and I watched the telly, and chatted about the day. We also looked around for his phone but it was nowhere to be seen. I gave up again!

Lar got up again for tea at half past six. After that he left the kitchen, while I tidied up. Next thing June said to me 'Where's Dad gone?' I said he's probably upstairs with the paper. 'No' she said 'He's gone out'. I never heard a thing, but June was in the sitting room and heard the front door closing quietly. I thought it was odd, but he was back within half an hour. I asked where

he went and he replied 'I just went to the pass machine for 20
euro'. Now that didn't make sense to me at all, because this was
Sunday, and two days ago on Good Friday I was with him as
he took 150euro from the pass machine then. He didn't go out
Friday night because all the pubs were closed and he bought a
few cans to drink at home. He never gave me any of the money
as I ran the house on my own wages. I was getting worried, but
kept my fears to myself.

He went out as usual that night and as usual I left his supper
ready and went to bed. I couldn't sleep, worrying about him,
and also my wrist was throbbing. I lay there promising myself
that after the 'long' weekend I would get it x-rayed, to see if
it was broken. Eventually, in the early hours he came home.
I was still awake when he came to bed but I pretended to be
asleep. He cuddled in to me and nodded off immediately. I, on
the other hand never slept.

Next morning I got up as usual at six. Half asleep I hobbled into
the kitchen. I then thought I was seeing things! There, in front
of the breadbin was his phone! He must have been so tired with
the drink that he forgot to hide it.

I still knew very little about mobile phones, but I franticly start
pressing buttons.

Then up on the screen came a text; I LOVE YOU TOO, WILL
RING U TONITE . I started to shake then ran into June. I
turned on the light and grabbed her glasses waking her up out
of her sleep! 'June' I said' Look at this and tell me who sent it'
She put on her glasses and checked it out. 'Mam' she said 'This
is a SENT text from Dad!'. I went straight into him and woke
him out of his sleep. 'Who is this woman that you sent this text
to?' I asked in an angry voice. 'What?, what are you talking
about' he said,' and why are you looking at my phone?'

'Who is this woman?', I screamed. Sheepishly he told me it was
a woman he met in The Village Inn, with his separated friends.
'She is very nice and I just got friendly with her'. What about
this 'I LOVE YOU TOO' text that you sent her?'Ah I was just
responding to her text' he said. ' Am I supposed to believe that?,
I want the truth', I said. But he wasn't capable of telling the

truth, because he kept contradicting himself with every sentence out of his mouth. I tried to calm down as I knew I would get more out of him that way.

Him; 'She really is nice you would like her yourself!'

Me; 'Where is she from?'

Him; She is originally from old Lucan like my mother but she lives in Leixlip now.

Me; What's her name and how old is she?

Him; Her name is Esther, and she is a grandmother like yourself with four grandchildren. In fact she too, has a daughter in a wheelchair who was in a bad car accident, and has to be cared for in a nursing home.

Me; Does she know you are a married man?

Him; Yes. She is separated two years, she had an awful life, I feel sorry for her, as she is a nice woman, and very holy. She goes to bed with her rosary beads every night, never misses mass, and does the church collection every week.

Me; 'Well she might be very holy, but she doesn't have any morals, if she is keeping company with a married man! How long is this going on when did you meet'?

Him; 'We started seeing each other eight months ago on my birthday' (sixty second birthday). What attracted me to her was that her accent reminded me of my mother,
being from old Lucan.

I couldn't take it in, my head was spinning. How could he? And worst of all, he wasn't a bit remorseful over what he was doing. By this time I was hysterical screaming and throwing things like they do in the films! I ran out of the bedroom and into the kitchen. June could hear the row, and called Val on her phone. Lar got up pretty fast and followed me. 'Don't tell the children', he asked looking very worried. 'Well it's too late for that' I said, 'It was the children who told ME that something was going on. I kept looking at him in disbelief. Here was a man so dutiful and loyal, like his father before him, pulling the rug out from under me.

I started talking about her again. What did she look like? What colour was her hair? Did she wear glasses, I asked the most ridiculous things. He talked lovingly about her, yes she did wear glasses, had dyed red hair, was not glamorous, just an ordinary woman, a grandmother like me. He admitted to seeing her every weekend, sometimes during the week, and texting in between times. He said over and over again, that she was very nice. My head couldn't take it in, how could a woman that goes after a married man be nice? According to him, she did the chasing. He told me that one night they were drinking together, and she said to him 'Larry, I'm afraid to fall in love with you in case you might leave me'. I said 'Why didn't you tell her that you're not free that you had a wife and children'. She knew, was all he said. Stupid things were annoying me now, like her calling him Larry. In our family, he was always Lar, or Laurence.

I thought about the text again. The 'I will ring you tonite' bit. I said to him, 'So that's where you went last night, out to ring her on your phone, and lying to me about going to the pass machine' 'No I really did go to the pass machine, I swear' he said. 'You did not I roared at him'. 'You're wrong' he said, I went up to the bank to get twenty euro'.

'Okay' I roared even louder, if you did, then the bank will have a record of it tomorrow morning. That changed his mind. 'Alright then I did ring her'. I calmed my voice again, trying to relax, I wasn't feeling too good, and my wrist was paining badly. 'What did you talk about on the phone' I wanted to know. 'She was asking me what I did today and I told her that we went to Valerie's for dinner with June. I was shouting again ' So you said WE went to Valerie's, does that not tell her that you have a wife living with you?' 'She knows', he said. I was having difficulty trying to take it all in. I stupidly thought it would be like the films and he would get on his knees begging forgiveness. But clearly his concern was for Esther. 'Does forty years of marriage mean nothing to you' I asked choking back the tears. 'It's not as simple as that', he replied. I said 'Do you not want me anymore?. Again he said 'It's not as simple as that'.

My mind was swinging from one thing to another, it was all over the place. I asked him what was her surname, and he said he didn't know. I knew this was another lie, as she knew my name, my children's names, where they were in life, and all about my little business. He had told me that earlier in the morning. Besides, if I was to believe the reason he was attracted to her, was the fact that she was from 'Old' Lucan like his mother, the first thing he would ask her was her surname. He said that she had the same accent as his mother, and all his relations still living in Lucan. In fact, Esther knew many of them.

It was now mid morning, and I was aware that June was patiently waiting on me in bed. She heard most of the row so kept talking to Valerie on her mobile phone. I went in to June with a heavy heart. We regularly had a hug every morning before she got up because its hard to give a real hug when she is in the wheelchair. The hug this morning was different. June was feeling my hurt, and it broke my heart that my life was falling apart. I did not know what to say to her. Normally on a bank holiday we did our 'Saturday routine' whereby we shopped, had lunch, then went to dialysis. But June said, 'Mam, why don't we get ready and go up to Valerie's first as she is very worried about you'.

She was right, so I helped June into her wheelchair, got her into the car, but let her drive. I wasn't capable of driving the way I was feeling. Valerie and Wayne helped us out of the car when we arrived.

Pamela was on the phone from The Isle of Man, and it was like a three way conversation! The children were concerned for me, and if I was to be truthful, I was concerned for myself.

I talked to my three wonderful children, and wondered where they got their wisdom from. True, they were adults now (36, 31, and June was almost 30.), but they were still my little girls. In all their years, they had never brought shame to our house, but now, their Dad, their hero, had shaken the very foundation of their world.

I know many men have affairs, but this was a man of loyalty, high morals, and a sense of duty like his father before him. I admit that he was difficult to live with but I did my best, and thought that now, in our sixties, it was hand in hand for the final part of the journey.

We stayed in Valerie's for a few hours, but June had to go to dialysis and get some lunch beforehand, so we left. June drove to The Square Shopping Centre, but our usual shopping was out of the question. We went for lunch, but I was having difficulty eating, thankfully June ate hers. I was in another world as I walked around. I remember being in the lift with two middle aged women. Although they were strangers to me, I wanted to tell them that my world had fallen apart, through no fault of mine! Of course I didn't, but I was screaming inside. Then I was aware of other couples walking around especially my own age, deep in conversation, laughing and joking. What was going to become of me?

I was having a hard job dealing with the fact that Lar was only disgusted that I found out. He never put his arm around me and asked for forgiveness. It was clear to me that he cared more for this woman. Yet I thought about him at home just now, and the fact that I left no dinner ready for him! That was not like me, knowing that he couldn't cook. Still I felt that I wanted to be alone right now with my thoughts. After I left June in dialysis, I drove around for a while, then decided to call to Connie. Connie and Lar were very close, and anytime Lar was in trouble, he went to her. But in my distress, I drove back to Lidl in Walkinstown, and sat in the car park, crying and reflecting on my life. After a while I turned back and went to Connie's. When I got there, she was out, so I sat in the car in her driveway, waiting on her. Her son-in-law Leslie came along and assured me that she would be back shortly. Two minutes later Lar pulled up in the car behind me and got out. 'What are you doing here', he asked. 'Clearly the same as you', I said, 'I need to talk to Connie, we have problems.

He gave a nervous laugh in front of Leslie, and continued laughing and joking with him. Then he got in the car and drove off. It would be a half hour later before Connie and Brian came home, amazed to see me waiting for them.

What's wrong? Connie said all concerned. 'Well Connie you will not believe what I'm going to tell you'. Her first concern was for June, and she asked if she was alright. 'She's fine, Con' I said. 'I found out that Lar is cheating on me with another woman. 'Oh no, not Lar' she said. I can't believe that,.... he wouldn't,... are you sure? ' Yes Connie, he admitted it when I confronted him'. Oh my God', she said,' never in a million years, would I have expected that from him'. 'Betty, the way he always talks about you, it seemed he thought the world of you. Then I told her the events of the day and how the children told me of their suspicions only four days ago. It was just as much a shock to her and Brian, as it was to me. They too were upset. We talked for a few hours, drank endless cups of tea, before I had to go home to be there for June. The hospital provide transport home after dialysis.

When I got home, Lar was still trying to justify the situation. He went over and over again about Esther chasing after him, and how he got to like her then because she reminded him of his mother. I again asked for her surname, but again he said he didn't know. I asked if his drinking buddies knew there was something going on with him and Esther. He said they knew there was something brewing alright. I felt like a fool, being the last to know. Then I asked him to ring her up to tell her that he could not see her again, and that he was going to work on his marriage. 'Oh I can't do that' he said, 'That would be very hurtful!'

'Do you not want to save our marriage?' I asked. 'Well we have issues' he said. I felt mad at that reply, and started yelling again. With that, he jumped up and grabbed his coat, 'I'm going up to Connie', and headed out the door.

Alone with my thoughts I reflected on my life again. It was only days before our 40th wedding anniversary. When did he stop loving me? I tried to think back, was it when my body changed from the rheumatoid arthritis? What was it? Oh how I wished he would tell me so I could make things better.

The girls were on the phone to me regularly to make sure I was all right, but although I chatted to them about my feelings, the truth was, I wasn't alright. In fact I thought I would never be right again! June came home from dialysis at eight o'clock, anxiously, looking at my face as she came in. She asked where dad was and if I was okay. I said no, I'm not okay but I'm hopeful that we can work things out.

Lar came home about half nine, with an angry face on him. I asked if he rang Esther and told her that he couldn't see her anymore. He yelled back 'No, and no one will make me. Another row followed, then he left, saying that he was going to stay in Pam's house in Mulligar for a bit of peace. He had a set of keys to Pam's house, as he went down regularly to cut the grass. Of course I believed him, and in my innocence worried if there was enough food in the house! I didn't realise that he was most likely going down to HER!

Next day I couldn't face going to the hospital for my wrist x-ray, I needed to be at home for Lar coming back. It was Tuesday, and Lar knew I always made stew for dinner which he loved, every Tuesday. I made the usual amount, but he didn't come home. I had no interest in going out to my workroom, for the first time ever. June was back in work so Valerie stayed most of the day. I was numb. My only conversation was Lar and Esther. The children listened patiently and continued to lavish me with love, praise and reassured me. Pam was constantly on the phone telling me that she would talk to him. She knew that if he was to listen to anyone, it would be her, they were very close.

At home that evening I was so sad. I don't know how June put up with me, talking about my feelings all night. After she went to bed, I tried writing it in my diary, but what I wrote didn't make sense, yet it was my true feelings. I wrote: Dear Diary, It is four o'clock in the morning, this is the worst time of my life. Only for the children, I wouldn't want to live anymore. Maybe time will help. But how can I forget this?. First the betrayal, then the lies. He says he lied to protect me, but they were to protect himself and this 'nice' woman. How can I ever start again when I don't know the real truth. Only two people know the truth, him and her. What should I do next? I wish my head would clear to help me make the right decision. I talk to the children because I have no one else, as no one else knows. I never realised what strong brave kids I have, loving me unconditionally too. What am I going to do?. She is healthier than me, so I can't compete with that. Would it help to see this woman, or even meet her, is that what I need, to see what I'm up against?. I don't know, if I got the real truth from Lar then maybe I could pick myself up and move on. Without the truth I can't cope. Should we break up? If we don't, will he leave me anyway? Yesterday during the row he said our marriage was in trouble anyway. But he showed me no affection, looked at me in disgust. Maybe my screwed up body didn't attract him any more, yes, that's it! But what was he doing years ago when I had a good body? Criticising me! When he came home from work he was more interested in what housework was done, than how I was. Now he asks HER how was her day!

During the eighties my self esteem was shattered when he continually told me what a useless wife I was, and how awful I looked.. Oh digging up the past is not helping me right now. Is this the end of my life as I know it, will I ever sleep peacefully again? Foolish me, I thought I had the one thing I was so sure of, so sure so sure. It is now 5.30 am and I have to face another day. I do not know how I can do it as I feel worse than horrible All Lar feels is disgust that he was caught out, and what other people will think of him. But he wasn't thinking of other people when he wrote 'I love you' to HER.

He has protected her from the truth' so she is sleeping soundly, while the rest of us are awake all night. I am such a fool..............

Next day he came home. Bright and cheerful as if nothing had happened. Like a fool I put the kettle on and asked how he was, and he said fine. We sat at the table and I asked if he told Esther that he couldn't see her anymore. 'No' he said, 'If you stop making a big deal out of it, it will just fizzle out'. Needless to say I wasn't happy with that! 'But if you are staying with me you will have to tell this woman where she stands' I said with enforced calmness. 'I cannot hurt her' he replied. 'She had a hard life and I feel sorry for her'. Although I didn't say it, I thought to myself that MY life wasn't a bed of roses either, and he never felt sorry for me!

Just then Valerie came in, and yelled at him for what he was doing to me. She let him know how disappointed she was that her Dad could lie and cheat. He tried to justify himself again but Valerie was having none of it. I hated seeing her so upset, as she was in the early months of pregnancy, so I did everything to calm her down. He went out again and headed up to Connie's. Valerie followed him and from what I heard there was a big row in front of Connie. It was breaking my heart looking at Valerie, she was such a good girl, always trying to help people. But now the very foundation of her world was falling apart.

Later that night Pam rang Lar as promised. Yes, he would listen to her, if anyone could get through to him, it would be Pam.

Later Pam told me that she first told him that she forgave him for making a 'mistake'. 'Dad lots of men make mistakes and make up with their wives and move on' she said. 'Now what you'll do is stop seeing Esther, and make it up to Mam' She said he listened, and promised he would. I remember thinking at the time that I knew he would listen to Pam, she had a special bond with him.

The next few days were awkward to say the least. Yes, we talked it through for hours on end, sometimes ending in another row. I found it hard not to get mad when he spent most of the time 'singing' her praises. The more he told me about her, the more uneasy I felt. Yet he loved to talk about how nice she was, over and over again, and like a fool I listened.

I got up every day, after a sleepless night, trying to get my act together. I could not sew, I had no heart, life was different now. I knew I was letting Valerie down as it left the whole business on her shoulders, at a time that she wasn't well herself.

'I have a mortgage Mam, I have to keep sewing' she said. Of course she was right and she did her best to keep going. I wondered did this man realise what he was doing to our family. We were all falling apart, while he was taking it all in his stride. I lay in bed every night thinking, what I would do if he left me. I often worried what I'd do if anything happened to him.

I remembered on his 49th birthday, he was in an accident that could have killed him. He was driving back to work at midnight down the Quays when there was a Garda chase going on with drug traffickers from Northern Ireland. He swerved to avoid a collision, the truck smashed the bridge wall and it almost went into the Liffey. The gardai quickly pulled him from the drivers seat and apologised to him for causing the accident. He came home that night very shaken even though it wasn't his fault. I got up out of bed and gave him a beer to settle his nerves. We talked for hours about what might have been, and I thanked God all night as I watched him sleep.

He went to the doctor next day just to talk, and our G.P. was able to explain to him why he still felt a bit shaken. I drove him into work, to make an accident report, and we stopped on the way to look at the bridge. It frightened me to look at the drop down into the river. Even though Lar is a strong swimmer, he was trapped in the truck until the Gardai rescued him.

I lay awake thinking back to that time, and here he was beside me talking in his sleep again, but only about Esther! I felt like shaking him but what was the point? The following Saturday, I was in The Square Shopping Centre as usual, when I decided to buy him new glasses. It was less than a year since he bought the glasses that he lost, so I knew that Vision Express would still have his prescription. They were 300 euro, and June kept telling me that I was mad to spend that much on them. But I thought it would be a nice thing to do and that he would be pleased. Well he was pleased, but said 'You shouldn't have, as he tried them on.' Nothing more was said about them after that.

He still stayed out late at the weekend, so I knew he was with her. I begged him to finish with her but he said over and over again that he couldn't hurt her. I threatened to lock him out if he came home late again. The children continued to yell at him, so finally, he said he would tell her in his own way.

Meanwhile June was taken into hospital for a serious operation on her bowel. I was worried about her and had a knot in my stomach, over the 'Esther' affair. Coming home from the hospital one night, I asked if he'd finished with her and he said he had. I told him that he should change his phone number so that she couldn't contact him now, and he agreed to this.

Next day he showed me his new sim card and assured me that he had changed it. I asked him to put back the old one so that I would know that it was the offending one before destroying it. He kept telling me I was ridiculous, but I was adamant that he show me the old one, because he changed it while I was at the hospital. So he put it back, 'Now are you satisfied' he said angrily, as he handed me the phone.

The next thing that happened was beyond chance! As I held the phone in my hand a text came from Esther. 'Miss you weekends' it said on the screen. He grabbed it, but I immediately wrote down her phone number as quick as I could. He stood up and with all his strength he twisted my sore wrist until he got the piece of paper. I was in so much pain, that I folded up and fell into the nearest chair. Only those with rhuematoid arthritis can imagine the pain. He knew that he hurt me bad and he was truly sorry. He ran to our bedroom to get my elastic bandage. While he was gone I wrote down Esther's number again from memory. I hoped it was right, but I knew that I had a good memory for numbers. I put it down my bra!

He strapped my wrist up tightly apologising all the time. It throbbed day and night for a few days, but then an amazing thing happened. The pain went completely and it hasn't pained me from that day since! Before he twisted it, I thought it was broken because of the pain, and had a form for to have it x-rayed. Now, whatever movement he did, seem to 're-set' it.

June asked me what happened to my wrist. I told her that the arthritis was acting up again, and she believed me, as it wouldn't be unusual.

After that, life was uncomfortable to say the least. I was the only one trying to keep things together. We spoke politely to each other, as the week went on. It would be another week before I got a chance to ring Esther. The phone call went like this:

ME; Hello is that Esther?

ESTHER: Yes

ME: My name is Betty, I'm Lar's wife.

Silence for a few seconds.

ESTHER: Oh yes

ME: Well Esther, I would like you to know that Lar and I are forty years married, not only that, but we know each other since we were five years old. Now what is going on here and where did you meet?

ESTHER: We met at the music session, and we haven't had sex.

ME: I have asked him to finish with you and he said he has, so what did he say to you?

ESTHER: He said that he was going over to do work for Pam in the Isle of Man, and
that he wouldn't see me for a couple of weeks.

ME: Well he was lying, he's not going over to Pam's, I have just found out the truth about you and him

ESTHER: I'm sorry, I thought he was separated

ME: Did he tell you that he was separated?

Esther: I'd rather not say.

Me: I can tell you that we are not separated, and never were.

Esther: I'm very sorry, believe me I know where you're coming from, I've been there, and now that I know the truth, you have nothing to worry about from me.

Me: Thank you for your time, goodbye.

I spent the next couple of weeks trying to be the best wife ever. I never sewed, just did housework and looked after my husband. I stayed up late every night with him and had his supper ready when he came home from the pub. In all my married years, I was too shy to make the first move in bed, ever. But I was trying to win back my husband now, so I felt that I had to change. I was so pathetic, that he had to say to me 'You don't have to change, just be yourself'. But the truth was, I was not myself anymore, in fact there were days when I didn't know who I was. I began to go out with him again on Saturday nights, only to keep him happy, but it always ended up in a row about Esther. Even if we didn't row, the conversation was always about her. I pretended to be interested but I got tired listening to how wonderful she was. One Sunday morning, we were lying in bed, chatting like we often did, before I got up to make the breakfast. He started to talk about her again. 'She said that I have a lovely smile' he said. I looked at him without his two dentures that he has in the front. I said 'Mmm..... if only she could see your smile now, without your teeth!' He had to laugh, because he knew it was the truth.

Another week went by before I told him that I rang her a few days after he hurt my wrist. He wasn't pleased at all, and I could see him squirming in the bed as I told him. He wanted to know exactly what I said to her, and what she said to me, and I told him the truth. He was extra quiet that day, and kept out of my way. That night, he went out on his own, telling me that he was going to the local for a drink. I believed him, because I thought he wanted to be with me, even though he never actually said those words. Alas, it was all in my head.

Even when it got very late that night I was worried in case he got mugged. I rang his phone about twenty times, but it was turned off.

I rang Valerie and told her how worried I was. I said that something must have happened because I knew he wouldn't hurt me again by going to Esther. Val agreed and said if he didn't come home soon, that she would get Wayne to drive around the local roads to see if he was alright.

At 2.15am I remembered, that any time he was late home during the last few months, he said he was in Mick's house. So desperately, I rang Mick's house.

I asked a very sleepy Mick if Lar was with him. 'No Betty, he said, I haven't seen him in ages'. Now I was really mad, and my blood was boiling. Valerie kept ringing me every fifteen minutes to see if I heard from him, but no I hadn't. I watched at the window until 3am, then finally he walks smartly like a soldier, up the road.

I quickly put the safety chain on the door as he put his key in. I looked out through the 'slit' and said 'Where were you?' 'I was in Mick's house' he said, so sure of himself. 'I rang Mick's house and woke him out of his sleep, and he said he hasn't seen you in ages.' 'Well let me in you are making a show of me' he said. There were a few more cross words before I let him in. I kept asking over and over again where he was but he wouldn't answer me. Finally I yelled 'You were with her but you haven't the guts to tell me'. He roared back, 'Yes I was with her are you happy now?'. I was far from happy, especially when Valerie rang to see if he was home, and I had to tell her that her Dad was with the 'other' woman.

Within minutes Valerie drove down, still in her pyjama's. She was so angry with him and so was I. I started throwing things again while he kept calmly picking them up. Valerie wanted me to go home with her but I stayed and locked myself in the bedroom. We had a spare bedroom and bathroom upstairs, but he kept knocking on our bedroom door for me to let him in, before finally going upstairs.

I cried all night and never slept. I was looking out of the window most of the time and eventually saw the morning come. When June is in hospital I always go up early to dress her pressure sores and help her into her wheelchair, and this day was no different. There wasn't a sound from upstairs as I left the house at 7.15am. I did my best to be cheerful to June but I wasn't fooling her for one minute. 'What happened Mam?' she asked I had to tell her the truth because she was nearly thirty years old, and besides, Valerie rang Pam so I couldn't leave her out'. She was so upset for me that I stayed longer than I normally do. I usually went home to make dinner at lunch time as Lar liked his dinner then. I would then spend the evening with her until 9pm every night.

My stomach was feeling sick now, so dinner didn't interest me, besides, I had to think of what to do next. My head was all over the place, but I knew I couldn't continue the way I was. I began thinking, what if he didn't see me for a while? Doesn't absence make the heart grow fonder? Yes, I decided there and then, that we needed a break from each other.

When I arrived home I sat down with him and tried to be calm. Valerie arrived too, worried about me after the night before. I said to him 'You really like this woman don't you?' He nodded his head in a yes. 'Right', I said 'I need to be on my own for a month to get my head together, so you can stay in Pam's house in Mullingar and decide what to do'. His reply was that he would stay home, live upstairs, and do the housework for me, but still carry on with his social life.

I had too much pride to agree to that, so I said no. Connie called later and tried to talk me out of it, but I stupidly thought that he would miss me so much, that he would come back before the month was up.

Later that evening he left, and my heart broke as he walked out of the door. I spoke to him on the phone every day, trying to make some sense of the situation. He told me that the doctors and hospitals were getting him down. I couldn't believe that as I looked after June's needs, and I went on my own to my hospital appointments, which was about four times a year, apart from the warfarin clinic every month, that was 8 o'clock in the morning, while he was asleep. I was usually back by 9am.

Then he said he was depressed, and that he had nobody to talk to. 'When did I become nobody?' I asked. As long as we were together I talked to him about the depression, reading every book I could get my hands on to help him. I would spend hours trying to talk him round on his bad days, and encouraged him to go to the doctor about it.

After two weeks apart, his mood seemed to be much better, so I thought the break was doing him good. In my innocence I didn't realise Mullingar was nearer to Esther, and now he had no one to nag him. Even when he was in great form on the phone, it still never occurred to me why. He said that he felt like he was on his holidays, and as luck would have it, the weather was great.

After three weeks, I asked him to meet me at a local hotel for tea and a chat. He agreed, so the following day I was hopeful as I got ready to go. Valerie came and had the house 'sparkling', expecting dad to come home with me, and knowing how clean he liked the house, she wanted everything right for him.

I arrived early for the appointment, looking my very best. I stood on the steps outside waiting for him. Next thing I saw our car pulling in, and he stepped outside. My heart missed a beat when I saw him looking so well and relaxed.

Hi! he said, 'I feel like I'm going for an interview for a job!' I laughed with him as we walked into the hotel and ordered tea. I asked how he was. 'I'm great' he said 'I feel like I'm on holidays and the weather is fantastic'. When we settled down and began to talk, I said 'Lar, we have been married for forty years, and apart for three weeks, how can we make things better?'. Without making eye contact he replied ' It can never be better, because June will always be there'.

I was shocked. I would have coped better if he had said he hated the sight of ME! Was it because he thought that I spent too much time with June? But she was now an adult and an independent young woman, who only missed work when she was in hospital. She did not depend on us finacially either, in fact she paid for her keep every week. I never asked him what he meant by that remark.

Looking back now, I should have walked away and never looked back, but I was weak, and kept hoping we could get back together. We went over everything again repeating ourselves, then we ran out of new things to say, but the bottom line was, that he was not coming back.

It was coming up to lunch time and the hotel was serving dinner. He asked if I would like some, but I was having a hard time swallowing my saliva never mind a dinner. He ordered one for himself, a large portion, and ate everything on the plate.

I was driving June's car, so he walked me over to it. I sat in the driver's seat crying. He held the door open and said ' Don't get upset it will work out right eventually' Sadly I drove home, dreading facing Valerie, because she was expecting me to come home with him. When I got there, I didn't have to say a word, she knew by my face he wasn't coming. Pamela and June were in work, waiting on phone calls from us. Valerie rang Pam and I rang June. I could never tell June his exact words, and I never did. All the children were hurting for me, even though they too were missing their Dad. I did not know what to do next. Somehow I struggled through the next few weeks still trying to make sense of what happened. But no matter what I did, I couldn't sleep or eat. Lar called in from time to time looking great, and clearly happy with his life. Many times he would say to me 'You look dreadful, and the weight is falling off you'. But my children kept reassuring me that I looked good and fussed over me continuously. Because I lost weight, my clothes were now hanging off me, so Valerie brought me shopping to buy a whole new set of clothes two sizes smaller. I remember standing in the dressing room of Marks and Spencers and looking at my belly folding over as I put on a size 10 trousers, with ease.

I realised then that I needed to go to the doctor to get back on track. Our G.P. was very sympathetic when I went to see him. I explained that I couldn't swallow so I didn't eat. He had a long talk with me and suggested a course of nutritious drinks, until my appetite came back. Also I wasn't sleeping, so he gave me something to help me sleep. I then tried to focus on my three wonderful children. At least they wanted and needed me in different ways.

Chapter Twenty Five
LOOKING FOR HELP

B y now all my sisters were aware of the situation, and shocked with Lar's behaviour. They were a great support to me and were in constant touch on a daily basis. I then decided to go for counselling to Accord. I first asked Lar if he would come with me but he refused. So I went on my own. When I made the appointment I asked if they had a counsellor my own age, because, at 61, I didn't want to talk to someone as young as my children. They obliged, and then I had my first meeting with Myra, a lovely lady my own age.

I will always remember her first words to me, she said 'Elizabeth, you WILL smile again'. I was in floods of tears, and of course, I did not believe her.

We spent an hour chatting, she asking questions about my life with Lar, me telling her more than what she asked. The time went in so quickly, and I was disappointed that she hadn't fixed it for me. I really needed to know how I could get him back! I did not realise that it was a slow process and that 14 months later I would be still in counselling, but getting stronger.

Meanwhile, Lar was staying in Pamela's house for months now, dropping in to me now and again when it suited him. Eventually, he decided to come home, but it only lasted three weeks as he was still seeing Esther. Pam came home when he came back and she was delighted. It was during that time that myself and the three girls decided to confront this woman, without telling Lar. We all met in the hospital, as June was still in recovering from a colostomy operation, and I was worried about her, besides, she loved to be involved in everything. We talked at length about our plan. how we could find Esther, and who would be the best person to approach her.

Pam offered and we all agreed that it would be better with just one person turning up at her door. We tried to get as much information as possible before she started but it was difficult. She asked me her name, but as Lar was always very careful to protect her, he never let her name slip. 'Ok' she said, 'Tell me everything you know about her and where she's from and I'll find her'. Pam left early, to investigate.

With very little effort she had a name and address! Leixlip is a small neighbourhood, and Lar told me what part she lived in, so the rest was easy.

That night with Valerie babysitting, Pam headed out to Leixlip, with her husband, Robert. She found the house and knocked on the door. Pam's description of Esther was that of an ordinary woman with glasses and spikey hair.

'Are you Esther?' she asked. 'Yes' said the woman. 'My name is Pamela, I am Lar's daughter'. Esther was shocked at first but invited her and Robert in.

When Pam sat down she said, 'I needed to see the face of the woman who turned my Daddy into a stranger'.

Pam said that she was a reasonable person and listened to her as she described life with Mam and Dad and our happy family, before she came along. Clearly, she had no idea of our family life, and she promised Pam, that she would not see Lar again.

She said that nothing happened, but it could have, and now that she knew the situation, nothing would. She also promised Pam that she would not tell her Dad that herself and Robert called. Alas, that promise lasted two hours!

Meanwhile, back home it was getting late and Lar was getting agitated as he was waiting for Pam to come home to go to the pub with her. Valerie had her baby Aaron up in her house, and was waiting anxiously too.

'It's very late to have that baby out' Lar said to me a few times looking at his watch. I reassured him that they would be home shortly. Sure enough, they were soon home, and Pam decided that she didn't want to go to the pub, so Robert went with Lar. After they left, Pam told me all about the woman and the evening. 'I don't think she will see him anymore' she said. I hoped Pam was right, but I had an uneasy feeling about the whole thing. When Robert and Lar came home, we made supper and sat around the table talking. As it got late into the night, I was falling asleep, and Pam said, 'Why don't you go into bed Mam?' I was so tired that I did, and said goodnight to everyone.

About fifteen minutes later, as I was drifting off into a welcome sleep, I was awakened by shouting. Next thing the bedroom door opened and Pam said 'Say you know nothing!' I was half asleep and didn't know what was going on. Lar came roaring down the hall to me in a mad rage. 'Did you know that Pam and Robert went out to Esther's house tonight?' Pam was behind him shaking her head in a 'no'. So I said no. Seemingly Esther had text Lar, told him about the visit, and said that she didn't want to see him again.

There followed an almighty row between Pam and her dad, the likes of which I never heard before. He called her terrible names, so I quickly came to her defence. Next thing he rolled around the bed holding his head saying 'Yisser driving me back into her arms' 'Oh' I said ,'So you have been in her arms?'

'You interfering bitch' he roared at Pam, then told her to get out of the house and get back to the Isle of Man. I was in a state of shock, and the whole thing went on for nearly an hour, I did my best to defuse the situation, but Lar was like a madman.

Unfortunately, because Pam and Rob were staying up in the spare room, I had no choice but to sleep with Lar. Pam was very concerned for me as we had never seen Lar so mad before. I was actually scared myself, but pretended to Pam that I was fine. June was still in hospital, so was unaware of the commotion at that time.

Esther's text turned him into a madman!

I never slept that night, wrapping myself up in a ball to keep away from him. He slept fitfully, talking in his sleep the whole night. Every word out of his mouth was Esther. He even woke himself up calling her! I thought the morning would never come, and when it did, I was up at six o'clock, like I do every morning. When June is in hospital, I always went up to her at 7.15am every day to help her with her personal care. This time however, I got out of the house earlier out of fear.

When I got to the hospital, I rang Valerie and told her to contact Pam on her mobile phone, and tell her to pack up and go to her house immediately. Pam and Robert were going home that day anyway, but I didn't want them there with him like a madman, especially as I was at the hospital. Valerie agreed and rang Pamela, so they left the house and went to her.

Meanwhile June wanted to know what was going on as I arrived at the hospital a half hour earlier. I told her the events of the previous night and we spent the morning talking it through. I left then and went to Val's to see was Pam alright, but she wasn't. She was very upset and swore that she would never speak to him again. It saddened me that it had come to this, because Pam had been his 'cuddles' all her life and she adored him.

I looked at how my three children were hurting for me and each other, and I silently cursed Esther. How dare she break up my family! But then I soon came back to reality and realised that it takes two, and that it wasn't her who said those horrible things to Pam! On the other hand I thought that any woman who went with a married man had no morals.

I dreaded going home. I said my tearful goodbyes to Pamela, and headed home with a heavy heart. When I got there he was still full of anger, still calling Pamela an 'interfering bitch', and he ripped up an important photograph of her. He completely disowned her and wouldn't listen to reason. I was terrified of him and told him so. I asked him if I was ' safe here' or should I ring one of my sisters. With an angry look on his face, he said 'I wouldn't touch you!'. I hoped he was telling me the truth, because I had never seen him like this before. I did not know how to handle the situation, but kept out of his way until it was time for me to go back to the hospital.

I took the car keys and was heading out the door, when he jumped up and said that he would drive me up. He often drove me to the hospital as the parking was bad, so I said okay. All the way up, he kept on and on about Pam. My mouth was dry from defending her, so I shut up until we got there. I was glad to see June, she was great company, and I could forget about Lar for three or four hours.

Even when June is unwell, she has a great sense of humour and always made me laugh! When it came time to go home, I left the hospital a bit anxious over her.Usually, when I come out Lar would wave with his hand out of the window, so I could see him. This time however I could see no wave, so I thought he wasn't there.

I looked around the car park for our car, then I saw him, with his head in his hands bent over the wheel. Silently, I got into the car and no sooner had I put on the seat belt, he started again. I was trying to think of something to defuse the situation, or calm him down, so when we were passing the Cuckoo's Nest pub, I said 'Let's go in for a drink'. He immediately swung the car in to the pub car park.

He stood at the bar and ordered a pint for him and a mineral for me, but he refused to sit down. He knew that I couldn't stand for long because of the arthritis, but he was so angry that he wasn't thinking of me. I looked at him drinking and knew this was a big mistake, I should have gone home. When I finished my drink I told him that I wanted to go home, so he swallowed his in one gulp, and marched out of the pub. I was worried and didn't know how I to get through this.

At home he didn't say much , but left the house again after a few minutes. It was now 9.45pm so I rang the hospital to check on June. She answered her mobile phone, not sounding very well, so I rang the main hospital number to talk to the night nurse, and she assured me that the medication had her drowsy and that she was fine. Even so, I felt uneasy, and kept ringing throughout the night. When he came home I asked where he went, and he said that he went into town 'just for a drive'. That sounded odd to me, but anyway, I told him about June. He spoke about her for a while, then went up to the spare room to bed.

Next morning at 7am I went to the hospital. I wasn't happy at all when I saw June. She was able to tell me about a feeling she had all over her body. I suspected that she was having a reaction to the drugs, but the nurses wouldn't listen to me. I asked to see a doctor, they said that they would ring one. One hour later, she was getting worse and still no doctor. By now I was getting angry, so I demanded to see a doctor NOW.

Within minutes he was there and immediately gave her an injection, for an allergy to the drug she was on. Half an hour later, June sat up in great form.

She recovered quickly after that and went back to work. She loved her work and only stayed out if she was in hospital. There was an unnatural peace at home. Lar was still staying out late at weekends and sleeping in the spare room. I asked him if he was still seeing Esther, and he said no. I wanted to believe him but I wasn't sure, and I had no way of finding out the truth. I really hoped he would come to his senses so that we could get back to normal. He and Pam no longer spoke to each other.

I was still going for counselling every week and continued to ask him to go but he refused. I continually had trouble sleeping and eating even after going to the doctor. I started to pray again for our marriage to be repaired. I even prayed to his mam and dad to help him see sense.

A couple of weeks later, Lar took June's dog 'Charlie' out for a walk on a Sunday afternoon. He came back in an hour and without thinking, threw his mobile phone on the kitchen table. He sat in the sitting room reading the paper while I was hand sewing a hem on my trousers. June had been in the kitchen talking on the phone to her friend, when she wheeled out and gave me a nod to follow her. I went into her bedroom after her, thinking that she wasn't well, as she would never say she felt sick in front of Lar, or anyone else for that matter, only to me.

She told me that she had been looking at his phone and that there was a call in the last hour. She rang the number, and a woman answered, so she quickly hung up. I went into the kitchen, got his phone, pulled up the number, and asked him who he was ringing when he took Charlie out. He got angry at me for checking up on him, but finally admitted it was Esther.

I was fuming. I knew things weren't right between us now, but I felt that he was betraying me over and over again. In my mind it was clear that he did not want to be married to me anymore, so what was the point in trying.

I told him to go because I couldn't take anymore, and he left that day. He went back to Pam's house in Mullingar. But now Pam wasn't speaking to him, so she was not very happy with him in her house. But for my sake she allowed it for now, because the alternative was back with me in the spare room, and I couldn't face him every day knowing he was still with 'her', and he didn't want me.

I soon realised that breaking up was causing a lot of practical problems as well as emotional. Simple things, like putting petrol in June's car, became a problem because I couldn't manage the pump with my crooked hands. June had a strong upper body, but it wasn't practical for her to struggle out into her wheelchair, to use the pump. I had to get Wayne to fill it up regularly, and if I was caught out, I smiled sweetly at any guy in the garage to help me! I had to force myself to look at the money situation, and check the bank account. We had a joint current account, and I had a savings account, where I put in money from my sewing. We also had savings in the credit union. We had no loans or debts as we kept to our promise in the early part of our marriage that we would never get into debt. While he was staying in Mullingar, he told me that he was withdrawing money from the credit union every week to live on. It was some time later that I checked the balance and realised it was dwindling fast, and he withdrew from our current account as well. But no matter what he did I made excuses for him.

A few times during our marriage, Lar was tempted to re mortgage our house but I would never agree to it, and I was glad now. It had been years since I managed the money and paid the bills, so I had to sit down and call a meeting with myself!

I went to the bank and got a current statement. I looked at it in disbelief! Clearly I had no clue as to our finances, because it was nothing like I expected. When Lar was at home, I never looked at the bank statements as they came in. I had no reason to, as I used my wages from my sewing to run the house. Lar paid the utility bills like ESB, etc. out of the current account.

I was real disappointed with the balance, although it was healthy, it was a lot less than I expected., even though we had paid over 9,000 euro to trade in our car, just before I found out about Esther.

I divided the account by two, and then left an extra 1,000 euro, and opened a new account in another bank. I never touched our joint account again. His work pension was paid into the joint account plus the money from the house rental. I could not concentrate on any sewing, although I knew that I would have to get some money coming in to run the house. But for now I had some savings, also June was handing up money every week.

I continued going to marriage counselling every week, but all I could talk about was would he get sense and end this affair? He called in to me a couple of times a week, and I gave him dinner, and chatted normally for a while. Then I would ask him to break with Esther, and come home. His answer was always 'No'.

In late summer, Pam had a long standing arrangement with friends of hers from the Isle of Man, to visit Ireland and stay in her house for a week. She asked me to tell her dad to move out for the week to accommodate her friends. She still wouldn't talk to him. So I told him what Pam said, and he said that he would stay with his sister Connie for the duration of the visit.

Pam's friends came and went and I never gave it another thought, besides, I hadn't seen Connie in ages. A few weeks later, our tenants in the rented house gave us notice that they were moving out. Lar said he would move in himself instead of renting it again. We had taken a deposit when the tenants moved in three years previously, so it had to be returned. We went up to talk to them, but got a shock when we saw the state of the house. It was wrecked! We had furnished it with beautiful furniture, fittings, curtains and a beautiful kitchen with all appliances.

What we were now looking at was beyond words! I could not believe it. I whispered to Lar that we could not return their deposit for this mess. He roared at me saying that I was the most disagreeable person he ever met. I just said 'Okay do what you want'. I got into June's car and drove home.

He came to see me the next day saying that he didn't have the money to pay them back, I knew he had, but gave him money out of my savings.

Four weeks later, they moved out, and he moved in. He asked me to come up and look around which I did. The house was almost inhabitable and filthy. I took another 1,000 euro from my savings account and gave it to him. I asked him not to tell the children about it as I knew they would not approve.

In the weeks that followed, I helped get some decent furniture from a free website, while he tried to get the house back in some kind of order. He continued to visit me regularly, sometimes touching me as I stood at the cooker. As the weeks turned into months, I gave him a few hundred euro here and there to get things back on track. He began to tell me that he might come back, but he had to get the rented house right so we could rent it again. The counsellor talked about it with me, and it was her expertise to look at the situation from another angle. She kept asking me how far away from our family home was the rented house. It was only ten minutes away by car. Clearly I was fooling myself, after all, if he really wanted me, he could have been at home and went up every day to repair the house. I was confused to say the least, and yet I believed him every time he called.

Months went by and I met Connie and Brian in the local supermarket. We chatted about the situation, Connie said she hadn't seen him in months. 'But' I said 'Didn't he stay with you for a week when Pam wanted her house'? Connie looked at me blankly not saying a word. I looked at Brian for answers, and he told me that no, he didn't stay at their house. I was upset that he continued to tell me lies. I asked

them if they knew where he stayed but they didn't know. So I promised Connie and Brian that I would not tell him, and I didn't. But I told Valerie, and she was fuming. A few days later he was visiting Valerie, and she got angry with him for lying to me. He left Val's immediately and came down to me. 'Hi!' he said, 'I heard you met Connie, and she told you that I didn't stay in her house'. 'So', I said 'Where did you stay'? 'In a bed and breakfast in Gardiner street'. 'And where did you park the car?' I asked. I could see he was squirming, as he said 'Ah down a lane nearby'. I knew he was lying but I wouldn't even admit it to myself! Like a fool I let it go, probably because it was the easier option. I made him tea and he stayed for about an hour. He was all chat , telling me what he was doing next in the house, even asking my opinion on things. I had myself convinced that he was coming back, and that he didn't see Esther anymore.

Chapter Twenty Six

FACING REALITY

A couple of months later the central heating in the house was giving trouble. He told me that he needed 1,900 euro for a new boiler. He had used up his credit union money when he lived in Pam's house, so now he could not afford a new boiler.I had 1,000 euro left from my savings, but needed another 900 to make up the difference. It was coming up to mother's day, and the children were asking me what I would like for a present. I talked about it with June, and told her that if I got money instead from each of them, I could make up some of the 900 euro for dad.

She wasn't a bit impressed with my plan, and reminded me of all the money that I had already given him. But I argued that at least the house would be finished and he would come home. 'Mam', she said 'I will give you 900 euro if it makes you happy, but in my opinion, I'd rather you spend it on yourself'. She went on to advise me not to tell her sisters, as they would be very angry.

So I'm not proud to say that I took the money from June and hated myself for doing so, but I promised that when he came home that I would start back sewing again, and pay her back. Of course she didn't want it back, but I couldn't live with the fact that I owed money, especially to my beautiful generous daughter!

On St. Patrick's day I met him in Valerie's and gave him the money as we left the house. 'Ah you're very good, thanks' he said then we bid each other goodbye. He called on a regular basis over the next few months telling me how the house was coming on, but not mentioning much about coming home. So one night I asked him about his plans. He replied ' If I come home it will always be thrown in my face what I did, and anyway you keep writing everything down in your diary'. I reassured him that I would get rid of some of the diaries and never mention Esther again.

Now he had no excuse, so he agreed to come home, 'When the house was finished'We had a long chat, and I said that I didn't want to start again with any lies between us. So I asked him again, where did he stay for the week that he was supposed to be in Connie's. Again he insisted that he stayed in a bed and breakfast in Gardiner Street. I asked him the name of it and he said, 'There you go again, questioning me, not trusting me'. Again, like a fool, I decided to say no more, he was coming back, that was all that mattered.

Next day I told Valerie that he was coming home as soon as he finished the house. She looked at me and said, 'Mam, he is not coming home, if he wanted to come home he would have come before now', and anyway it's my opinion that he is still with Esther'. 'Well' I said, 'His guitar is still upstairs, and you know he wouldn't go anywhere without it, he even brought it on our honeymoon!' Val looked at me again, and said, 'Mam, the guitar is not upstairs, it's been gone for months, along with some of our family photographs'. It seems so silly now, but that shocked me, as I knew how much the guitar meant to him. Then I remembered him asking me for some family photographs to hang on the wall of the rented house, and I said that would be ridiculous if we were renting the house, to which he replied, 'Oh yeah'. Clearly, I had no 'Cop on' until it was spelled out to me. So, after that, anytime he called in to me I never mentioned a thing about him coming home.

He still collected June on Mondays and Wednesdays from work to bring her to dialysis. June continually told me that there was a strong smell of perfume in the car. I hadn't been in our car since he left, and it was irritating to me that 'She' was enjoying our family car, that we paid for! He had told me that she didn't drive, so now he was available to bring her anywhere she wanted, while I had to get a bus, if June was in work. Many times I had to go to my hospital appointments on the bus with great difficulty because of my bad knees. Thankfully, Valerie was able to bring me most of the time.

Meanwhile June was having serious problems with the pressure sore. I was getting worried about it but I would never let June know. Because she couldn't feel or see it, she had no clue of how bad it was. I tried to be as honest as I could when she asked me what it looked like. I knew if I didn't tell her, that the doctors would, after all she was an adult. The truth was, the cavity was so deep after surgery, that you could put your fist in it. I set about learning everything I could about high grade pressure sores. I had meetings with the tissue viability nurse in Tallaght hospital. She was a lovely lady, very kind to June, and reassured her that it would get better, but it was a long road.

They showed me how to put in a vacuum dressing. This was a dressing attached to a long tube and small motor. Needless to say, June wasn't happy about it at all, and told me she didn't want it, and was going back to work. I got around it by making a 'handbag' for the motor so that she could hang it on the back of her wheelchair, and I made a thing like a 'scrunchy' to put the tube in, then she went back to work. Her favourite doctor, Dr. Catherine Wall, told her that it was important to clear the pressure sore as quickly as possible as she could not have a kidney transplant while it was there. So bravely, June co-operated with the doctor, and endured six months on the vacuum dressing. Then Helen, the tissue viability nurse agreed to stop it after June got fed up with it. So I had to learn how to dress it with cavity fillers every day before she went to work. It took almost an hour at first, washing it out, filling the cavity with special dressings, and padding it all out so it didn't move when she moved. June had to 'bum' when transferring from bed to wheelchair, and in and out of the car, so it was important that she was padded securely, so that the dressing wouldn't move. My days were filled with concern over June, and she worried about me. We would talk endlessly about her dad, still trying to come to terms with the fact that when we needed him most, he was gone. She still saw him on dialysis days, but his visits to me were getting fewer.

I was now in a situation whereby I had no money coming in and my savings were gone. June was handing up money like she always did, but I felt that it was unfair on her, to depend on that every week, although she would have given me anything.I decided to go to our local welfare office to see if there was anything I was entitled to. There was about six in front of me when I arrived. Within a few minutes the place was packed to capacity with young couples with children, many of them non-nationals. I quickly became aware that I was the 'oldest' person there. I looked around me and thought 'O my God, is this what I'm reduced to?'. I reflected on my 'cushy' life, and how smug I was, because I was financially comfortable. I could hear people arguing with the welfare officer and indeed raising their voices, and I dreaded my turn. I was almost in tears when it came. I was expecting the welfare officer to be cross with me too, so I was shaking going in.

I sat down in front of a kind looking lady, I couldn't believe that she was the welfare officer. I went to open my mouth, but it all became too much for me and I just burst into tears. The lady handed me a tissue and said 'Take your time, I'm here to help you'. She was so nice to me when I told her the story, and even filled in the necessary forms with me. She immediately organised a payment of 160 euros weekly social welfare. I will never forget her kindness to me and I was to learn later that her name was June too. Because of my severe arthritis, she said I was entitled to a bus pass and fuel allowance. This was of great help to me, especially the bus pass, because I couldn't hold small change in my crooked hands.

I quickly learned to cook budget meals to stretch the money for the week. I used what June handed up for utilities, and mine for food. We managed quite well, even though June had to have a special renal diet. At first I ate the same as her, but I soon realised that I was running low on potassium, as she had to have a low potassium diet. With my heart problem, I needed to keep my potassium up. Also, I needed to have plenty of calcium for my weak bones, while June's had to be more balanced.

June kept insisting that she give me more money, but I refused. Besides, I was now enjoying budgeting, especially knowing that if I hit a brick wall, June would help me out. Our heating bill was the highest because June suffered greatly with the cold. I didn't like the cold myself but June's circulation was poor. I recall when her Dad lived with us there was many a row with him because he always accused her of hanging out of the radiator. 'You'll pull it out of the wall' he would yell at her. After he left, she hung out of the radiator in peace, and to this day it is still intact!.

I still lived in hope that Lar would come back to me. I still loved him and would have taken him back with open arms, but as usual, I was fooling myself. I was hearing rumours that he was staying in Esther's a few times a week. When June had the 'Vacuum' dressing, I had to drive her to and from work as she could not transfer from her wheelchair with the motor attached to her. So, as 'his' house was not far from June's work place, I would drive by early in the morning to see if his car was there. I soon saw a pattern of the days he was in Esther's. I began to realise that he truly no longer wanted me and it hurt. And yet I thought about him day and night. I could not walk around to his side of the bed, I just pulled up the duvet from my side. Valerie helped me change the bedclothes with me standing on my own side! There were still clothes in his wardrobe, and when no one was at home, I stood there smelling them. I was still in counselling because I knew I needed help.

Friends were telling me that they saw him with her in the same music session every week, where he had met Esther. I began to fear for the future, about our family home. I knew my health wasn't great and I feared if anything happened to me that he would move back home with 'HER'. So I tried another tactic. Visits from him were now few and far between, so when he rang me I asked if he would put our family home in my name. I had to hold the phone away from my ear, he yelled so loud. 'No way' was the bottom line. 'Why can't you leave things the way they are and you and June can stay until the end of your days?' he said.

This was totally unsatisfactory to me, as all I could see was HER in my house, and I couldn't stand it and neither could the children. Besides, I considered the will we had made many years previously to be null and void, now that he was with another woman.

I made up my mind to find out for sure what kind of relationship he had with Esther. He refused to tell me anything, even telling me at times that he didn't see her anymore, so I decided to do some searching my self. I hired a private detective, because Lar wasn't capable of telling me the truth. I needed to know the truth, and from someone who didn't know us. Less than twenty four hours later, the detective rang at midnight to say that Lar's car was outside a house in Leixlip, giving me Esther's exact address. He was able to tell me that the car was parked outside until midnight and then driven into the drive way. My first reaction was anger at his lies. I felt justified in hiring the detective, because this person didn't know him from Adam, he was just doing a job. If he had told me the truth, I never would have done it, knowing what a private person Lar is. But desperate times call for desperate measures. With the help of friends I continued to watch out for them.

One night we watched as he sat at the bus stop in Leixlip with her, waiting for the bus. When the bus arrived, they got on the bus together like an old married couple. No one looking at them would believe that this was an affair. With great difficulty we followed the bus, but we couldn't drive in the bus lane, even so, we kept the bus in view until they got off. Clearly they were heading for the music session, but they had a drink in another pub across the road from it first. I was very angry and wanted to confront him that night, but I had a better idea.

Chapter Twenty Seven

FACE TO FACE WITH THE TRUTH

Next morning I asked Valerie to drive me over to Esther's house in Leixlip. I had a chat to June about what I was going to do, and she gave me great encouragement to find out the truth, once and for all. She stayed in bed with the phone beside her as we set off at 7am. When we arrived at the house, his car was parked neatly in the driveway. I felt sick with the thoughts of her enjoying our new car. The house was in darkness, as was the whole road as it was very early, and in October. I thought to myself, that if he doesn't come out when I ring, I would either keep my hand on the horn of our car (I had a set of keys) or I would drive the car home! A security light came on as we walked up to the door. I rang his mobile from my own phone. It rang for a while before he answered it, in a sleepy voice.

'Hello' he said

ME: ' Hello, I'm outside the door and I need to talk to you urgently'

HIM: 'What? You're outside what door? (I think he thought that I was in Tallaght)

ME: 'Leixlip'

HIM (in a loud whisper) 'Jesus Esther, she's outside the door!'

HIM: 'Okay hang on'.

A good five minutes went by before he came down fully dressed. I could see him coming down the stairs through the glass porch. Then he cleverly went in to the sitting room to make it look like he had been there! Valerie and I could see it clearly through the glass. Anyway, he opened the door, and before he could say a word, we marched into the woman's house! This is so unlike me to go anywhere that I'm not invited, but the anger was overtaking me.

What struck me most about the house was, that it was everything he hated. There was clothes everywhere, clutter, and I almost fell over shoes in the middle of the floor. If I left shoes on my bedroom floor, they were put on my pillow, in other words I could not go to bed unless I put them up!

'So' I said, 'Talk your way out of this! He was gob smacked, to say the least, and I nearly got drunk with the smell of drink from him. 'What are you doing here'? he kept asking. 'I need to talk to that woman, call her down now'.

He replied ' I'll get her in a minute, what are you going to say to her?' 'You can listen, and if you don't go upstairs and get her now, I will go up myself!'.

He had never seen me so angry before, in fact I've never been so angry. I kept thinking of the money I gave him to do up the house so that he could come home, and all the time he was living a double life. I was now worse than angry! He took the stairs two at a time to get Esther. I've no doubt that she was probably listening from the top of the stairs, but at this moment I feared nothing.

Sheepishly she appeared in her dressing gown. I looked long and hard at this woman that wrecked my life. My first words to her were ;'Have you anything to say to me?.

'No Betty, except I'm very sorry', she said. I let a roar at her telling her that I was a good wife and mother. 'I know' she said, ' he told me'. I asked her how long the affair was going on, and she said two years. I thought to myself this woman has no morals, but unlike him, she tells the truth. I then asked if he stayed with her during the week that he was supposed to stay in Connie's, and she said yes. The guilty look on Lar's face said it all. If he had told me the truth about this affair, I wouldn't be here. I watched how they interacted with each other, and knew then that I didn't stand a chance. He had a whole different persona with her, speaking very gently.

Valerie too was angry and told him so. She went on to tell Esther what life was like for us. I don't know what she made of us, but right now I didn't care.

Any questions we asked her she answered truthfully. Then we asked her if she had ever been in our other house in Tallaght. She said yes, and I hit the roof.

'You bastard I screamed at him, how dare you have another woman in our house!'.

I could not believe I said that. I hated bad language of any description. In a gentle voice he said 'I didn't think you liked that house'. I could not believe what was coming out of his mouth, what a childish thing to say.

Esther got up and made tea. As she walked into the kitchen he said to me 'She's nice, isn't she?' almost like he was looking for my approval!

Then he began to show us photos of her family on the wall. Exasperated, Valerie said, 'Dad we didn't come here to look at photos!' Esther came back with the tea.She handed him his. For a minute I resented the fact that she knew exactly how he liked it. Clearly they were very cosy with one another, and I was getting uneasy, but Valerie wasn't finished what she needed to say. Here was a man, she loved all her life, her hero, living a different life with another woman.

I then asked him to sign over the family home to me, and to my disbelief he very gently said ' Oh yes, I was going to ring you about that'. (Little did I know that he only said that for Esther's benefit and twenty four hours later, he would yell on the phone 'I'm not giving up my home for anyone!.)

Now calmer, I told him how disappointed I was with him for taking my money on the pretence that he was coming home. In front of Esther, he replied 'I never said I was coming home'. I reminded him of his exact words on the night I destroyed the diaries, but by now it was a useless exercise, he had made his choice, and he chose her. Meanwhile June was getting worried because it was now over two hours since we left home. She rang Valerie's mobile phone. Val reassured her that we were fine and would be leaving for home shortly.

We stood up to go, I went over to Esther, said goodbye with a hug, and told her to look after herself. The reason I did this was I didn't want to leave her with the impression of a mad wife. I held my head up and walked out. His last words to me were, 'Does this mean I will never see you again? I said in reply, 'Maybe one more time in court'. With a heavy heart I walked to the car with Valerie. I looked at 'our' car parked so neatly in her driveway like it was meant to be there.

I knew now that it really was over. I had seen it with my own eyes. All the second hand information I got up to now, was true. As sure as night follows day, he had chosen another woman. I never thought that this man, for all his faults, would be unfaithful. I left that house feeling at rock bottom. My thoughts went back to another house where it started nearly forty two years earlier. The beginning of a love story, when there was ' a rainbow around the moon'.

I took off my wedding ring when I got to Val's car.

There is something about knowing the truth that makes you responsible for what to do next, and I knew what I had to do. So back to reality.

On the journey home, Valerie rang Pamela, who was sitting by her phone in the Isle of Man, waiting to hear how we got on. Valerie related how the visit went and that she was disgusted with her Dad. She had no plans to ever speak to him again since the big row, and she was still angry with him.

During our three way conversation in the car, the girls agreed that I would need to go to a solicitor about the house. There was no other way. Even though in front of Esther, he said he would sign it over, I knew now that he couldn't be trusted. June was waiting anxiously as Valerie dropped me home. I sat on the bed with her and told her the whole story. I had to describe in detail what Esther looked like as now June was the only one of us that hadn't seen her. She felt more sorry for me, than herself. We had our 'hug' as usual, before I did the dressings, and bed bath.

I was feeling both sad and angry. I came from a generation whereby we were virgins getting married. I could not imagine any man touching me other than my husband, now here he was sleeping with another woman. I felt a need to get in the bath immediately. The thoughts of him touching her after touching me, made me cringe. June loved reaching over from the wheelchair to wash my back. She loved getting her back scrubbed and wanted to share the experience with me. She was trying to make me laugh, and for a while she did. She was so good humoured that it was infectious. I looked at this remarkable girl who now needed me more than ever, with her failing health. I knew that I had to put aside my own feelings for the sake of the girls, especially June. It is a tragedy when a marriage breaks up, especially when the children are young, but it is my experience that it is no less painful when the children are adults. The three of them were very upset. Life as they knew it was gone. Daddy was their rock, always there to sort all there problems, fix there houses, bring them anywhere, but now he was caught up in his 'new' situation with Esther, and she came first. Before me, before them, before anyone.

We all had a wake up call. But you don't go through an experience like this without changing. I could feel myself getting stronger almost by the hour that day. I had seen them both with my own two eyes, and I needed that.

I had not told many people that Lar left me, except my four wonderful sisters who gave me great support. My lovely next door neighbour Tom (who was eighty something) had asked where Lar was in the beginning. I lied, telling him that he was doing work on Pam's house in Mullingar. Every time I was lifting the wheelchair in to the car, he would look over the wall and tell me I was a great woman. I used laugh and have a brief conversation with him before I headed off.

One morning as I lifted the chair as usual, he called me over. 'Betty', he said 'I don't care what Lar has to do in Pamela's house, he should be here helping you'.

I was in a hurry to bring June to work, so I said I would have a chat with him when I got back. 'How am I going to tell him?', I asked June on our journey. 'Well Mam' she said, 'We cannot hide it any longer, anyway, the neighbours must know something is happening when he hasn't been around for ages'. I knew she was right, so I decided to tell the truth if I was asked.

Tom was gone in when I got back, so I knocked at his door. He opened it and I told him the truth that Lar had left me for another woman. He was shocked. He reassured me that I was a great woman and that Lar was a fool not to see it.

I felt a sense of relief after telling him. He and his wife Mary were so kind and offered to help me in any way I needed it. Our other neighbours Sonny and Ida, were very kind too, and I felt that all the neighbours had great sympathy for us when word got out.

June rang me from work telling me that she had just sent dad a text telling him she no longer wanted him to bring her to dialysis any more. In fact she said that she didn't want to see him again. She was determent never to look at him again, and made me promise, if ever she was in hospital, he was not to be told. I wasn't sure if it was the right thing to do but I respected her wishes. Anyway, June seemed to be happier since he left. She certainly appeared more relaxed at home, doing what she wanted, when she wanted. She would be hours on the phone talking to her friends, without having to look over her shoulder, worrying if dad was there. It never bothered me at all how long she was on the phone, as a matter of fact I was delighted to hear her laughing and joking with her friends.

I chose to go to the solicitor that looked after our business affairs in Sally's Alley. I was familiar with him through the business and also when we bought our second house. I worried about the cost, but the children offered to pay between them. Even so, the twelve thousand quoted seemed a lot to expect them to pay.

However, it had to be done and the sooner the better. I refused to answer any phone calls from Lar, and I changed the locks on the door of our family home. I knew that doing so was against the law as technically it was still his home, but as it happens, he never came near me after that. He had his 'new' lady now. But he was getting irritated with me for not answering the phone to him, so he started to sending me text.

I never answered those either, because it was all about him losing the family home. He never asked how I was or how the girls were, it was all about himself. Then the text turned nasty, telling me I was 'vindictive' among other things. I tried to ignore them especially as my self esteem was still low, but I was getting stronger every day. Besides, I had no time to wallow in self pity as June needed me now.

Chapter Twenty Eight

OUR BEAUTIFUL BRAVE JUNE

June began having trouble with her fistula. A fistula is a procedure, whereby an artery is joined to a vein through which the patient gets dialysis. It is usually in the arm but occasionally in the leg. In June's case, the leg couldn't be used because of her lower limb paralysis. She was brought into hospital again to make a new one. They tried both arms without success. They even tried both wrists. She went through a lot of painful surgery, but she never complained. The only thing that upset her was getting her dressings changed on her pressure sores because of where they were. I made an agreement with Helen (the tissue viability nurse) that I would go up every morning and change the dressings myself, when she was in hospital. She now had three pressure sores, one on her thigh (arising from plaster of paris for a broken leg), one on the back of her knee, and the big one in the sacral area.

I loved going up early to the hospital, getting the dressings done, helping her wash and get dressed. She always refused to stay in bed all day, unless she was very sick. I got to know all the nurses, and they gave me everything I needed for June. When she was in hospital, I stayed there from seven in the morning until nine at night. I had no one to rush home to, so I was happier in June's company. She made me laugh every day, so I was able to put my broken marriage out of my mind unless I got correspondence from the solicitor. During her hospital stays, we made friends with everyone. All the medical staff, catering ladies, porters, security, and cleaning staff. We had a laugh and a joke with them every day.

Meanwhile a new star lit up our lives in the shape of Niamh, my newest grandchild. Oh what joy she brought to us when she arrived into this world, so beautiful and cuddly. June and I lavished attention on her, and indeed argued about who held her the longest! We loved fussing over the grandchildren, but it's fair to say that June spoiled them the most. June told me once that she would love to have a baby. In fact she asked me if I thought it was medically posible, and I told her it might. I hated the fact that she was missing out on something else in life, after all I knew the feeling of longing for a baby.

The fistula situation wasn't looking good, so they had to go directly into her heart for dialysis. She had a tube permanently left in her chest for access. She hated the fact that she could no longer wear certain tops anymore because the tube could be seen. But it was no problem to me to re-shape them to look better.

So now she was back in work with the dialysis working fine for now. Meanwhile I continued to get letters from my solicitor regarding the case. He sent me a copy of an affidavit that Lar swore to. Lar claimed that the last five years of our marriage was very stressful, so much so, that he was prescribed anti-depressants by his doctor. I couldn't believe what I was reading. First of all I felt that the last five years before the affair, was somewhat calmer than the previous thirty five. But what really upset me was the fact that he was saying the depression only started during the last five years of our marriage.

I could go back almost to the day that I realised he suffered from depression, because of my diaries. I wondered why he would say that. Is this what he told Esther? What other lies did he tell her? The thoughts were going round and round in my head. I was embarrassed talking to the solicitor, in case he thought I wasn't a nice person. He reassured me that this was 'par for the course' in trying to justify his actions. I made up my mind to let the solicitor get on with it and put it out of my mind. I was desperately trying to come to terms with the rejection. But I had to face it. He didn't want me anymore, he had chosen Esther.

June told me that she felt more comfortable with Lar out of the house. It is true to say that he was always annoying her in one way or the other. She suffered terribly from the cold, sometimes even in the summer. She got the 'rigors' regularly, (that is a sudden feeling of cold followed by a temperature). She would hold on to the radiator for heat, but he would get angry with her, telling her that she would pull it off the wall. Many times he came home complaining that he was too warm, and turn off the heat. In fairness, I don't think he realised the seriousness of 'the rigors' at that time. I probably didn't either but I would let June have the heat on all day every day if she wanted it. Now it was different. She turned on the heat at will without having to ask. She was a very tidy girl, and kept her own room spotless and indeed helped me clean the house. The year before Lar left, we got huge work done in our kitchen. We got a disabled person's grant for half, and June paid the other half. We had the sink and cooker hob on a 'motorised' counter top, whereby she could lower it right down to her level, and cook for herself. There were no presses underneath so she could wheel right under. Oh! the fun we had when she could see into the pan!

I had forgotten that June had never seen an egg frying in a pan, even though she was now almost thirty years old! Her face was priceless as she watched it sizzling. She insisted on trying another one, then another, until we were floating out with fried eggs! I wouldn't mind but June hates eggs, so Lar and I had to eat too many eggs that day. She then went to cookery classes with Valerie every Monday night and learned to make a variety of things. Alas, many of them she could not eat herself, as she was on a renal diet for her dialysis. So I am the one that put on the weight!

I was starting to accept that we were permanently on our own now, and although I felt sad at times, I was for the most part, contented. I realised that for the first time in years I could be ME, without criticism. I liked being ME, but it took longer to feel like a worthwhile person again. I could not have done it without the love of my children, and my sisters. Living with June was great fun, except for the worry of her pressure sores and failing health. She bravely went to work every day, many times in severe pain. She loved working in South Dublin County Council, and the only time she stayed out, was when she was in hospital.

My son-in-law Wayne helped us with the maintenance of our house. He had so much to do in his own house, but he would help me out no matter what time of the day or night. One day

June said 'Ma, the hall paints are gone shabby, they need to be re-done'. I stood in the hall agreeing with her and wondering what I could do. Then she said quite seriously ' How about you paint the top part and I will paint the lower part?'. I had a good laugh, and for a brief moment I considered it, but much to her disappointment decided against it, mostly because I'm afraid of ladders, I knew she would be quite capable of painting. She had a strong upper body and strong hands. Indeed we were right when we said that between the two of us, we made one good body! There were many things that I couldn't manage with my crooked hands, like opening bottles, jars, and tightly wrapped packages. But it was no problem to June, and at times I would sit on a low stool and she would dry my hair for me.

She had such a wicked sense of humour. She was always following me around the house turning off lights whenever I forgot. She would laugh and say 'No wonder he left you!' She made me laugh every day so much so that I missed her when she was at work. Often she would send me funny e-mails from work She loved to send age related ones on the joys of growing old. They always brought a smile to my face, although in my mind I still felt twenty one!

One day she sent me one that said (among other things) " Laughing is like a massage to the inside of your belly". So ever after that, we decided to laugh every day, and we did. One evening after dialysis she was concerned about her vision in one eye. She said that there was a 'blackness' covering the front part of her right eye, but she could see around the edge. Next day she took time off work to see Dr. Wall, her consultant. Immediately she arranged to see a specialist. After numerous tests, she gave us bad news. Because of June's general health and continuous low blood pressure, the blood wasn't pumping to the back of the eye. There wasn't anything they could do about it. I asked her if the blood pressure improved, would it come back. She did not sound too hopeful, but said it might . June was so disappointed, and my heart broke for her, because now there was a question mark over driving. She loved the independence that driving gave her, and she was an excellent driver.

She had to do a 'field test' to see if her vision was good enough to drive. This is a test whereby you look straight ahead into a machine and identify objects in your peripheral vision. Amazingly she passed it and was allowed to continue driving. Apparently, we were told, that there are many people who are driving with only one eye. We comforted ourselves in the fact that June had one and a half eyes! I was hearing rumours regularly, about Lar and his new lady. He was no longer 'hiding her away' as everyone now knew that he had left me.

Sometimes I would get angry when I'd hear of him at parties and pubs with her and them both full of 'jollifications'. He had no idea of June's failing health, and anyway she didn't want him to know. But I could not shake off the feeling of rejection. The emotional pain of not being wanted was, at times unbearable.

Living with June helped me put my own sadness to the back of my mind. She truly was an amazing young lady, with a wisdom beyond her years. Regularly, she would tell me that everything happens for a reason, and that we were happier now on our own. In some ways she was right because I was starting to laugh again. I was so caught up in caring for June that the only time I thought of Lar was when a letter came from the solicitor. I was starting to live again in spite of myself.

One Sunday afternoon June asked me to go to the cinema with her. It had been many years since I had been to the cinema, in fact, for the forty years that I was married, Lar and I went no more than five or six times, and that would have been in the early years. On occasions, I asked him to bring me to a theatre for a change, he would always say no, telling me instead to go with one of my sisters. So I gave up asking him, and went with him to the pub, even though I didn't drink.

June laughed at my reaction in the cinema. I was like a child, looking around me in amazement, at the 'modern cinema' compared to when I was last there. There was a special place for a wheelchair person at the back row where a seat had been removed, and their companion could sit comfortably beside them. We got our tubs of popcorn, and I sat wide eyed in anticipation. I was so excited that my popcorn was almost gone before the film started! We had the most enjoyable afternoon, and laughed all the way home, at the way I took the whole experience, at sixty three years old!

That was the first of our regular trips to the cinema, and in no time at all, we were up to date on the latest films. We then started to go to the theatre from time to time, watching out for anything new. June still went out with her own friends, sometimes driving, more times driven and collected by Wayne. I loved to see her enjoying herself, even though I worried about her health.

She looked younger than her years. Although she was in a wheelchair, her body was in proportion, like an able bodied person, she had a good shape, and was not over weight. Many times when people thought she was a lot younger, she would get annoyed. I recall one such time when she was twenty six, we were coming out of Tallaght hospital, heading for her car. There was a lady sitting on a seat near the car looking at us. She looked at June, then at me and said 'Ah she's lovely, how old is she?' Before I could say a word, June said 'I'm twenty six, how old are you?'

The lady didn't know what to say, and I felt a bit sorry for her as I am sure she was trying to be kind. Then June whispered to me, 'Don't help me into the car in front of this woman'. So I stood there as she transferred in, then I put the wheelchair in the boot, and jumped in the passenger seat. The poor lady's face was priceless as June drove away waving to her in the process!

Another time we were out with the family having a meal in a hotel. The waitress came along to take our order. We each gave our order one by one including June. Then the waitress looked at me and said, 'Would she like chips with that?' June replied, 'I can speak! Just because my legs don't work, doesn't mean I cannot talk!'. There was silence for a minute, but everyone burst into laughter, including the bewildered waitress. Unfortunately, there are still many who speak over the heads of disabled people, not realising that a wheelchair, does not affect your brain!

As time went on, June spent many hours talking me through my 'down' days. She would point out the positives, and there were lots, like not having to worry if I didn't get as far as cleaning every room, every day. And the best part was I didn't have to listen to criticism day after day either. Also my three children showered me with affection, telling me what a wonderful mammy I was. I could now watch day time television if I felt like it without him telling me that I was wasting my life, and should be doing housework. The negatives were of a practical nature, as I'm not very strong. I now had to pay to get my windows cleaned, and the gardens, front and back, were beyond what I could manage. But Wayne kept them tidy for me, and my lovely neighbour Mr. Moylan, (a man in his eighties), looked after my bins.

When Pam and Robert came home, they too helped out. I was desperately clinging to my children even though they were hurting too. I suppose we were all in a state of shock for a long time, as it was the last thing we expected to happen. I continued with counselling for 14 months, and the counsellor was right, I did smile again!

Although I worried constantly about June's failing health, I marvelled at her humour and sense of fun. She saw the funny side of everything. I frequently stayed for the three hours of dialyses, where she even had the nurses laughing. Many of them had unusual names, like Fessy, Blessy. Gi-Joe, and Jibby. Of course June made up her own names. She called Gi-Joe; Ginnyjoe. Oddly enough there were three Marys. Then there was the nurse that never took off her surgical mask, so June called her 'halloween'. The whole dialysis unit, both patients and staff were like one big happy family. When anyone was called for a transplant, everyone rejoiced. I soon realised that my marriage problem was trivial compared to what many of these patients had to endure on a daily basis. There are no words to describe the dedication of the staff, who were on there feet from 7.30am until 8.30pm. Also the drivers (Ronnie, Paul, and Gerry) were wonderful with the patients, and always had a laugh and a joke. They were so kind and reassuring, when the patients were at their weakest on the way home. June loved them all, and I know they were very fond of her.

June and I soon settled in to a routine. Much to her disappointment her sight got a bit worse, so I drove her to and from work every day. She wasn't happy about not driving, but she loved my company on the journey. She made me laugh every morning as we drove along. When we were stopped in traffic she would look at the faces of the on coming drivers. She would remark 'Look at him Mam, he's had a hectic time last night and should be still in bed!' Then she would count the amount of gloomy faces on a Monday morning, and the smiles on Fridays.

I remember one morning a 'boy racer' overtook us at speed going to the wrong side of the road in the process. 'Ma', she said, 'I hope that idiot carries a donor card, because if he doesn't want his kidneys, I know plenty who do!' I laughed at her humour in the danger.

The first year after Lar left, June's beautiful natural blonde hair began to fall out. She was very upset as even hairdressers admired it. We asked her consultant about it, so she changed her medication to see if it made a difference. Alas it didn't, and the doc thought it might be stress from her dad leaving. I was saddened as I thought June was the least affected by his leaving. Now I began to blame myself for not being aware of it. But she kept telling me that she wasn't stressed, and that she was glad he was gone. She was always at loggerheads with him, and she got upset when he yelled at me. If I didn't bother yelling back she would do it, so that he wouldn't get away with it! Anyway, I was never going to let her get stressed again, but she was a worrier, especially about me. I made sure she knew that I was fine and happy again, and I was. After wearing wide hair bands for a few weeks, her sisters and I researched hair pieces and were lucky to get one near enough to her real colour. It was held on with clips to the top of her head as it blended with what was left of her real hair.

She felt confident again. No matter what happened, she dusted herself down and started all over again. She still went with her friends to lots of concerts, and Wayne brought her to and fro'. She loved Wayne lifting her, he had a knack of lifting her in a sitting position, so she could keep her dignity and be comfortable.

One morning when I was dressing her pressure sores, I noticed the start of another one right on her bottom. I was so disappointed, as I thought that I was doing well with the other ones. I did not tell June at first because I was confident that I could clear it up, without her knowing. But I was forgetting that June was a clever girl, and even though she could not feel it, she asked me why I was dressing 'somewhere different'. So I lied and said that it was just a tiny sore and I was clearing it up before it got any bigger. But the truth was, that it was heading down the same road as the big one in the 'sacral' area. I discreetly rang the tissue viability nurse and told her about it. Of course I knew what she would say, 'Bring her in tomorrow and I will have a look at it'. Now I had to admit to June that I was concerned about it, but she took it better than I thought. She was so brave, because it had to be 'debrided' in her senses as because of her low blood pressure, she couldn't have an anaesthetic, but thankfully she couldn't feel it.

Like before, after surgery, you could almost put your fist in it, and again it was back to the vacuum dressing again. But nothing would faze June, she was back in work as soon as she came out of hospital. So each morning it took longer now to do all the dressings and bed bath. I tried my very best to keep chatting as I did them so that she wouldn't feel embarrassed. Many mornings we would laugh the whole way through, talking about anything and everything. She loved when I told her what life was like when I was growing up in the nineteen fifties. One morning she said 'Ma, why don't you write your life story?'. I replied, 'Yes, maybe I will, do you think it sounds interesting?' She thought that everyone would love it, but then she would wouldn't she?. We laughed, but she was serious, and insisted that she teach me how to use the computer. Alas, I had only one 'straight finger' for typing, but it was just another funny aspect to my life. Anytime I would try to do something, she would say 'Ma, use your favourite finger!'. And so, this story began...............

June became my editor-in-chief! She read it as time went on, and told me if I said something that she didn't like, so I removed it. I laughed at her reaction to the part where I came back from my honeymoon, still a virgin. 'Ma,' she yelled 'Too much information!' We giggled, but agreed it had to stay in, to show how different life was then. Writing gave me long hours of enjoyment, and June made sure I kept at it. Even when she was in hospital I brought her laptop with me, and if she wasn't too sick, I worked on it.

Meanwhile, the date for the court case was getting near. Occasionally, I got a text from Lar telling me that we may have to sell the two houses and divide the proceeds.I began to have sleepless nights again as I couldn't bear to be out of our family home. June too kept asking me could it happen, but I kept reassuring her that no judge would put us out. I worried night and day and wished it was over. The solicitor assured me that because we had two houses, and in view of June's needs, that we would get the family home as it's a bungalow, and Lar would get the other one. I hoped and prayed he was right. With my health and at my age, I didn't want to be uprooted.

On the day of the court case, I arrived with Valerie, feeling very nervous. I was worried too about facing Lar, as it was now nearly two years since I had seen him. I looked around me at the family court that was packed to capacity with couples breaking up. It seemed like we were the oldest couple there!. I searched the faces looking for Lar's, but couldn't see him anywhere. We went into a small room with the solicitor and a lady barrister. We discussed the case again and I listened carefully as the barrister explained what would happen. They were so confident that I would get the family home, and I hoped they were right.

It seemed like ages before we were called, and I shook with the thoughts of seeing Lar again. I wondered what emotions would surface, after not seeing him for so long. Finally the time had come. We were led into the court and told where to sit. Next thing Lar walked in with his solicitor. I did my best not to make eye contact for fear I would go to pieces. But I briefly looked at him. The only thing I felt was fear when I saw his angry face. A few times he whispered my name but I pretended not to hear. The judge considered the case, after asking me details of living with June. He then asked me if there was any chance of reconciliation. I only had to remember that day in Leixlip, and how cosy he was with Esther, so there was only one answer. 'No'. The judge then made a decision, and I got the family home. I was relieved but in truth there were no winners. I was somewhere that I didn't want to be. I truly believed in my marriage vows, and if it weren't for the house I would never have agreed to a separation even though he didn't want me. I was glad that I didn't have to worry about the house anymore, but I still left the courtroom with a heavy heart. I thought of all those young people in there whose marriages were breaking up at such a young age. Many times in the past long before mine broke up, I often thought that young people did not give their marriages a fair chance.

It seemed to me that after the first hurdle, they got out. Now I know not to judge anyone, because their struggle is as real as mine. Even so, I cannot live with the word 'separated'. It was never part of my plan. When I have to fill in forms now I hate having to 'tic' separated, I would much prefer if they had 'deserted wife' written on the form, as that's what I am.

I wrote to Lar after the court case as I couldn't have any contact with him while it was going on. I needed to tell him how I felt now that every thing was final, and wished him well. Also I was instructed by the court to return the remainder of his belongings, so I rang an advert from the paper for a van driver to deliver them. It was better that he received them from a stranger, rather than a relative or mutual friend. In quiet moments at home for a weeks after, I shed a few tears whenever I reflected on our marriage. I was so sure of myself in thinking he would never leave me. Now it was well and truly over. Forty years meant nothing, but I had my children and grandchildren. It was time to try to look forward, not back.

When I finished the counselling, Myra (the counsellor) suggested that I join a group for people like myself, from broken marriages. She told me about one in the city centre, so Wayne drove me there as the parking was bad. It was a big hall filled with men and women, although probably more women than men.

It struck me straight away that I was one of the few 'older women', however I sat around chatting with those near me who all had a story to tell.

Then the facilitator told us to sit in groups of ten, and one by one tell our story. There were all women in my group. I would have been number nine, so I listened to a lot of stories. All of them caught their husbands cheating, and although one woman's husband was now deceased, she never got over the rejection.

Each and every one of them said that their husbands excuse was 'I was depressed'. I couldn't listen anymore, and mumbled an apology then walked out.

It was the depression that floored me, the same old excuse, from all of the men. I thought back to the years I tried to help Lar through his, now he was with another woman, and no more talk of depression. I knew then that I could never trust another man, after all I was married to the most loyal man on earth for forty years! (Or so I thought.) I never went to anymore group therapy sessions after that.

June frequently told me to go out and socialise and get a new man in my life, but I just laughed. Besides, my life was full, looking after her and enjoying Val, Pam, and my grandchildren.

June's sight was getting worse and she was frightened. She was a wizard on the computer, typing very fast without looking. I bought her a collection of magnifying glasses so that she could check what she had written, but her workmates were super, and kept an eye if she needed help. The connection to her heart for dialysis blocked four times in as many weeks and it had to be re-set in her senses. She told me that it was an awful sensation, like someone pulling at 'strings' in her chest. Each time she went to theatre, I sat in the ward praying. She always gave me a big smile when they wheeled her back. She was now having a lot more hospital stays than she liked, with one infection after another. The choice of antibiotics became limited as she developed an allergy to two of them. It was a worrying time for all of us but I kept reminding her that she was in safe hands, with Dr. Wall, her favourite doctor in all the world. They often had long conversations about life in general, in fact June looked on her as more of a pal. She was young for a consultant, in fact younger than my daughter Valerie, but she had a way with her patients, like nothing I have ever seen.

Chapter Twenty Nine

Devestating News

O ne day during the morning visit, Dr. Wall, took me aside and discreetly asked me to come to her office in the afternoon. I told June that I was going home for an hour to feed her dog, and she believed me. I had an uneasy feeling about this, so I rang Val and asked her to come with me. A nurse from dialysis accompanied Dr. Wall. When we sat down she got straight to the point. She said; 'June's heart is badly scarred from trying to get access for dialysis, and when this connection goes, that's it'. She said June had a lot of medical problems, so the prognosis wasn't very good. With a dry mouth I mumbled 'How long?'. She replied 'Months'. Val and I had to support each other in shock. 'Please don't tell her' I heard myself saying 'I know there are ethics, but I will take full responsibility. Dr. Wall replied 'June is an adult, she has a right to know, besides she will notice herself that she is not getting better, she is an intelligent girl. My argument was that no one knew June like I did and she wouldn't want to know. So Dr. Wall agreed to say nothing for now, assuring me also that she would do everything in her power to make her as well as possible, and she did. This news was the worse thing ever. I thought the bottom fell out of my world when Lar left me, but I now realised that it didn't even compare to this.

Val didn't want me to drive home, she wanted me to leave June's car in the car park and go home with her. But I needed to go home and compose myself, before going back to June. I fed Charlie, but couldn't eat myself. I now had to ring Pam to tell her the awful news, but Val had already rang her and she was in the process of booking a flight. I allowed myself a few tears, but quickly 'got my act together'.

After all I had to go back to the hospital with my usual smile on my face. Even though June and I were having great fun together, I vowed, if God spared me that the rest of her life would be the best yet. Her sisters already spoiled her but they said the same.

Valerie was always like a second mother to June and they were very close. Pam was only a year older than her so they were like pals. They emailed each other every day, catching up on the gossip. June loved Pam's outgoing personality and sense of mischief, forever making her laugh.

I went back up to her at 5pm and stopped at McDonald's on the way, buying her favourite snack. She was allowed 'cheat' on her diet every Saturday, three hours before dialysis. This was Thursday, but what the heck!. 'Ma' she said, 'I'd better hide this'. 'Ah no, I said, 'Dr. Wall said a few treats now and again is okay'.

June came home from hospital the next day in great form. She was not a bit suspicious of Pamela arriving home as she often had to meet clients in the course of her work, both in Belfast and in Dublin, so it wouldn't be unusual for her to make a surprise visit. We had a fun filled weekend, so much so, that even I could put Dr. Wall's words to the back of my mind. When Monday came June went back to work and was delighted to do so. We all continued on as if nothing had happened, because June was in great form apart from her low vision which upset her deeply.

As the weeks turned into months, and the connection to her heart was working well, I kept telling myself, that maybe the doctor was painting the worse case scenario, and besides, June was a fighter. At that time it never even occurred to me to tell Lar, as he never contacted us and he seemed to be happy without us. Anyway June always made me promise that I wouldn't tell him when she was sick.

We seemed to get back to normal in no time, with June working away, keeping well at least for now. Every day we found something to laugh at, seeking out funny television programmes, joke books, and funny emails. But it was June herself who made me laugh the most with that wicked sense of humour.

From regularly lifting her , I had developed a muscle on my right arm, while my left arm was as flat as a pancake. June thought it was hilarious looking, and kept encouraging me to try and develop the other arm to match! But no amount of exercise made a difference. No one else noticed, as I covered it up most of the time, but in the summer June would say 'Ah go on Ma, put on a tee shirt and show off your muscle!' It was great the way we could laugh at ourselves and our limitations.

We could never visit Pamela in the Isle of Man because of June's dialysis. The hospital over there had dialysis machines but June had complications because of her low blood pressure. Also, she was now getting blood transfusions on a regular basis, while she was on dialysis, because her blood count kept dropping.

So, we made arrangements whereby she got her dialysis, early on Thursday morning, we got the ferry to the Isle of Man at 2pm, spent the weekend there, and arrived home at 2pm on Sunday, then drove straight to Tallaght hospital for more dialysis. Just to see the delight on her face when we got to Pam's house, made all the rushing around worthwhile. The weather was great and we had a ball.

We were all together, Val, Wayne, Ciara, Emma, Niamh, Pam, Robert, Aaron, me and June. It was great to have all the family together, even if it was only for the weekend. The following months were up and down, the down days were when June had to go into hospital, but we made the most of the up days when she had a good spell. Sometimes when she had a good spell for a couple of months, I would forget what Dr. Wall told me. Then when it came into my head, I would acknowledge that she was a brilliant consultant, but she wasn't God.

In 2009, June was in hospital very unwell for a few weeks and her best friend Nicola was in the next ward. When June began to recover she went into Nicola everyday. It was clear that she was sicker than June, but she had always been stronger, so I thought in time she would bounce back like June. Usually, it was Nicola doing the visiting as June was more often in hospital. Sadly June came home, Nicola didn't. She passed away after a painful illness and we were all devastated.

It was in the month of May, when June and I were in the car heading up to her work in the morning. My phone was connected to the 'hands free' loudspeaker. When Nicola's Mam Helen rang me very upset, and wondering how I could break the news to June. 'Helen', I said, 'She is sitting beside me and heard you'.

When Helen hung up I pulled in at the next available opportunity. We had a clumsy hug and a few tears. We sat there for a while, then I asked her would I turn around and go home. She thought about it for a while, but said 'Mam, I'd rather go to work and be with my friends right now' so we continued on our way. Again as I lifted the wheelchair out of the car, I asked was she sure that she wanted to go to work, but she was adamant. I rang regularly during the day to see if she was okay and she assured me she was. But when she came home she was still upset. Herself and Nicola were friends since they were four years old. They spent hours on the phone if they hadn't seen each other for a while. June hadn't spoken to her Dad since he left so I was surprised when she text to tell him about Nicola. I thought to myself, here is a golden opportunity for him to lift up the phone and ring her as he knew how close she was to Nicola. But no, he sent a text back asking what happened, and said he was sorry to hear that. I really thought he would ring, even briefly to console her.

The funeral was sad, the church was packed, the service very moving. Many of their disabled friends attended so there were quite a few wheelchairs. Another close friend was there, Donal Allis. Everyone loved Donal, he was the joker in the pack!

He had an amazing 'telephone' voice, always sounding like someone important. One day he rang June in work, but June was gone to her break. Another girl took the call and asked if she could take a message. Donal replied, 'This is Michael Flately, if you could get her to call me when she gets back, I would appreciate it'.

You can imagine June's workmates, they fell for it hook, line and sinker! As she wheeled back to her desk, she was told that Michael Flately called and asked for her. Without blinking an eyelid she said 'Sorry girls, it's only Donal again putting on one of his voices'. Alas eight weeks after Nicola's funeral, Donal also passed away. June was devastated, losing two friends in eight weeks. Where once there were four pals, now there were only two, Declan and June. Herself and Declan were always real close, but not boyfriend/girlfriend, at least I don't think so! They went everywhere together, concerts, snooker exhibitions,(which they both loved). June often got annoyed with him for paying for everything. He was very generous, and bought her beautiful presents. Many times I asked if they were 'an item' June said no, Declan said yes. But I know he was her very best friend, and she cared deeply for him. She was in a relationship with an able bodied guy for eight months. She really liked him and they went everywhere in her car. He had a motor bike, and used to park it in our garden, while she did the driving. Then he won a large amount of money on the lotto T.V. show, and a week later he was gone. He needed a break he said.

Six months later, he got in touch again but I was delighted when June refused to have anything to do with him. 'Mam, he showed his true colours when he won that money', she said. I kept my feelings to myself but deep down I felt that she was well rid of him.

Once again June text her dad when Donal passed, but it was the same as before, a text back sympathising. I couldn't understand why he never picked up the phone. All I could think of was that he was involved in his 'new' family, and no time for anyone else. If June was hurt by it, she never said, and I didn't dwell on it, keeping my feelings to myself. I was so absorbed in getting through every day one at a time, that I never thought much about Lar or his new lady.

Occasionally I would hear stories of him seen out with her, and my heart would skip a beat. Especially when one of our mutual friends met him and her at the airport, as they were heading off for a holiday. It was at times like that, I would feel anger. Him going off on holiday, and he couldn't lift up the phone to June. In fairness, he didn't know what I knew about June's prognosis, but he did know that her health wasn't great. Sometimes I wondered what was going on inside of his head.

June's hospital stays were getting more frequent, now every couple of months. But in between times, she was back at work, even though her sight was still deteriorating. We got around it in many ways, like putting large letters on her computer, buying a bigger television, and new curtains with a remote control.

It was sad for her that she was now in her thirties, and I had to do so many personal things for her. From my point of view, it was a pleasure, but I understood how she felt. She said it to me many times, but I told her over and over again how much I loved helping her, and I did. She brought so much joy into my life that it well outweighed the hard work.

She developed two leg ulcers, one on each leg, that had to be dressed every morning along with all her pressure sores. The tissue viability nurse in the hospital gave me instructions on how to treat them and the local community nurse gave me the extra dressings. June and I would have a good laugh as I was dressing them. 'What am I like' she would say, 'I'm like a wounded soldier!'.

Thanks to the nurses I was becoming an expert on dressings, from the smallest wound to the biggest pressure sore!. The hospital praised me constantly for my efforts, and June was happy that I did them all.

One morning, I was doing all the dressings as usual, when I came to the last one on her leg. She couldn't see it from the way she was lying, so I was giving her a running commentary on each sore, always telling her the truth. 'I'm delighted with this last one June, It's almost cleared except for a tiny black dot in the middle' I said. 'Great ma, at least it will be one less to do', she replied. Next I gently washed it with a saline soaked swab, and as I dabbed it dry, blood shot up in to the air like a fountain! I grabbed a bunch of swabs and pressed with all my strength for ten minutes. There was blood everywhere, but as I was pressing it seemed to stop. June was asking me what was going on as she couldn't feel a thing, but she could see the blood. I told her what happened but that I think it's okay now.

I carefully lifted the swabs, but the minute I took the pressure off, it shot up into the air again. This time June could see it and got frightened. I grabbed her mobile phone off her locker and handed it to her so she could ring Valerie. I figured that she would be stronger than me and could maybe stem the flow. In five minutes Valerie arrived and again I slowly lifted up the swabs, and again the blood shot up into the air. I was now covered in blood, as was June, the bed, and bedding.

No amount of pressing could stop the flow, so we decided that we would have to go to the hospital. But we had a problem. We couldn't stop putting pressure on it to get herinto her wheelchair and then the car.

So Valerie rang Wayne. June yelled! ' No I'm not letting Wayne in here without my trousers on! In the panic I had forgotten that she wasn't dressed as I always do the dressings first before helping her into her clothes. 'How are we going to get trousers on while keeping the pressure on the leg' Val asked. (June only wore trousers) 'I don't care' said June 'But he's not coming in here until I'm dressed!

Well what happened next was hilarious, as well as worrying. We took turns pressing on the leg while trying to get the trousers on. Remember June's legs were totally limp with no feeling in them so 'fishing' the legs through, was like trying to put tight jeans on a rag doll! In the middle of it all, June roared laughing! 'Ma this is like Mr. Bean squeezing into his trousers on the beach!'. Somehow we got them on without releasing the pressure before Wayne arrived.

We tried again with Wayne's strength to press on it for another ten minutes, but when we looked at it again it was still shooting out. I was now starting to get worried as I could see that she was losing a lot of blood.

Anyway Valerie kept up the pressure as Wayne carried her in his arms to the car. Wayne then sat in the back continuing with the pressure while Valerie drove to the hospital. I sat in the passenger seat reassuring June that the doctor would sort it out. When we got to A and E, with great difficulty we got June into her wheelchair. I wheeled her, while all six foot of Wayne was bent in two trying to keep pressure on the leg. The receptionist could see that we were in big trouble and had us seen to straight away.

The diagnosis was a burst artery so she had to have it stitched. There was another pool of blood on the floor as two doctors worked on her. Of course June felt nothing only annoyance that she would be late for work! But the doctor told her that she would have to have a blood test and wait, because chances are that she needed a blood transfusion. The doctor was right, she had two units of blood. But as usual, next day she was back in work relating her ordeal to her work colleagues.

After that I used a syringe to flush saline on her legs while washing the sores, blaming myself for what happened, even though the doctor assured me that it was nothing to do with the dressing, and more to do with her general health.

Over the next few months it happened twice more. One of the times, we were sitting watching television, when I stood up to go into the kitchen, I stood in a pool of blood, and looked at June. One of her beige boots was red so I pulled it off. The boot was half full with blood and as usual June felt nothing. I got a bunch of swabs, rolled them in a tight ball, placed it on the wound and wrapped a tight elastic bandage on it. I got her into the car and went straight to the hospital and rang Val from the car. At the hospital, the staff knew us, and knew June wouldn't be there unless she had to. Immediately we were seen to, and it was the same as before, including another transfusion. Of course June's biggest worry was that her favourite beige boots were ruined! But she was back at work two days later in her black boots!

In between bad times, life with June was uplifting to say the least. She saw the funny side of everything, often laughing at herself in the process. We were regular visitors to the opticians, trying to improve what sight she had, and even then she would have a laugh with the assistants. Much to the amusement of the optician, when she tried on a new pair of glasses I would say to her 'Well am I looking any better?' and she would reply 'Ma you look gorgeous!'.

Even in the hospital we were always joking around, seeking out fun wherever we could. The staff called us a 'double act!' as we got them laughing as well. We continued our sing-songs in the car going to and from work. June taught me the words of 'I will survive' and we sang it at the top of our voices. When we came to the part 'Now go, walk out the door, don't turn around now, 'cos you're not welcome anymore,' we sang louder then burst into laughter. Sometimes she liked to sing 'The Rose' and I would join in, but she kept telling me that I sang it too quick, while I insisted that she sang it too slow. We would start off together singing in harmony, but by the end of the first verse, I was already on the second verse. She never gave in and neither did I. Perhaps I was singing Bette Midler's version, and she only knew Westlife's. Whatever it was we never agreed, but we enjoyed arguing about it and blaming each other. I was now laughing more than crying these days. Only occasionally would I think of Lar, if I came across something that reminded me of him. I no longer grieved for him because I realised that he clearly didn't care about me. If he did, he would have chosen me instead of Esther. Besides, from what I heard, he was happy in his new relationship.

Sadly, June's sight got so bad that she could not look after her colostomy bag anymore. She had been looking after it herself since she had it done at age thirty. I remember the excitement after the operation when she realised that she would no longer have to wear pads for her incontinence, as she already had a bag for the waterworks. So for the first time in her life she was free from pads, totally independent, and loved wearing fancy pants! But now, she couldn't see properly to empty the colostomy bag. The waterworks had stopped altogether since she started on dialysis

We developed a new routine whereby I would empty it completely before she left for work, in the hope that it would last the day. For the most part it did, but occasionally she had to ring me during the day if it got too full. It was less than a ten minute drive from our house, so it was no problem to go up. Also, Valerie was familiar with everything if I was at the hospital. So, while she was disappointed, she never had to worry. I also noticed around this time that she was putting on her make up 'skew' ways because she was having difficulty looking in the mirror at herself.

So I let her do what she could, then went over it before we left the house. She had beautiful skin in spite of her illness, but like most young people, still loved to wear the make up. Her own hair started to grow again, much to her delight. But her general health was getting worse. The dialysis was no longer removing all the fluid, and she was swelling up. We had to get more new glasses because the frame was stretched to capacity. She didn't like the look of her swollen face and complained regularly about her 'double chin'. One day we were going in to the hospital for dialysis and she was worried about her low blood pressure stopping the dialysis machine. I kept telling her it would be fine, and she gave me a big smile and said 'Ah well ma, two chins up!'.

For three years running, her hospital stays fell on Christmas week. She would be fine and working away until about a week before Christmas, she would get another bad infection. But Dr. Wall was great and let her home for a few hours on Christmas day. One year they let her home for a few hours on St. Stephen's day too, so we had Christmas dinner in Valeries, and St. Stephen's day at home.

I remember lifting her on to the settee and feeling a bit breathless. We sat watching television for a few hours, and eating sweets. Then we had a nice tea and it was time to go back to the hospital. I tried to lift her back into her wheelchair, but my breath went again. I did not want to ring Val as she was visiting her in-law's in Blanchardstown. So with a super human effort, I eventually got her in the wheelchair and then into the car. At the hospital, I struggled real bad to get her out of the car. Then when I got to the ward. I still had to get her into bed as the hospital now have a 'no lift' policy to protect their backs. June knew I could hardly breath, and she was worried. I assured her that after a good night's sleep, I would recharge my batteries! Alas, through the night, even in a resting position, I couldn't breath, so I had to ring Valerie. I was taken off to A and E, and put on oxygen, and medication.

The following day my breathing stopped altogether, and I was put in intensive care and my family were sent for. Apparently it was 'dodgy' if I would ever wake up, but I did! I remember opening my eyes, with a ventilator down my neck and wires and tubes everywhere. Obviously I could not speak, but I was aware of all my family there. On the funny side I thought, this is not heaven, with this lot here!

But to be honest, I was scared as I knew this was serious. My first thoughts were of June, in Tallaght hospital, waiting for me to come as usual early, to look after her personal care. I looked anxiously at Valerie, and she knew what I was thinking. She assured me that she was talking to the nurses in Tallaght hospital and everything was under control. I felt helpless. I was in St. James's hospital, and June was in Tallaght. The nurses in intensive care were so kind and gave me an alphabet board so that I could communicate with my family. Poor Valerie, she was running from one hospital to another, wearing herself out without complaining. Then Pam flew home and it eased the burden on her. It was great having Pam home, she spent most of her time with me while Val was with June. My only concern was for June as I knew how much she worried about me. I told Valerie to tell her the truth about what happened, and reassure her that I am on the mend.

After three days I was back in an ordinary ward and I could ring June. She was delighted to hear my voice and me hers. I kept the conversation light hearted and funny so that she would know that I really was getting better. I was even able to send a photograph of myself on the mobile phone, and she sent me one of her. A week later I was allowed home. June could have come home sooner, but without me being there, the doctor kept her for another few days. So, I came home on Wednesday night, and June came home on Thursday afternoon. We had one of our awkward hugs when we saw each other, (at times like this I hated the wheelchair as I couldn't get close enough to her), but when she was in bed that night, we had a 'real' hug.

Valerie had arranged a home help with the community nurse, because I was so weak, so next morning I was able to look after June's personal needs, while our lovely home help (Linda) did the housework. I had rang the chemist about my medication and they offered to deliver it. So, I was standing at the front door talking to the chemist lady when June's dog Charlie ran out. We live on a very busy main road so I yelled at her to come back. She ran across the road dodging traffic and away with her out of view. I could barely walk, never mind run! Linda ran after her, but came back for her coat as it was snowing and she was now out of sight. She ran to the field behind our local church with Linda in hot pursuit! Alas, she kept running away from Linda any time she got near. Linda rang me keeping me updated on what was happening.

Valerie was on her way down and I felt sure that Charlie would come to her, so I rang her in the car and explained. She drove straight to the church and met up with Linda, and both of them tried in vain to grab her. Then Val rang me, suggesting that she come back for me in the car as he would definitely come to me. So we tried that, but every time I went to grab her she ran away. Then she ran in the direction of home, so Linda ordered me back into the car and she would follow him. As we got near our corner, June rang asking did we get him. Before I could answer I looked up and saw him lying on the road outside of our house! Linda was so upset standing there and the poor guy who hit him, was in shock. I went in to console June who was very upset.

It was clear that he was dead, so poor Val brought out a blanket and wrapped Charlie up and brought her to the vet. It was a sad day for all of us as we had her almost fourteen years. I bought her for June's 18th birthday.

Again June text her dad to tell him about Charlie, but he just text back to say he was sorry. It never ceased to amaze me why he made no attempt to get in touch with any of the children. I tried helping them to cope with their hurt, but it wasn't easy, as I was trying to come to terms with it myself. They were all adults, so I thought that he would sit down and tell them that he still loved THEM, even though he found a new lady. But it seemed that we were just not part of his life anymore.

The tube going in to June's heart was still working, but her blood pressure was a big problem. It was very low so consequently the dialysis machine kept stopping. The nurses kept trying so that she would get some dialysis, but without the proper amount she was filling up with fluid. It would bring on another bad infection, and hospitalisation again. Tallaght hospital was now like our second home. Our lovely neighbours knew when June was in again, because the car was gone from 7 am until 10 pm, each day. Sometimes I brought a packed lunch for myself, other times if June was well enough, we went to the canteen.

One day we were on our way up to A&E as June had a severe pain in her stomach. As we turned into the hospital there was a strong smell of burning, and fire brigades everywhere. 'Ah Ma' June said 'Someone has burned the toast!'. I laughed out loud and so did she in spite of her pain. When we did manage to get to A&E they were in the process of closing it because the canteen had gone on fire.

The porter was turning everyone away, but then he saw June, and brought us in. All the staff knew her and loved her, and worried when she was sick. It was impossible to walk in to Tallaght hospital without everyone waving to her. I told her that she was like the queen! I occasionally felt sad that Lar never really knew June. I could see that she was very popular with everyone she knew, and to her family, and extended family, she was more than popular.

Each time June recovered, she went back to work, but she now had very little energy.But once she was sitting at her computer, she was happy. I usually called to collect her at 5pm, and 4pm on dialysis days. Sometimes I went earlier to go to the public library that was in the same grounds as South Dublin County Council. I would browse until it was time to meet her in the lobby.

Chapter Thirty
A Voice From The Past

One day I was coming out of the library, heading over to the lobby, when I heard 'Betty'. I recognised the voice and turned around. I got a fright when I saw him, as this was the first time since the court case. I felt embarrassed and uncomfortable.

'How are you?', he asked, and I sensed that he too felt embarrassed. I told him that I was fine and doing well. He asked if I would go for a cup of coffee with him, but I told him that I was collecting June. He then asked how she was. So I told him the truth about her prognosis, and that the dialysis wasn't working as well as it used to. I kept walking towards the lobby while I was talking, so he asked if he could come with me to see June, and I agreed to let him. We sat where I usually wait and I text June. I always text one word every day; Lobby, and she would text OK.

But today I text; I am talking to your dad in the lobby! She text back; O MY GOD! I laughed out loud and Lar said 'She probably won't come out now!'. We chatted while we were waiting, and I still felt uncomfortable, even though I had lived with this man for forty years. The first thing that struck me was he still couldn't be truthful. He claimed that the 'new relationship' was no more, even though he had been seen out and about with her, days previously. I asked why he couldn't tell the truth now that it didn't matter any more, he continued to reply,'I AM ON MY OWN' He said it slowly and loudly as if I didn't understand, but I kept accusing him of telling me lies again. In any event, June came wheeling out. Clearly Lar was visibly moved at the deterioration in her, and wept as he hugged her. June appeared embarrassed by the whole scene, with work colleagues still around the lobby. When we calmed down again June was just her funny self, laughing and joking. Then she brought up the subject of Esther, again he repeated loudly and clearly as if we didn't understand, 'I AM ON MY OWN'. I changed the subject, as it was no use, he would never tell us the truth. We excitedly told him about our new granddaughter that he had never seen, our beautiful Aine Elizabeth, born to Pam and Robert, six months previously. 'Dad' June said, 'She is a miniature version of Pam, another cuddles'. He smiled and said that he would loved to see her, and all the grandchildren. He asked me if I thought that Valerie would allow him see the children. I could not speak for Val, so I suggested that he ask her.

We continued chatting for another thirty minutes or so, then I stood up to go. I asked him to call over to the lobby the following day, so that I could give him our yearly V.H.I. health insurance, that was due, and that we usually send to him every year, as the family policy we took out when Lar worked for the oil company, was still valid. The money was stopped out of his pension every week, but June and I paid him yearly in advance. At that time it was almost 1000 euro each, so June wrote a cheque for hers, but I had to get a bank draft as I did not have a checking account. Because June was in hospital so often, I worried that he might cancel the policy, but he reassured me that he would never do that. I believed him.

Next day as arranged he came and we gave him the money. But before June came out, I brought up Esther again. I couldn't help myself as there were so many unanswered questions. It was clear that I was only annoying him, he didn't want to talk about her, only about me. He told me that he still felt the same about me as he always did, and that he would die if anything happened to me. 'But', I said, 'Something did happen to me, it didn't bother you at all when my world fell apart after you left'. He blamed drink on the whole affair, but he was cold sober when he walked out of my door!

No matter what I said about Esther, he never said a bad word about her, it was like he was protecting her. I was of the opinion that he cared deeply for this woman, but when he was with me he told me a different story. I was tempted to ring Esther to ask if it really was over, but what was the point? What if it was? I was in a different place now, and at peace with myself, so it didn't matter to me if they were still together. It was the lies that bothered me.

I changed the subject again when June came out, so we sat together, laughed together, and chatted together. A few more times after that he came over to the lobby, and by now June was getting fed up with him coming so often.. Besides, while we were waiting on June every day, we ended up rowing again over Esther. He wanted to know everything about me and what I was doing with my life, but he told me nothing about his. I knew that this contact wasn't good for me as it was only opening up old wounds, and when June asked me to stop it I didn't hesitate. He still kept in contact by phone to me regularly, but only text June on dialysis days. She never answered him, and I don't know why. I never questioned her as I felt that as an adult, she was entitled to her own decisions. My friend who lived close to Esther continued to see his car in her driveway a few times a week. When I asked him about it he said that he knew guys out there that he drank with, so it was a handy place to stay.

I decided never to talk about anything else but our children, from now on if he rang. In September 2010, June got seriously ill, and the doctors, thought that this was it. She then had a seizure and went into a deep sleep. I had this awful feeling that she would never wake up again. I slept in a chair in the hospital all night, and at five o clock in the morning she woke up and looked at me. I said 'Do you know where you are?' She replied Tallaght Hospital'.I asked if she remember what happened. 'I think I had a seizure' she said. She was right, but when she didn't wake up after it the doctors told me they were worried. Amazingly, she bounced back and she was back in work within a week!

But I could see work was a struggle now so I persuaded her to arrange a four day week until she got stronger. She agreed, and her 'boss' in South Dublin County Council sorted it out for her advising her the best way to do it to protect her pension.All she needed, he said was a letter from the hospital and that was no problem. The doctors were amazed that she still worked, even if it was a four day week. June wasn't one for sitting around doing nothing, she had to have a purpose to her day. Her sisters too could see that she was deteriorating day by day. Because Pam wouldn't see her for six weeks at a time, she noticed a huge difference each time she came home. Pam would laugh and joke with her when they were together, but got very upset in private. In spite of her suffering she continued to make us laugh. She loved her nieces and nephew dearly and had fun with them when they visited. It is true to say that they loved her in return, and they always asked her to play with them and she did.

She loved buying them presents, indeed she spoiled them rotten! She spoke about them constantly to her workmates and regularly brought in photographs. On the days that June was in work, Val and I continued with our sewing. I mostly helped when she was busy, but I had no interest in making money now. Yet I knew Valerie had a mortgage to pay so she had to keep the business going. I love sitting at my sewing machine so it was a pleasure to help Val. In fairness, she also loved her work so on days that June was okay, we would have a ball, stitching and sewing to our hearts content.

In Oct, four weeks after June went back to work, she was taken back into hospital again. Clearly she was very ill and in pain and her body kept filling up with fluid. The dialysis removed some of it but when her blood pressure dropped, the machine stopped, and she would pass out. I sat beside her throughout all the dialysis sesions holding my breath, but yet chatting to her 'matter of factly' as if I was sure everything was alright. Even at her lowest, she was great company, and tried to make me laugh. One day we were watching one of the 'soaps' on television, when one of the more devious characters in the soap said 'Everyone in the world has a secret, and I'm going to find this guy's one'. June turned to me and said 'Do you believe that Mam, that everyone has a secret? 'Ah I don't know, I said, 'At least I don't have one anyway'!

'I have a secret' she said. 'Oh really' I replied, amazed that June would keep a secret from me, after all we told each other everything. I was afraid to ask what it was, besides, she was entitled to keep secrets if she so wished. 'Do you want me to tell you?' she asked. I wasn't sure if I wanted to hear this, but she sounded like she wanted to share it with me. 'Okay, go on then tell me' I said.

'Well Mam, I am the one who cut a hole in Sr. Mary Francis' jacket! I was dumbfounded to say the least, I could not believe it! She had a miscievious grin on her face as she told me. For twenty five years I blamed Pamela even though she always denied any knowledge of it.

It happened when Pam was ten years old and June was nine. Sister Mary Francis had taught me in school and I was terrified of her. Then she came to teach in our local school, and had heard about me and the dressmaking. She asked if I would make her a new suit for her golden jubilee. I wanted to say no as even as an adult she frightened me, but there was no way out of it. So she gave me a suit to copy, instructing me to make sure that I had sixteen stitches to the inch!

I carefully gave the suit my undivided attention, checking every inch that I sewed. I was delighted when I was finished and she was pleased. But I left the suit that she gave me to copy, on the settee in the sitting room. When I went to wrap it up to return it there was a cut in the top of the sleeve. I was shocked! Pam was the only one who was there with her friends, so I confronted her but she was adamant that she knew nothing about it. I knew I could not face the nun and tell her the truth. I was awake all night worrying about what to do. Then I got inspiration! I got up early and ripped out both sleeves,made them both one inch shorter, and reset them! They looked perfect, but shorter. But I was hoping against hope that it wouldn't be noticed. The next Sunday at mass, (Sr. Mary Francis was a minister of the eucharist) she was giving out the holy communion with the 'short sleeve' jacket on, and yes, I noticed the sleeves were shorter, but did she? Well if she did, she never said, and I heard no more about it. But for years after that, I brought up the subject with Pam and she still denied it. It never occurred to me to even ask June if she knew anything about it, but she would have heard me blame Pam over and over again!

What puzzled me most was that when they had grown and it didn't matter any more, Pam still wouldn't admit to it. The conclusion I came to was that I left the scissors open on top of it and someone sat on it.

June's confession made me laugh, and it solved a twenty five year mystery! She told me that she deliberately did it because she was mad at me over something that she now cannot remember. I had to ring Pam from the hospital and tell her. You could hear her laughing her head off with the thoughts of June doing anything wrong. It was always poor Pam that got blamed for everything.

June was now getting blood transfusions monthly. She got them while on dialysis as it was quicker that way. One day we were watching the blood going in and she said to me, 'Mam, just imagine some stranger put themselves out to give blood so that I could have a better life'. That got me thinking. She was right, there is no reward for giving blood, and yet thousands of people walk in off the streets, and put themselves out to help others. I looked at the bag of blood hanging over June's bed. I remember thinking that the person who gave this was in fact saving June's life. People who donate blood are our unsung heroes, and are not praised enough. At June's suggestion we went later that day to the hospital chapel to offer up a prayer for all those who generously donate blood. June loved going to the chapel when she was in hospital. It was non-denomonational, and very peaceful. We seldom saw anyone else there unless there was a service or mass on. On every seat there was a book with bible stories. Because June could not see too good anymore, I read out some of the stories, if we were alone. She loved this and we would discuss them at length later, back in the ward. One day I came across the story of John the Baptist. I had learned about this many years before when I was in school, but June hadn't. The story goes something like this;

An angel appeared to Elizabeth (Our Lady's first cousin) and her husband, telling them that they would have a son, and he would be John the Baptist. The husband disbelieved the angel because they were elderly, and passed child bearing years.

Because he would not believe, the angel said that he would be struck dumb, from now until the baby was born. And so he was! After finishing the story I looked at June's face. It burst into laughter! She laughed so much that I wheeled her out of there quickly before the chaplain heard us!

All the way back to the ward she had me laughing too. I had known this story all my life, but June made me see it in a new light, and yes I now wondered if it could be true. She had an amazing ability to find laughter in everything, and she liked nothing better than relating it all to Wayne. Wayne and June had the same wicked sense of humour, so she told him all about John the Baptist when he came in to see her.His laughter was as loud as her's!

Once again she recovered and went back to work at the end of October. She really wasn't well and had broken out in painful sores on her hands. The tissue viability nurse gave me some sort of 'gel' to put on them. So every morning after all the main dressings were done, I would spend quite a while dressing her fingers to get them looking decent for work. Her little finger was the worst as the sore was right on her knuckle, limiting her movement of it. I suggested to keep it as still as posible to curtail the pain. 'Ma', she said, 'To do that I would have to leave out all the "A's" in my typing!' She was so funny, and never missed an opportunity to get a laugh.On dialysis days she came home from the hospital shattered, only wanting to go to bed. It was hard trying to lift her in as she was too weak to help me. Most times I managed, but occasionally I misjudged, and she ended up across the bed instead of the length. It was imposible for me to swing her around when she ended up like this, so we would ring Valerie to rescue us while we lay there laughing!

She wasn't eating well at this time, but I got around her to have a snack at least. No matter how tired she was, she liked to watch her telly lying in bed, so, every night I sat in her wheelchair beside her and we watched telly together.

She was now having sleepless nights with severe pain in her stomach. Most of the nights I sat with her rubbing it and sometimes using my portable massage gadget that she bought me for the arthritis. At three or four in the morning she would pretend it was better so that I could get some sleep, but I knew it wasn't.

Dialysis was now a real struggle, and almost every time she passed out when her blood pressure dropped. The nurses in dialysis were amazing, reasurring her each time, and watching her closely for the three hours. Her doctor once again took me aside and told me that she wouldn't live beyond Christmas.

I shed my tears when I was alone, but I never gave up hope. Her sisters knew the prognosis, but like me, they didn't want to believe it.

And yet I looked at her suffering so much, it was breaking my heart, but still I prayed and hoped for a miracle. We had come too far to let go now.

On November 17th she had a bad turn on dialysis and was kept in hospital again. When she was settled in the ward, we were chatting and she got serious and said 'Mam, I worry in case something happens to me because you won't be able to cope without me.'

I got a shock at her seriousness and gave her a hug. I said 'Will you stop talking like that, I need you to get better, we have a lot of shopping to do for Christmas!'.

'Do you ever see me well enough to go shopping with you again'? she said. 'Of course I do, just make sure you're out of here for Christmas, not like last year!' I replied, with my heart breaking. I spent all my time in the hospital, sometimes sleeping in a chair, sometimes on the floor.

I rang Lar and told him how bad things were, and he called over to the hospital to see her. When he walked in she said 'What are you doing here?'. He replied 'I heard that you weren't well so I thought I'd come over to see you'. 'Well' she said 'I must be dying!' She was smiling saying it but it got to me and I think to Lar as well. I left the room to give them time on their own, and stayed out for half an hour. Then June text me to come back. When I returned she was showing him her laptop and how it worked as he had no clue about computers. So I thought that they got on well, but after he left June told me that she felt uncomfortable with him, and thought I'd never come back. It was sad that she didn't feel comfortable with him, but then they never had a close relationship with each other. He rang me a few times to ask if he could call again, but I was in a difficult situation now. June didn't want to see him, and her sisters refused to come if he was there. The strain of trying to do the right thing, and please everyone was getting to me. I sought out the lovely chaplain, and explained the situation to her. Her main concern was for June's feelings, and she was right, nothing else mattered just now. So each time Lar wanted to visit I checked with June, sometimes she said yes, but more times it was no.

If I mentioned Esther's name to him in front of June, she would tell me off after he went. Of course she was right, but it maddened me that he knew everything about what was happening in our lives, while he told us nothing about his.

Although most of the time his life now didn't interest me anymore. He had left us when we needed him most, he knew it would be hard on June and I without practical help. But with the support of our extended family, we were getting by. I often wondered if we ever came into his mind at all, even occasionally. If we did, he never said so. Many years ago he said that he wouldn't be able to live with the guilt if he left me, but it wasn't troubling him now. Perhaps his love for Esther far outweighs the feelings of guilt. Whatever was in his mind, didn't matter to me anymore, June was my biggest concern right now, and her sisters couldn't do enough for her.

They loved her to bits and their hearts were breaking looking at her suffering. It was getting harder for June to see her food on the tray, but she had very little appetite anyway. Even so I spoon fed her and encouraged her to eat as much as she could stomach. Much to her frustration, she was now knocking over drinks that were in front of her. Things were looking real bad, and yet neither her sisters or I gave up hope. When she was sleeping I strolled down to the chapel to have a word with God. I begged him with all my heart to help June, making all sorts of promises in the process. Each time I went there I got great comfort and renewed strength to stay cheerful in front of her. She knew that I loved listening to the tail end of other people's conversations as I passed them by, so each time I heard something new, I would relate it to her, especially if it was funny. Like the day I overheard two young doctors talking in the corridor. One said 'The rash is three days coming, three days on, and three days going'. 'Oh', said the second doctor, 'How do you know?' First doctor replies 'My mother told me!'.

Another day I was in the lift with two very large ladies, so big that only one other could fit in. One said to the other,'What do you think of what the doctor said?' 'Well, the doctor is right, he'll have to lose a few stone, he is way over weight!' June laughed whenever I told her new tit bits I'd heard. One day when I was relating another, she said 'Ma, when you are finished your book, you should write another one entitled 'Overheard in Tallaght Hospital!'

It was coming near Christmas, and the doctor said that June could come home. I knew that she wasn't well enough, but I also understood the doctor's reason for it. So I thought when I got her home, that she would be more comfortable and happier, and I looked forward to fussing over her myself.

She had a lot more pressure sores, one of them now up her back to where she could feel. I did my best to pad it out but she was only comfortable for a while, then the pain started again. I figured that when I got her home I could do a 'masterpiece' on it like many times before.

Thursday,16th of December was the day for leaving the hospital. It was clear to me that she was in terrible pain. The nurses were extremely kind and gave her the painkillers that the doctor ordered. With great difficulty I got her washed and dressed and into her wheelchair. I asked her if she was sure that she wanted to go home, and she said yes, but I wasn't so sure.

We were waiting for the nurse to return with the paperwork, when June decided to look out of the door to see if she was coming. She wheeled towards the door, but misjudged it and crashed into the frame. I knew her sight was bad, but I thought that she could see enough to go through the door, and I think she could, so I realised it was her balance. I was getting more worried by the minute.

I had her car outside, but I rang Wayne to help me lift her into it. Within minutes He arrived and insisted on putting her in his car so that he could help me at the other end.I was glad, as they both had a similar sense of humour and always joked with each other. Alas, he would tell me later that she was very quiet all the way home.

At home Pam had just arrived home for Christmas. She came earlier than usual as I had to tell her that things weren't good. When we got to the house it was full, with the grandchildren all excited to see June. Bravely she tried to laugh with them and answer all their questions, but I was aware of her pain. When no one was looking, I asked her would she like to get into bed and she said yes. With Valerie's help we got her in and tried to make her as comfortable as posible. Val was great at lifting her forward and fluffing up the pillows. After that Pam and Val took the children up to Val's house, realizing that June needed to sleep. Alone again, I let her sleep as long as she could, giving her painkillers, as frequently as I was allowed. She had an uncomfortable day, eating nothing, sleeping little. I sat in her wheelchair beside her bed as I often did watching telly with her. This time she had no interest in television at all. By midnight she was so uncomfortable that I rang Val to come and help me turn her and fluff the pillows. We got her comfortable again and Val stayed until the early hours. After she went, I tried to sleep, but I knew June was awake and in pain, so I went back in to her.

By morning she told me that she was more comfortable in hospital, and felt she needed to go back. Immediately I rang Val and within minutes she was down.We couldn't move June because she was in so much pain, so we had to ring an ambulance. Unfortunately, our house is in the catchment area for St. James' Hospital, but I told the ambulance men that it was vital that I get her back to Tallaght hospital. They said that they would have to get permission from Tallaght. When they rang A&E, they told them to bring her in immediately when they heard it was June. When we arrived at the hospital, everyone was so kind. Her doctor came along and called Val into her office discreetly out of view of June. She told Valerie that the main thing now was to keep June out of pain, that there was nothing else she could do. I knew this, but I didn't want to believe it, that is why she spoke to Valerie. I could see Val trying to hold back the tears, but I kept talking to June, telling her that the doctor was going to give her something for the pain. Val was so upset that she had

to go outside to ring Wayne and Pam.

Meanwhile, the doctor spoke to June, I held my breath as I still didn't want her to know. 'How are you feeling'? Dr. Wall said. 'I have terrible pain' June replied. Dr. Wall assured her that the injection that she was giving her would take it all away.They brought her back up to the room that she vacated the day before and gave her the injection. The pain went almost immediately much to our delight. She looked so comfortable now and dozed off into a welcome sleep. Val went home to pack a bag for me as I was staying with June. A machine was attached to June's side that portioned out the drug at regular intervals. It certainly kept her out of pain and she was smiling again. That evening she woke and said 'Ma sing me an oul song'. I laughed and sang Dublin In The Rare oul Times. It was my party piece because it was the only song I knew all the words. In her beautiful voice she sang the whole song with me, and at the end, as we always did clapped ourselves!

I was so happy to see her out of pain that I put everything else out of my mind, and lay on a mattress on the floor and had a few hours sleep. In the silence of the night I was aware of this 'wooshing' sound of the machine, every so often. It started to annoy me as I knew what it meant, and it was upsetting to say the least. At about 5oclock I got up to go to the toilet, she said to me 'You alright Ma?', 'Yes I'm fine June, I'm just going to the toilet'. This was the last time she spoke, and typical of her to be concerned for me. The next day, Saturday, she was in a deep sleep, although she managed a grin when Valerie put vaseline on her lips. They always had a laugh about it as everytime June went in to hospital, Valerie arrived up with the vaseline! Lar came to visit for a while when her sisters weren't there. I had given up trying to keep them apart because the situation was too serious now. Nevertheless, they still avoided each other, and never arrived at the same time.

Chapter Thirty One
OUR SADDEST DAY

When Lar was leaving on Saturday, he said that he would call again on Sunday morning. I knew Val and Pam weren't coming until the afternoon, so again, they would not clash.

I spent another sleepless night, listening to the 'swoosh' of the machine. No matter what I did, I was wide awake lying on the floor, listening. The night nurse was great. Twice during the night she came in with a mug of hot tea, and chatted to me for a while. I got up at 5.30am, chatted to June although I wondered if she could hear me.I stood looking out of the window at the falling snow, yes, it would definitely be a white Christmas. Almost every year for the past five, June was in hospital for Christmas, this time I knew that she wouldn't make it. I sat in silence for a while beside her, then the phone made me jump. Val was anxious too and couldn't sleep, so she was waiting for morning to ring. Pam was staying in her house so they were a comfort for each other, at this unbearable time. They asked if I needed anything brought up, but I could no longer eat. I shed a few tears reflecting on the thirty four and a half wonderful years that God gave me with June.

She brought out qualities in all of us that we didn't know we had. I thought back to the day that she came into the world, midsummers day, in the heatwave of 1976. It was now almost mid winter's day 2010, and we were having the worst snowfall ever. I stood at the window looking over the vast area of Tallaght. There was a blanket of snow as far as the eye could see. June loved looking out at the snow, but as every wheelchair user knows, it is imposible to wheel on.

I thought back to the first time that she saw snow. I remember bringing a shovel full into our kitchen so that she could feel what it was like. Then Lar took the wheels off her shasbah trolley, put a rope on it, and pulled her through the snow. The squeals of delight could be heard for miles around, which amused our neighbours.

My thoughts were interrupted by the lady chaplain coming in the door. She was a lovely lady with whom I became friends over many years. We chatted for a while and drank tea until we ran out of words, then she prayed that God would help me today. I spent the rest of the morning talking to June, telling her that I was determined to finish the book, but there was no sign of recognition on her beautiful face. I looked at my watch, it was now almost lunch time, and no sign of Lar. I felt angry at him as he only lived five minutes away from the hospital, even in the snow.

I was angry because if he didn't come now, he would be embarrassed meeting my sisters who were coming in the afternoon. They hadn't seen him since he left me, and, while I knew they wouldn't be embarrassed, he would. So I rang him. I was so angry that I yelled down the phone at him, reminding him of his promise to come over that morning. He had no excuse and mumbled that he would come straight over. Half an hour later he arrived. I started to yell again, he yelled louder, then I looked at June, and realised that this was neither the time or the place. I quietly shed a few tears. Just then the priest came to bless June with the holy oils. He stayed a while consoling us and talking about God. After he left, we spent the next hour talking quietly and reminiscing June's life. Then Lar left, again promising to call back later. My sisters came in the afternoon and were a great support and comfort to me. We tried to talk normal conversation hoping that June could still hear us, as she loved all her aunties and always had a laugh with them.

Val and Pam were waiting until the crowd had gone, before coming up as the room was very small, with only three chairs. When everyone left, I spoke to them on the phone, giving them update on how things were. They said that they would come up when they fed the children. Meanwhile, the lady chaplain came in again and I felt a compelling need to confess about my anger that morning to Lar. She was so kind to me, and after talking for quite sometime, I was able to forgive myself, but not before I turned to June and apologised.

Sitting alone with her again, I felt a peace coming over me. I was watching her steady breathing when I noticed that it was no longer steady, but laboured. I rang the nurse's bell but it didn't work. I ran out of the ward screaming for a nurse, but it seemed some of them were gone on tea break, so I banged on doors until I found one.

Immediately she put on the oxegen mask and said to me, 'I think you should ring your family.'

My hands shook as I rang Val, luckily they were already on their way, so I told them to ring their dad. Within minutes we were sitting around the bed holding her hands. This was the first time in five years that the complete family was together. I was pleased that we could support each other at this sad time. Fifteen minutes later, through her tears, Pam said, "Mam, she's stopped breathing'.

We called the nurse again, and she confirmed that June was gone to heaven. I cannot recall who said what after that, as my body seemed to go numb. We sat there in tearful silence looking at our beautiful June, now at peace, but leaving behind, broken hearts. The nurses were so kind and couldn't do enough for us. They gave us a family room with tea etc. while they did what they had to. Valerie rang everyone including my sisters and Lar's sister Connie. My sisters were on their way back to the hospital with their welcome support. Lar whispered to me 'What do you think your sisters will say to me?'. He was worried as this would be the first time to see them since he left me. I told him that they would treat him with respect and dignity at this sad time. And that is exactly what happened. I knew my wonderful sisters.

We piled back into the room were June was but my heart and mind was somewhere else. How can I live now without my beautiful fun loving daughter, who filled our house with laughter for thirty four and a half years? How can I go back to an empty house? I asked Lar to remove her 'talking' watch that I had bought her the previous Christmas when her sight got worse. Oh how she loved that watch. I put it on me, promising to love it now, as much as she did.

Later when it was time to go, the girls wouldn't let me go back to my own house, so I went home with Valerie. Connie and her husband Brian went home with Lar to give him support. I had never slept in Valerie's house before, so nothing felt real that night, nothing felt right. As I expected, I never slept, and Lar text to say that he couldn't sleep either. Somehow I stayed in bed until 5.30am, then I got up and made tea. It wasn't long before everone was up confessing that they didn't sleep either! I did a lot of thinking during the night and came to a decision. So I told Valerie and Pam what I had decided.

Because I thought it was the right thing to do, I wanted to include Lar in the funeral arrangements. I wasn't sure how the girls truly felt about it, but I knew they would do it for me. I had kept the money in the credit union for this, as I could not get June insured since she was twenty one years old, when her childhood policy matured, because of her ill health. Anyway, the money didn't matter, I just wanted to do everything right. My only worry was that Lar's partner would turn up at the church. As it happens she didn't and I was glad because we were upset enough without that. Meanwhile, I was having difficulty getting through this day. I stood at the window watching heavy snow falling silently, covering everything. I watched the birds pecking at the food that Valerie had hung on her trees. They were oblivious to the pain that we were feeling, chirping, hopping from tree to tree, then flying away over hedgerows out of view. The thought of never seeing June again was overbearing. I was her Mam, how could I let this happen? My body felt like a shell called 'Betty' an emptiness beyond discription, with an ache for my youngest child. I could not think about God and His plans, He had lost my address again, just when I needed him most. Where are you now God what were you thinking? From a distance I could see the main road with the traffic reduced to a crawl. I remember wondering why life was going on for everyone else, while mine had come to a standstill. I wanted to shout Stop the clocks, turn out the lights, my world has come to an end'. But of course I didn't, this was no time to upset my two remaining children who were also deep in grief. I prayed to God for guidance, to help me through the coming days.

Later that morning Lar arrived for our meeting with the funeral director. All four of us sat with him going over the arrangements, and choosing a casket. I couldn't focus, all sorts of emotions and even confusion was going through my head. I wasn't Me. No, ME was somewhere else, I wasn't here just now. Strangely, I was aware that I was saying the right things, but it was almost like I was on the outside looking in. Yes, Betty was doing everything right as usual, but the real Betty wasn't there. I needed to be somewhere else, June was in the chapel of rest, and I never left her alone.

In the afternoon we went back to where she was in the chapel. I could not believe how many of her work colleagues were coming and going paying their respects, and also the lovely staff from dialysis. It was a great comfort to me to know that when I was not there, she wasn't alone. I felt a gratitude to them for the way they reached out to us at this most horrible time. June looked like she was in a peaceful sleep, so pretty, with an expression on her face like her dads. 'Oh! Look', Valerie said, 'She's got dad's face!' I could see Lar's face breaking into a smile, he could see it too.

We went back to Valerie's house and continued making plans for the interment. Clearly the weather was extremely bad, so we were not sure how it would work out. I let everyone else worry about it, because in my mind, nothing mattered anymore. Valerie was great, and kept us all fed, even though her world too was falling apart. Pam couldn't stop crying, and she needed a sign from June, that she was okay. Already they were missing their sister, feeling an overwhelming sense of tragedy.

Next day, with all the arrangements in place, we set out for the chapel of rest for prayers and the removal to our own church. On arrival we felt great support when we saw the crowds there. It showed us that June was well loved, and respected for so many to turn up in the worst winter ever. June was laid out in her favourite red top, that she had bought for her friend's wedding. She looked beautiful, and at peace. The lovely lady chaplain said the prayers. She knew June for many years, and talked about visiting her regularly when she was in hospital. 'But' she said, looking over at me, ' June didn't like my visits!' I had to smile and said 'I never thought you noticed!' June was always nice and polite to her, but secretly she told me that she hated the religious chats. She called the chaplin 'Holy Mary'.

I recall many times she would see her coming and say'Oh no, here comes holy Mary' To think that we never fooled the chaplain for one minute, in spite of our best efforts.But this revelation brought a smile to everyone there.

My everlasting memory of that day was to see her work colleagues from South Dublin County Council stand knee deep in snow to form a guard of honour as we left the chapel of rest. What a tribute to their special friend.

When we arrived at the church, we were greeted by many many people. It was consoling for us that so many had braved the weather to be with us.

Lar and I walked down the aisle behind the casket carrying our beautiful youngest child. The last time we walked down the aisle together was on our wedding day, full of hopes and dreams. Alas, now our marriage was broken,our youngest daughter dead. I felt a bit uncomfortable sitting next to him during the prayer service, but then I knew I was doing this for June, to keep things right. Besides, I was still feeling 'in the third person' a kind of out of body experience at that time. After the service, we spent an hour talking to friends, neighbours, and relatives that we hadn't seen in years. We then went back to Valerie's house, where she allowed her dad stay the night for the interment the next day.

The snow was still falling heavily the next morning, and clearly it had snowed all night. I again reflected on midsummer's day in 1976 when June made her entrance into this world in a heatwave. Today, was midwinter's day 2010, with one of worse snowstorms we had ever seen. All of us as a family got into the mourning coach to go to the church for the funeral mass. We had only got to the end of Valerie's road when the car got stuck in the snow. The men got out and pushed but the wheels kept pinning around, going nowhere. I sat in the car getting more upset by the minute, then I thought of June's wicked sense of humour, and imagined her saying 'It could only happen to us Ma!'.

A passing motorist came to our rescue. He had a shoval in the boot of his car and kindly lent it to us so we could get on the move again. On arrival at the church I was again taken aback by the hugh crowd there in such bad weather. We sat in the front row as a family, too numb to think of anything else but June. The year before she died, she bought Valerie a silver photo frame engraved,'Sisters by chance, Friends by choice'.

Valerie had put my favourite photo of the three of them in it, and now she placed it on the casket. Every time I looked at it during the mass, I felt overwhelming pride of my three girls. Alice, a close friend and colleague of June's joined Pam on the altar to say the prayers of the faithful, with her godmother Tina. Pam was struggling to talk, but she bravely got through it.

We had lovely music, many of the songs favourites of June. Indeed she told Valerie a few months previous about one song in particular, that she would like at her funeral! It was a lighthearted conversation at the time, but she told Val, what C.D it was on, and where she would find it. When Val looked, it was exactly where she said it would be. Towards the end of the mass Valerie and I went up on the altar to share our memories of our beloved June. It was emotional for both of us, but it was important that everyone should know how wonderful it was to have June in our lives.

When the service was over, Wayne requested to carry June one last time. He knew that she loved him lifting her, so this would be the last time. So with the help of her dad, Wayne, Robert, and my brother-in-law Noel, carried her out of the church.

The crowds came with us to the graveyard for the interment. I remember standing nsteadily at the graveside, and was glad to feel the arms of my brother-in-law Noel behind, supporting me. There was a blanket of snow as far as the eye could see. I was somewhere that I didn't want to be. The only way I could cope was to imagine that we were all standing outside of Heaven's gate, but only June was allowed in. We would all make this journey, but today it was June's turn. The flowers were like a kaleidoscope of colour, against the white snow. As the priest began to say the prayers, a little fat robin hopped out of nowhere and hopped from flower to flower. It seemed to look around at everyone, then it went under the flowers, into the grave, and out again.

Everyone watched in amazement as it continued to do so for the duration of the prayers. Ironically, June loved robins. They were on her favourite Christmas cards. Every year she would buy a box of cards and pick out the robin ones first, to send to her friends. Alas, this year there will be no Christmas cards, in fact Christmas will never be the same for any of us again. Standing there in my grief I marvelled at nature providing us with proof that God was all around us. And how strange was that robin...............?